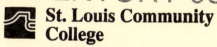

The Velvet Revolution

The Velvet Revolution

Czechoslovakia, 1988–1991

Bernard Wheaton
and Zdeněk Kavan

Westview Press

BOULDER · SAN FRANCISCO · OXFORD

Copyright © 1992 by Westview Press, Inc.

Published in 1992 in the United States of America by Westview Press, Inc., 5500 Central Avenue, Boulder, Colorado 80301-2847, and in the United Kingdom by Westview Press, 36 Lonsdale Road, Summertown, Oxford OX2 7EW

Library of Congress Cataloging-in-Publication Data
Wheaton, Bernard.
  The velvet revolution : Czechoslovakia, 1988–1991 / Bernard Wheaton and Zdeněk Kavan.
    p. cm.
  Includes bibliographical references and index.
  ISBN 0-8133-1203-5. — ISBN 0-8133-1204-3 (pbk.)
  1. Czechoslovakia—Politics and government—1968–1989.
2. Czechoslovakia—Politics and government—1989-   . I. Kavan, Zdeněk. II. Title.
DB2228.7.W47   1992
943.704'3—dc20   92-8442
                                                                  CIP

Printed and bound in the United States of America

The paper used in this publication meets the requirements of the American National Standard for Permanence of Paper for Printed Library Materials Z39.48-1984.

10   9   8   7   6   5   4   3   2   1

Contents

Making a Clean Break: Purges, 179
Unsettled Economy, Uncertain Future, 182

Illustrations

Acknowledgments

Many people contributed to this book in one way or another even before writing got under way, and we would like to express our gratitude to them. Our thanks go first to the British Council, which sent one of the authors off to Prague in November 1989 on a two-month postdoctoral fellowship to work on Czech-German relations. This was an opportunity to experience a revolution firsthand. The preparatory work for this book was assisted by the English Language Centre Educational Trust, which provided a small grant for a further two weeks in Czechoslovakia in May 1990.

Prof. Dr. Litsch, formerly director of the historical archive at the Charles University, Prague, donated a wide selection of runs of all daily newspapers for the weeks covering the revolution. Inženýr Starý and Paní Hrušková of the Prague Information Service and their staff at very short notice supplied the newspaper cuttings that formed the basis of a significant section of Part Three. In addition, thanks go to Dr. Svatoš, also of the historical archive, and to Dr. Petr Kučera, member of Parliament and adviser to the president, who found time to discuss aspects of the post-Communist government and Citizens Forum when more important matters were pressing.

Dr. Vladimír Kaiser, director of the county archive in Ústí nad Labem, and Dr. Kristina Kaiserová reported on their experiences during the revolution in northern Bohemia. Vlasta Jaroš of Most kept information flowing from the Teplice, Most, and Litvinov regions and likewise from local and regional newspapers. Petr Němec, an erstwhile employee of the Semafor Revue Theater in Prague, provided contacts with members of the theatrical community (especially at the Vinohrady Theater) who were personally involved in the revolution from the very outset. Jeník Jařab, then a final-year student at the medical faculty, offered the benefit of his experience as an organizer of a so-called circle during the crucial first weeks.

In addition to newspapers, the media, and records of personal experiences, Part Two, on the revolution itself, is based on original documents gathered in the Špála Gallery, one of the nerve centers of the revolution.

We would like to express our appreciation for the help given by all the people who worked downstairs, especially to Tomáš Cejp, an artist who manned the improvised archive single-handed. In difficult circumstances, he provided originals and photocopies of all available documents of Citizens Forum and the students, letters from the public, and protests from the basic organizations of the Communist party and the trade union movement; he also donated a complete run of Citizens Forum's alternative newspaper, *Informační servis,* from the first four weeks of the revolution.

We also owe a debt of gratitude to Jan Kavan, who worked in the dissident movement for two decades and was a member of Parliament for Citizens Forum in Prague. His information was invaluable, especially for the chapters dealing with the new state. Jiří Kappel's business experience helped us greatly in working out the complexities of the present economic conditions. Stephany Griffith-Jones of the Institute of Development Studies at the University of Sussex also gave us the benefit of her knowledge of the economic reforms.

A word of thanks, too, to Vladimír Jiránek and Jiří Lochman, whose cartoons adorned the walls and press publications in Prague during the revolution; a sampling of their work is reproduced in this book.

Finally, Romy Damian deserves a special vote of thanks. She did a great deal more than provide expert advice when the computer went down.

Bernard Wheaton
Zdeněk Kavan

A Rough Guide to the Pronunciation of Czech and Slovak

In both Czech and Slovak, the first syllable always carries the main stress, but the unstressed syllables are not neutralized as they are in English. Rather, each one is pronounced more or less clearly, whether stressed or not. Vowels are short unless marked with the diacritical ´ or (over a *u*) °. Háčeks (literally, little hooks) in effect soften consonants. An *ň* thus sounds like the "gn" in "monsignor"; *č* like the "ch" in "chop"; *š* like the "sh" in "shirt"; *ž* like the "zh" in "leisure." A *d, t,* or *n* before the vowels *i* and *ě* takes on a similar softness (that is, a *t* in such a case would become a "ty" sound as in the British pronunciation of "tune").

Certain consonants have an altogether different pronunciation from their English counterparts. The *c* is equivalent to the "ts" in "cats"; *ch* is much like the Scottish "ch" in "loch"; *j* is pronounced as is the "y" in "yes"; *r* is trilled. Perhaps the most difficult sound for a nonnative speaker is the *ř*, which is something like a compressed "rzh" (thus Dvořák = DVOR-zhahk).

Following are a few examples:

Letná = LET-nah
Bat'a = BAT-ya
Dubček = DUP-check
Václav = VAHTS-lahf
Beneš = BEN-esh

Acronyms

AR	Association for the Republic (Sdružení pro Republiku, or SR)
ASD	Association of Social Democrats (Asociace Sociálních demokratů, or ASD)
CCTU	Central Council of Trade Unions (Ústřední rada odborů, or ÚRO)
CDA	Citizens Democratic Alliance (Občanská demokratická aliance, or ODA)
CDM	Christian Democratic Movement (Slovak) (Křesťanské demokratické hnutí, or KDH)
CDP	Citizens Democratic party (Občanská demokratická strana, or ODS)
CDP(C)	Christian Democratic party (Czech) (Křesťanské demokratická strana, or KDS)
CEH	Common European Home
CF	Citizens Forum (Občanské fórum, or OF)
CFP	Farmers' party (Česká strana zemědělců, or ČSZ)
ČKD	Kolben-Daněk industrial plant
CM	Citizens Movement (Občanské hnutí, or OH)
Comecon	Council for Mutual Economic Assistance
CPBM	Communist party of Bohemia and Moravia (Komunistická strana Čech a Moravy, or KSČM)
CPC	Communist party of Czechoslovakia (Komunistická strana Československa, or KSČ)
CPP	Czech People's party (Česká lidová strana, or ČLS)
CSCE	Conference on Security and Cooperation in Europe
CSD	Czech Social Democracy (Česká sociální demokracie, or ČSD)
CSP	Czech Socialist party (Česká socialistická strana, or ČSS)
CUSC	Prague City University Students Council of the SUY (Městská vysokoškolská rada, or MVR SSM)
EEC	European Economic Community
GDR	German Democratic Republic

HCDM	Hungarian Christian Democratic Movement (Mad ǎrská křest̆ anské demokratické hnutí, or MKDH)
IMF	International Monetary Fund
IPA	Independent Peace Association (Nezávislá mírová iniciativa, or NMI)
KDU	Election coalition of CDP and CPP in 1990
KGB	Soviet secret police
MDS	Movement for a Democratic Slovakia (Hnutí za demokratické Slovensko, or HDS)
MSGD	Movement for Self-Governing Democracy—Society for Moravia and Silesia (Hnutí za samospravnou demokracii: společnost pro Moravu a Slezsko, or HSDSMS)
PDL	Party of the Democratic Left (Strana demokratické levice, or SDL)
PHM	Party of the Hungarian Minority (Egytéllés/Spolužitie, or ES)
RPC	Republican party of Czechoslovakia (Republikanská strana Československa, or RSČ)
RTUM	Revolutionary Trade Union Movement (Revoluční odborové hnutí, or ROH)
SCDU	Slovak Christian Democratic Union (Slovenská křest̆anská demokratická unie, or SKDU)
SDP	Social Democratic party
SNP	Slovak National party (Slovenská národní strana, or SNS)
SPIC	Student Press and Information Center (Studentské tiskové a informační středisko, or STIS)
StB	Czechoslovak secret police (Státní tajná bezpečnost)
STUHA	Students Movement (Studentské hnutí)
SUY	Socialist Union of Youth (Socialistická svaz mládež, or SSM)
TAMA	Theater Academy of Musical Arts (Divadelní akademie muzických úmění, or DAMU)

PART ONE

The Long Decay
of the Communist System
in Czechoslovakia

~1~

Normalization and Soviet Foreign Policy: Brezhnev to Gorbachev

The Soviet invasion of Czechoslovakia in August 1968 ended the optimum chance for a fundamental reform of a socialist regime and started the long process of the decay of communism that was to culminate in the Velvet Revolution just over two decades later. It dashed the hopes of a substantial section of the population, whose active involvement in public affairs had reflected a revitalization of their beliefs in both socialism and democracy. The main purpose of the reforms in 1968 was to revitalize socialism in its political and social dimensions by bringing in democracy and, in the economic field, market principles. The reformist program of the Communist party of Czechoslovakia (CPC), the Action Program of April 1968, was the culmination of a series of studies and reflections on the crisis in the socialist system throughout the 1960s. This program was based more or less on an influential study published by Radovan Richter under the auspices of the Czechoslovak Academy of Sciences that concentrated on the issue of how a socialist society should cope with the new conditions of the so-called scientific and technological revolution. In particular, it emphasized an increased role for the individual. Hence:

> Far more is expected of individual activity . . . and the growth of the individual acquires a wider social significance. Hitherto . . . individual initiative has been curbed by a mass of directives. We now face the necessity of supplementing economic instruments with sociopolitical and anthropological instruments that will shape the contours of human life, evoke new wants, model the structure of man's motivation, while enlarging and not

3

interfering with freedom of choice, in fact relying on a system of opportunities and potentialities in human development. An urgent task in this field, in which scientific and technological advance can make an especially hopeful contribution, is to bring into operation a variety of ways in which the individual can share in directing all controllable processes of contemporary civilization and to do away with some of the restricting, dehumanizing effects of the traditional industrial system.[1]

The Action Program sought to reestablish democracy not by the introduction of political pluralism but by the revitalization of the elective organs of the state, guaranteeing a full range of human rights (including, in particular, freedom of expression), while restructuring the leading role of the party. The CPC no longer intended to maintain itself by the monopolistic concentration of power in its own hands but by constantly winning over the people. This new stress on public support led directly to the abolition of censorship and the freeing of the public discourse from political controls, a process that helped generate various civic initiatives, including organizations of a political and social nature beyond the direction of the party. In effect, this development contradicted the notion of the leading role of the party as expounded and practiced by the Soviet Communist party and ultimately clashed with the Soviet view of what constituted socialism. This was the most significant factor in the Soviet decision to intervene.

Alexander Dubček's subsequent and enforced acceptance of the Moscow Protocols—an agreement between Soviet and Czechoslovak leaders to station troops in Czechoslovakia indefinitely—amounted to the legitimation of the Soviet invasion. It marked the acquiescence of the Czechoslovak government in a process that began with the gradual abandonment of the reforms worked out in 1968 and ultimately led to a period of full-blown "normalization." Insofar as the Velvet Revolution was the working out of public reaction to the normalized regime in changed international conditions, in this chapter we consider certain of its internal and external aspects that contributed to the crises leading to the subsequent undermining of Communist rule.

The first steps in the abolition of the gains brought about by the Prague Spring were taken with the surreptitious introduction of measures to reassert control over the media and to facilitate the abandonment or dilution of reforms. The manner of retreat from reform was an essential part of the strategy that aimed at preventing the open mobilization of public support for the preservation of reform. Though Dubček gave an assurance that the policies of 1968 would not be abandoned,[2] the Moscow Protocols effectively impelled the leadership to cancel the April Action Program on which many were based. Other reforms relating to federalization, however, were not abolished. Such conciliations, along with the temporary continuation of rehabilitation procedures and the drafting of the Enterprise Bill and a law for a system of workers councils, were an attempt to attract public attention away from the major reversals that froze out the Prague Spring. The central elements in the reform of the Communist party of Czechoslovakia and the decisions of the Vysočany Congress[3] of the party were declared void. Political pluralism was thwarted by the banning, largely at the instigation of the Soviets, of organizations such as KAN and K231.[4] The removal of the heads of television and radio was followed up after what party heads considered a decent interval by the abrogation of the law abolishing censorship in September 1969. Informal guidelines for publications had already been drawn up in January 1969, complementing various forms of direct pressure on journals and magazines. The abandonment of reforms went largely uncontested as the continued presence of Dubček at the head of the party helped reconcile, not to say pacify, the public to an acceptance of this eventuality. This held true, though in a shakier fashion, even at times when the emotional temperature of the population was raised by such events as the removal, under Soviet pressure, of the popular chairman of the National Assembly, the radical reformer Josef Smrkovský, early in 1969, the threat of a general strike, and, especially, the public suicide of the student Jan Palach in protest against the Soviet invasion. In April 1969, Dubček himself fell victim to the advance of normalization when he was removed from his post as first secretary of the party.[5] Nevertheless his having formally, if only nominally, helped initiate the normalizing process played a part in delegitimizing reform communism as a long-term proposition.

The apparent ambivalence surrounding the continued presence in office of Dubček and his colleagues, which amounted to the performance of a play designed to deceive the public, has long aroused controversy. Milan Šimečka, for example, rejects the view that their presence was essential in the attempt to rescue something from the wreckage of the reforms, which Smrkovský suggests in his memoirs. Šimečka believes it a part of Communist tradition and notes:

The art of leaving gracefully has never been the strongest suit of Communist politicians. Perhaps it is because real socialism never allows its politicians to leave with honor . . . and nobody has ever been very enthusiastic in wanting to be dumped on the rubbish heap of history. . . . Their slow retreat made them experience the bitterness, drop by drop. It was a long and probably pointless agony. Like everybody else, I was simply a spectator at this game, but like everybody, I was left with a feeling of embarrassment, moral disgust, and shame. Many people thereafter formed a permanent and unshakable conviction that politics was a filthy business. This sad spectacle has had a profound influence on the origin of mass apathy and in the choice of private preoccupation with personal well-being bought by formal agreement toward the civil power, though with the illusion of decency within the realm of private existence.[6]

This statement, which seems a fitting epitaph to the Dubček government, also hints at conditions contributing significantly to lasting public disillusion with Communist reformers, which virtually ensured that they would never be given a second chance. Indeed, this was borne out by events twenty years later in November 1989.

The Features of Normalization

The process of normalization introduced in 1969 was completed in its broad outlines by 1971. Though changes were made over the following years, its main features remained more or less constant. The protagonists of the new regime regarded the reforms associated with the Prague Spring as amounting to a counterrevolution that therefore justified Soviet intervention as a necessary act of socialist internationalism. Needless to say, this was in outright conflict with public feeling. The post-Dubček Czechoslovak government hence had no legitimacy and was underpinned by the force and threat of force whose most conspicuous embodiment was the permanent presence of Soviet troops. Yet the use of internal security forces and other instruments of state power also helped ensure civil compliance. The complete negation of the reforms of 1968 went beyond the political and applied equally to the economy. It was expressed in the move back to recentralization and was sweetened by modest economic growth supporting a reasonable and slightly improved standard of living.

The normalized regime rested on three main foundations. The first related to the purge of all major social and economic institutions, including the CPC itself, enabling the party leadership to reimpose central control and thereby reverse the trend to pluralization initiated in 1967. The system was maintained by the continuous threat or actual application of punishment for nonconformist behavior. The second element of normalization was strict control over the spread of ideas, involving a purge of all institutions engaged in the dissemination of knowledge and culture and especially of those, mainly the media, that provided the framework for public discourse. The media in fact became a mouthpiece for the regime, publicly proclaiming an ideology that though largely empty of meaning, helped to institutionalize and ritualize agreement and public acts of compliance for the purpose of justifying the developments of normalization. The reacquisition of centralized control over the economy provided the third pillar on which the regime's power rested. This involved a rollback of reforms, modest performance goals regarding the planned economy, and the evolution of a tendency to ignore major structural economic weaknesses in favor of dealing with short-term economic problems.

By the Fourteenth Congress of the CPC in 1971, the purge of leaders and all party members at every level involved in the reforms had been completed. The hard-line leadership elected at the congress established the complexion of the primary organs of the party, which remained more or less unaltered for the subsequent two decades. The purges did not abate, however, but continued throughout the 1970s. Though estimates vary, roughly half a million members, or one-third of the party, either resigned, were expelled, or were "deleted."[7] Of these, about 65,000 to 70,000 represented expulsions. However, it should be added that this did not represent an attack only on leading reformers in the party but also on the economy, for those affected often held prominent managerial positions in the institutions of state administration, especially in commerce. To cite only a single example from many, the director of the prestigious fine art publisher Odeon was dismissed and his position given to a card-carrying ex-waiter. The punitive economic and social sanctions, very often associated with loss of suitable employment, visited on those driven from the party could not fail to stir up bitter, if private, resentment that was added to the incipient apathy. This was soon reflected in attempts to emigrate to the West. When successful, these escapes prompted another round of sanctions directed at the relatives and immediate family of the departed; when not, they triggered the similar practice of informal punishment and, not infrequently, a custodial sentence. The period characterized by the "cleansing" of the party was followed by a recruitment drive, and by the end of 1977, the loss had essentially been made good with the admission of 400,000 new members. Despite the odium in which the public held the CPC, this was clearly a response of a careerist character to the party's establishment of a norm involving a strict ceiling on job opportunities for non–party members.

The purge of the institutions of knowledge was in some ways the most deleterious for society as a whole in that its stranglehold on education and the arts resulted in a "cultural desert," as the intelligentsia later described it. The regime found itself unable to control artists' associations and accordingly disbanded them, founding new artists' unions in their place. As the price of publication, writers were required to publicly disavow the events of the Prague Spring, which also became a condition of membership in the union. Refusal brought registration on a blacklist that not only made publication impossible but also served as the pretext for the disappearance of all previous works from public libraries and other institutions. Some of the best-known contemporary Czech writers, such as Václav Havel, Milan Kundera, and Ludvík Vaculík, were thereby erased from the literary scene. The control the CPC exercised over the media allowed no latitude whatever for the presentation of alternative views, and the public discourse that had burgeoned in 1968 was crushed into a lifeless and unmitigated monotony.

The universities, research institutes, and the entire educational spectrum of Czechoslovak society suffered in much the same way. The appointment of an extreme hard-liner as minister of education brought about the wholesale dismissal of academic and administrative staff who had been active or shown sympathy with reform communism. The education minister's campaign even involved the circulation of questionnaires requiring detailed information on the activities of both faculty and students in 1968 and 1969.[8] The purges went beyond their immediate targets insofar as they also touched the families of those directly affected. The normalized regime did not regard dismissal from employment or notice to quit accommodation as sufficient punishment but also exacted retribution from,• for instance, the children of targets, who were not infrequently barred from secondary and higher education. Ensuring compliance by using relatives as pawns in a game of blackmail became an established method of dealing with all opponents of the regime. The effects of this policy on Czech culture and education rapidly became visible not only in the profound decline in standards but also in the scale and social composition of illegal emigration. The number of such emigrants has been estimated at 170,000,[9] which, in that it was drawn largely from the intelligentsia, amounted to a significant brain drain. •

The purges in effect laid down general principles for establishing centralized control and social conformity. Within a few years of the suppressed revolution of 1956 in Hungary, the regime of Janoš Kadar felt confident enough to liberalize and substantially widen its framework of tolerance operating on the basis of the slogan, "He who is not against us is with us." The Czechoslovak government, in contrast, remained rigid and intolerant. Although Gustav Husák, Dubček's successor as first secretary of the CPC, repeatedly hinted at liberalization, all opponents of the regime, defined as much in terms of cultural as political nonconformity and including groups in the youth counterculture, became the subject of police attention. Interrogations, house searches, phone tapping, the interception of private correspondence, unlawful detention, and eventually arrests, trials, and imprisonment were added to the social sanctions available to the security forces in one way or another. Though the value of labor, and especially manual labor, was everywhere extolled by the regime, a favored form of coercion was to set recalcitrant members of the intelligentsia to work as unskilled laborers. Members of the Communist establishment obviously regarded this as degrading—further illustration of the emptiness of the government's official propaganda, which was entirely at odds with what the leaders believed.

Public Compliance

The public reaction was reflected in a mood of disillusionment and retreat into the private sphere (usually the family), as captured in the contemporary term *inner emigration*. An apt if symbolic example of this state of affairs was the preoccupation with country cottages. These modest, mainly wooden structures represented not simply temporary flight from city life in which urban pressures were exacerbated by the relentless confrontation with the ideological, but also a target for the meaningful investment of the work ethic that the public conspicuously failed to deliver in its economic performance during the week. The mushrooming of these "cottage reservations" attests to the debilitating effect of official ideology. On a more prosaic level, it also suggests widespread support for small-scale corruption in conditions of official scarcity of building materials.

The ideology of the normalized regime, though devoid of content, attempted more or less successfully to involve everyone in the system. Ritualized conformity with public ideology, often achieved under pain of social sanction, drew the individual into helping reproduce the system, thereby lending some credence to the regime. It enabled people in effect to collaborate in their own oppression. Havel has illustrated how this ideology operated. He uses the example of a greengrocer's putting up in his shop window a slogan—such as "Workers of the World, Unite!"— that does not represent his opinion. Havel explains his action as being in keeping with tradition and likewise as a hedge against trouble with the authorities. Putting up the sign is a token of compliance with the regime's demand for conformity, the real meaning of the act. The *content* of the slogan is unimportant; the greengrocer can refrain from contemplating its real significance. At the same time, this and similar ritualized acts of allegiance helped strengthen the regime and generalized a particular behavior pattern. Departure from this approved conduct was rare and treated as deviancy.[10]

The ideology of "actually existing socialism," as the normalized regime described itself, removed the developmental aspect of the concept of socialism and contradicted the Marxist notion of the withering away of the state. It was designed to underpin the central role of the state and provide some degree of crude legitimacy for the system. In practice, the public did not accept the doctrine at all, though insofar as they engaged formally in the rituals of the system, they conducted themselves publicly as if they did. This "as-if game," as it has been described,[11] involved those preaching the doctrine behaving "as if the ideological kingdom of real socialism existed in 'what we have here and now', as if they had in all earnestness convinced the nation of its existence; the nation behaves as if it believed it, as if it were convinced that it lived in accordance with this ideologically-real socialism. This 'as-if' is a silent agreement between the two partners."[12] Both sides benefited from this arrangement. The regime gained the nation's compliance with the rules it had laid down; in return, the people did not have to behave in the way the ideology prescribed. For instance, they were not required to work hard, a blind eye was turned to their pilfering and stealing, and free rein was given to the exploitation of patronage, which became more or less endemic. This state of affairs generated a monumental moral corruption that left few untouched. The game of pretend and pretense was nicely captured in one of the slogans of the revolution in November 1989 in Brno:

• The Seven Wonders of Czechoslovakia

Everybody has a job.
Although everybody has a job, nobody works.
Although nobody works, the Plan is fulfilled up to 105 percent.
Although the Plan is fulfilled up to 105 percent, there's nothing in the shops.
Although there's nothing in the shops, we've got enough of everything.
Although we've got enough of everything, everybody steals.
Although everybody steals, nothing ever goes missing anywhere.
And the Eighth Wonder of the World is that it has been working for forty-one years.[13]

Two other factors deriving from this ideology strongly influenced public morale. First, the public monopolization and perversion of the concept of socialism had deprived it of any constructive meaning, which ultimately induced leading dissidents to cease using the word altogether. Second, the existence of large-scale corruption among the Communist elite, who felt no inhibitions about misappropriating state funds, despite their privileges, high incomes, and guaranteed access to high-quality goods and services, became a justification for corruption among ordinary people. For instance, leading government and party officials commandeered labor and materials to construct their villas, whereas less-privileged citizens would filch what they could for their cottages. Miroslav Kusy puts it nicely: "Where leading members of the Nomenklatura stole from the nation wholesale, many ordinary citizens stole retail."[14] Another writer presents the moral corruption in starker terms: "People say, 'Where could I, my family, this country have been, if it hadn't been for Them! Surely that gives me the right to take back everything they've stolen from me.' A person's decision to relinquish his honesty is presented as a virtue. All inhibitions evaporate because people are free to imagine simply anything they have allegedly been deprived of by the regime—regardless of the fact that they may be incompetents, layabouts or thieves."[15] Implicit in the game of "as-if" was a social contract in which the regime in effect exchanged a guarantee about a reasonable living standard, unconnected to performance, for the public's grudging compliance with the normalization.

The only reform of 1968 to survive was federalization, by which both the Czech Lands[16] and Slovakia assumed republican status and contributed to the appearance that the Slovaks had gained from the normalization. The first secretary of the CPC from 1969 to 1987 was a Slovak, a matter of great symbolic importance. Further, Slovakia had done well economically. Consumer spending had risen from 68 percent of the level of the Czech Lands in 1953 to 93 percent by 1983. This relative equalization of living standards was due mainly to disproportionately higher levels of investment in Slovak industrialization,[17] though this kind of preferential treatment ignited some resentment among the Czechs. It was not allayed by Slovak resistance to ideas of economic reform in the early 1980s, which was based on fears of the social and economic consequences of the rationalization of their industrial structure, especially in the areas of heavy industry, armaments, and petrochemicals.

Organized Dissent: The Emergence of Charter 77

The relatively high level of public conformity should not be taken to imply that the normalized regime went unchallenged in the twenty years of its existence. Opposition can be traced back to those both within and outside the party who had retreated from the reforms. Some groups were relatively well organized and indulged in overtly political activity. On a broader and looser front were those operating in the cultural field whose push into opposition activity was related to the incidence and effects of the purges in the cultural sphere. Prominent were blacklisted writers who engaged in organizing the illegal publication of their own and banned foreign works through samizdat networks. By the mid-1970s, they had established links with the representatives of another main area of nonconformist activity, the youth counterculture, notably the rock group the Plastic People of the Universe and the jazz section of the Musicians' Union, the official organization of the country's professional musicians. Despite a widespread assumption that the state would not go to the lengths of invoking the judicial process to rein in the opposition, the first trials of opponents of the regime took place in 1972, and these were extended within a few years to take in the counterculture. This provided the spark for a section of the dissidents to organize themselves into Charter 77, which in a later reincarnation played a key role in the revolution. In its first declaration, it described itself as

> a free, informal, open community of people of different convictions, different faiths and different professions united by the will to strive individually and collectively for the respect of civil and human rights in our own country and throughout the world. . . . It does not form the basis of any oppositional activity. Like many similar citizens' initiatives, West and East, it seeks to promote the general public interest. It does not aim then to set out its own programme for political or social reforms or changes, but within its own sphere of activity, it wishes to conduct a constructive dialogue with the political and state authorities, particularly by drawing attention to various individual cases where human rights have been violated, by preparing documentation and suggesting solutions, by submitting proposals of a more general character aimed at reinforcing such rights and their guarantees and by acting as a mediator in various conflict situations and so forth.[18]

The issue of human rights enabled Charter 77 to form a broad coalition including reform Communists, Social Democrats, liberals, and conservative Catholics who, though quite disparate politically, all agreed on this question and on the need for an ethical basis to politics. It is worth mentioning, too, that because it was an organization run on democratic lines, no single group could take over. Its statement that it did not engage in overtly political activity, however, must be regarded as disingenuous in that Charter 77 had to be considered a serious challenge to the regime, which was obviously in violation of human rights. Many dissidents recognized and articulated this view themselves. Havel argued that the moral example set by refusing to live according to the official lie was sufficient to show the public that playing the government's "as-if" game was not necessary. This combination of "living in truth" and "antipolitical politics" operating through citizens' initiatives, was, as he successfully predicted, to provide a potent force for change. The regime overreacted to the implied threat of Charter 77, its campaign of vilification in the media bringing the group to the attention of a general public who had been largely unaware of its existence. This exercise did not prevent the dissidents from extending their reach geographically: They established connections with similar groups in Poland and Hungary, and their interest in the Helsinki process brought them into touch with groups in the West who recognized the importance of human rights in the peace process. Neither did they confine themselves to human rights, however, but also became involved in issues appealing more to the common folk, such as ecology. Environmental damage caused by the nature of the economy and reflected in certain regions in, for example, high child mortality and low life expectancy brought into existence citizens' initiatives that, though not overtly dissident, saw their natural allies in the dissident movement.

The significance of Charter 77 lay not simply in its message that it was not necessary to conform to the mores of an amoral state but equally in the personal example of the courage of its individual members, who withstood everything the state threw at them. Yet the organization was affected by a number of limitations, not least that its roots were largely, though not exclusively, in the intelligentsia of the major conurbations, principally in Prague and Brno. Because the dissidents were unable to publicize the movement widely and recruited members mainly through personal contacts, it is not surprising that Charter 77 was relatively isolated. Its message also complicated its efforts to broaden support nationally. In calling into question the bargain with the regime, the Chartists posed a challenge not just to the regime but also to the general public. This stirred up some resentment as it in effect represented a threat to people's livelihoods. Nevertheless, in the latter half of the 1980s, the generation gap provided an impetus to greater dissident activity, the young being much less subject to the control of the regime and accordingly neither demoralized nor sunk into apathy. Yet the fundamental challenge to the regime in the 1980s arguably lay in the oft-delayed solutions to structural economic problems that could no longer be put aside, whose nature and process would in fact cause the government to collapse.

The advent of internal normalization, as we have noted, followed from the Soviet invasion of 1968. The justification for this armed intervention into the internal affairs of a fellow socialist country derived from the Brezhnev Doctrine, the basic precepts of which had been formulated long before. This principle governed relations between the USSR and the countries of Eastern Europe and was based on the assertion that the interests of the socialist commonwealth of nations had perforce to take precedence over the sovereignty of each member state. This policy changed over time, particularly after Mikhail Gorbachev came to power in April 1985. These changes, which in their impact on the CPC and society in Czechoslovakia made a vital contribution to the collapse of Communist power, are the focus of the second part of this chapter.

Brezhnev and Beyond

The purpose of the Brezhnev Doctrine was not simply to justify the invasion; it was also designed to resolve some of the problems the de-Stalinization of the mid-1950s had caused for Soviet–East European relations. In 1955, and particularly at the Soviet party congress in 1956, the party leadership had publicly acknowledged that there was more than one road to socialism and recognized the right of each party to decide upon its policies and programs according to specific national differences. However, this posed the question of the acceptable extent of these differences of policy and the cognate problem of how to preserve the unity of the socialist camp under Soviet leadership. One of the crucial difficulties related to the uncertainty of where the boundaries of acceptable divergence and reform actually lay and, similarly, who decided them and on what basis. This lack of doctrinal clarity tended to induce the leaders of socialist states to believe that instances of Soviet reactions to past developments in Eastern Europe constituted, in effect, the laying down of guidelines informing their future decisionmaking. The course the Czech reformers took in 1968 reflects this ambiguity. In dealing with increasing Soviet criticism and pressure, the reformers did not readily believe they would invite Soviet intervention provided they refrained from repeating the policies of the Hungarians in 1956, namely, withdrawal from the Warsaw Pact and declaration of neutrality.

Although the Brezhnev Doctrine addressed some of these questions, it generated others. Applicable only to the members of the socialist commonwealth, it emphasized the leading role of the Soviet Union based on its military might and therefore its central role in the maintenance of socialism, as exemplified in the following statement: "Even if a socialist country seeks to take up an 'extra-bloc' position, it in fact retains its national independence thanks precisely to the power of the socialist commonwealth—and primarily to its chief force, the Soviet Union—and the might of its armed forces. The weakening of any link in the world socialist system has a direct effect on all socialist countries which cannot be indifferent to this." The doctrine also attempted to resolve the apparent contradiction between national sovereignty and allowable intervention by proclaiming:

The five allied socialist countries' actions in Czechoslovakia are consonant with the fundamental interests of the Czechoslovak people themselves. Obviously, it is precisely socialism that, by liberating from the fetters of an exploitative system, ensures the solution of the fundamental problems of national development in any country taking the socialist path. By encroaching on the foundations of socialism, the counter-revolutionary elements in

Czechoslovakia were thereby undermining the basis of the country's independence and sovereignty.[19]

Nowhere in the doctrine was socialism actually defined. It was therefore difficult to specify what could constitute a threat to it, or who and what procedures could identify such a threat. It was clear, however, that the doctrine could not be applied to the Soviet Union itself. Though useful as an instrument underpinning Soviet hegemony, the doctrine could not successfully imbue it with socialist legitimacy. If it did not establish the doctrinal boundaries to socialist divergence, it did imply that the Soviet government was in practice the arbiter of these matters. Problems relating to the lack of clarity hence remained, especially given that neither doctrine nor subsequent Soviet practice presupposed uniformity. Throughout the 1970s, there were indeed significant differences between the socialist countries. Even those of a neo-Stalinist character, such as Romania or the normalized regime in Czechoslovakia, were not identical, and these in turn were strikingly different from the reformist regime in Hungary. Some genuine mediation and bargaining of economic interests did indeed take place, though within relatively firm limitations. Nevertheless, the doctrine provided the ideological underpinning for the latent threat of Soviet intervention in any of the East European countries in case of either the initiation of unacceptable levels of governmental reform or the development of radical popular movements. It therefore served as a crucial external prop for maintaining unpopular governments in Eastern Europe. Though the advance of the Solidarity movement in Poland did not prompt Soviet intervention, it can be argued that a Soviet crackdown was averted only by the Polish government's declaration of martial law in 1981.

The doctrine also fit well with the Soviet conception of détente, involving superpower global management and the maintenance of spheres of influence in which each superpower recognized the other's hegemony. Détente, however, collapsed with the invasion of Afghanistan, the non-ratification of SALT II, and the advent of a new arms race in the early 1980s. The arms race in particular was an important contributory factor to the process of change in the Soviet Union, as the massive expenditures it would require could only exacerbate the problems of an already overstretched and stagnating economy. The most conspicuous reforms were initiated by Gorbachev, who on coming to power responded to the conditions of economic, political, military, and moral decline in the Soviet Union by building on the basis constructed under the administration of his predecessor, Yuri Andropov. Gorbachev's political and economic reforms, which came to be associated with the terms *perestroika* and *glasnost,* involved modernization, the introduction of a system of self-management, and moves toward the utilization of the market in the economic sphere. A democratization of public life was planned through the revitalization of the legislature, measures enabling a relatively free public discourse, and recognition of at least some form of pluralism. It is striking that the language of perestroika and glasnost in many ways resembled the language of the Czechoslovak reform movement of the 1960s. Because of this similarity, both the normalized regime in Czechoslovakia and the Soviet government found it difficult to maintain the claim that the Soviet invasion had been entirely proper and legitimate.

Gorbachev's "new thinking" also affected Soviet external relations, not least those with the socialist countries. The gradual abandonment of Marxist-Leninist dogmas regarding international relations was linked to a recognition that the position of the Soviet Union in the world had altered. Its stagnating and uncompetitive economy had fallen far behind the capitalist states and was incapable of providing the wherewithal for maintaining military parity with the West. In foreign policy, the proposal to revitalize détente was an implicit recognition that the Soviet Union was intent on ending its isolation from the world economy and on ultimately availing itself of opportunities in world markets.

The economic factors underlying the formulation of perestroika also generated pressure on the Soviet government for change in foreign policy. The drive to cut costs prompted a reconsideration of the benefits of maintaining a role as a military superpower. The new arms race threatened by the United States' Strategic Defense Initiative, and the crippling expense of military and economic aid in areas of the Third World (for instance, maintaining a military presence in the Horn of Africa) strongly suggested that the USSR could no longer afford superpower status based on military might. Recognizing the necessity to move away from an overdependence on military power, Gorbachev embarked on a series of both nuclear and conventional arms control initiatives as soon as he came into office. He himself noted in May 1988: "In our bid for military-strategic parity, we occasionally failed to use the available opportunities to attain security for our nation by political means and, as a result, allowed ourselves to be lured into an arms-race which could not but affect this country's social and economic progress and its standing on the international scene."[20]

The overall strategy of reducing costs generated an incentive to conflict reduction and an emphasis on peaceful coexistence. In contrast to the old notion formulated under Nikita Khrushchev and Leonid Brezhnev, the new perspective stressed the importance of peace over that of socialism and, in accepting that there were values humanity shared, introduced the concept of common interests. This in effect was an official recognition that Soviet security required the security of the United States.

An easing of the strongly competitive elements in East-West relations was expected to reduce military spending and, as a positive spin-off, to encourage economic cooperation, including the transfer of Western technology. "On a mutually beneficial and equal basis,"[21] the USSR would "become involved in the world division of labour and resources in a way never known before. Its great scientific, technological and production potential [would] become a far more substantial component in world economic relations."[22]

The replacement of class interests by common and national interests as the basis for Soviet international relations suggested the potential for cooperation with any other country.[23] Gorbachev floated the novel idea of the Common European Home (CEH), which he suggested involved "above all, a degree of co-operation, even if its states belong to different social systems and opposing military-political alliances."[24] This, however, did not prevent his acknowledging the special relationships between the great powers and their allies. As he observed, "the historical relations between Western Europe and the USA or, let us say, between the Soviet Union and the European socialist countries are a political reality. They cannot be ignored if a realistic policy is to be pursued. A different attitude could upset the existing equilibrium in Europe."[25] Gorbachev's statement indicates the dual importance to the Soviet government of reducing divisions in Europe yet protecting its unique position within Eastern Europe.

Soviet policy toward Eastern Europe showed no sign of massive and radical change on or after Gorbachev's accession to power. For the first few years, he stressed the need for economic reform as the primary means to increasing efficiency and to achieving a higher level of economic integration essential for developing the unity of the bloc. This was informed as much by the Soviet leaders' desire for improvement in the quality of goods exported from Eastern Europe to the Soviet consumer as by their goal of lowering Soviet costs of supplying Eastern European countries with cheap energy and raw materials. Economic efficiency implied reform, and this in turn meant growing diversity that could not fail to have important implications for the Brezhnev Doctrine. The tension between the recognition of diversity and the demands of unity was not lost on Gorbachev: "Today, the socialist world appears before us in all its national and social variety. This is good and useful. We have satisfied ourselves that unity does not mean identity and uniformity. We have also become convinced that there is no model of socialism to be emulated by everyone."[26] The dilemma for him was clear: To what extent should satellite socialist countries follow the Soviet Union in going reformist? Because the governments in those countries were not at all legitimate in the eyes of their populations, it was a moot point at that stage whether reform was possible without running the risk of its leading to the disintegration of socialism. This problem was particularly acute in Czechoslovakia, as the adoption of perestroika-type reforms by the government in Prague would imply that Dubček's policies of two decades earlier had been essentially correct. The very rationale of the normalized regime hence would disappear. This also helps to explain the USSR's great reluctance to publicly disassociate itself from the 1968 invasion and the Brezhnev Doctrine. Gorbachev noted in 1987:

> The evaluation of the events of 1968 in Czechoslovakia is above all a matter for the Czechoslovak comrades themselves. Since that time, the leadership of the CPC headed by Gustav Husák has completed a massive amount of work. Czechoslovakia has made great strides in many different ways. I personally became convinced of this during my recent visit. We have seen that the Czechoslovak comrades in accordance with their own conditions are also looking for ways of improving socialism. They have their own problems and are solving them.[27]

Gorbachev was treading a fine line between, on the one hand, supporting and encouraging these kind of reforms in Eastern Europe and, on the other, hoping to prevent instability and upheaval. The governments in Eastern Europe did not react in the same way to the possibility of reform. Some, like Hungary and to some extent Poland, were enthusiastic; others, like Czechoslovakia and the German Democratic Republic (GDR), displayed outright opposition.

By mid-1988, Gorbachev's policy statements had indicated the shift toward a de facto abandonment of the last vestiges of the Brezhnev Doctrine. The qualification placed on national sovereignty by common socialist interest was gradually jettisoned and, if anything, an emphasis was placed on international law:

> In a situation of unprecedented diversity in the world, the imposition of a social system, a way of life or policies from outside by any means, let alone military, are dangerous trappings of past epochs. Sovereignty and independence, equal rights and non-interference are becoming universally-recognized rules of international relations which is in itself a major achievement of the 20th century. To oppose freedom of choice is to come out against the objective tide of history itself. That is why power politics in all its forms and manifestations is historically obsolete.[28]

Toward the end of 1988, this shift was reflected in policy allowing and even supporting major changes in Hungary and Poland; in the case of the latter, for example, Wojciech Jaruzelski had opened negotiations with Solidarity. In a further emphasis on glasnost, the Soviet government expressed its willingness to allow a public reexamination of past events that had bedeviled relations among socialist countries. The investigation of the Katyn massacre[29] and the subsequent public acceptance of responsibility showed this commitment to be genuine. Given the changes in Poland, this also required a greater response from the Communist government to the demands of its people.

The economic situation and the deepening nationality crisis in the Soviet Union were reflected in the early part of 1989 in further shifts in Soviet policy. Violent clashes between Soviet troops and civilians in Georgia, for example, and the massacre of students in Beijing by the Chinese army raised the possibility that public dissatisfaction could lead to loss of control by unpopular regimes. Gorbachev thereafter became much less willing to prop up the more unresponsive, conservative regimes, as he indicated in a speech at the end of February 1989 that amounted to a reversal of the Brezhnev Doctrine:

Complete independence, full equality, absolute non-interference in internal affairs, the correction of distortions and mistakes resulting from the previous history of socialism, more profound and scientifically-based analysis of mutual interests, solidarity and mutual assistance implies the responsibility of the parties and governments of all socialist countries to their peoples. Encouraging these processes in one's own country means furthering the cause of world socialism and advancing the general progress of mankind.[30]

Yet the accelerating changes in Poland and Hungary added to the reluctance of Czechoslovakia and the GDR to respond to popular demands, and the USSR's need for Western aid caught Gorbachev in an impossible dilemma. He wanted neither a loss of Soviet control in Eastern Europe nor changes of regime involving antisocialist movements. He could not, however, countenance the use of force by either the Soviet or national armies, as this would have brought about the collapse of the entire policy of perestroika. Still placing his hopes in reform communism, he believed the ideal solution, in theory, would be to sponsor the emergence of flexible, Communist reformers capable of coping with and responding to public demands. These were not readily available, and, in any case, there was no guarantee that this arrangement would have been acceptable to the peoples of Eastern Europe. Nonetheless, when Miloš Jakeš, the first secretary of the CPC, visited Moscow in April 1989, Gorbachev warned him that though "the specific status of every country implies differences in the character of the policies and the choice for the optimal pace of reform, what is common to all is the need to make continuous headway to keep pace with the requirements of society and the sentiments of the mass of the people."[31] In October Gorbachev offered similar views to Erich Honecker, head of the GDR: "Life is setting ever-new tasks and the main thing for communists is to respond to current social needs and the feelings of the masses."[32]

Provided that the changes in Eastern Europe would not result in major instability and strongly anti-Soviet regimes, the Soviet leadership was ready to accept nonsocialist governments—which it subsequently did with some grace. For example, Gorbachev informed the new Polish prime minister that: "We have different views, our life experience differs as do our world view and political orientation. But the realization of the most important fact that the Soviet Union and Poland are both interested in good-neighbourly relations creates a basis for mutual understanding on a broad range of issues."[33]

In the course of the revolutions in Eastern Europe, Gorbachev made a statement that was far removed from the Brezhnev Doctrine and amounted to an epitaph to Soviet rule in the region:

What is taking place in socialist countries is the logical outcome of a certain stage of development which made the peoples aware of the need for change. This is the result of internal developments, the result of choice by the peoples themselves. For all the specificity of profound changes in socialist countries, one cannot deny that they proceed in the mainstream of our perestroika, although we have in no way encouraged these processes. In some socialist countries, the situation has been out of the ordinary. Fraternal parties are no longer ruling in Poland and Hungary. Our friends in the GDR and Czechoslovakia have largely lost their positions. New political forces have emerged. They include those who support the socialist idea and those who seek other ways of social development. . . . The situation arising demands from us the elaboration of a clear-cut approach to the processes and the way there and to our contacts with the new political forces and organizations. . . . We welcome positive changes while fully realizing both the domestic and international difficulties accompanying them. The Soviet Union is building its relations with the East European countries on a unitary position of respect for sovereignty, non-interference and recognition of freedom of choice. We proceed from the fact that every nation has the right to decide its own fate including its own choice of system, the paths, the tempo and the methods of its development.[34]

With some qualification, his statements can be taken at their face value. His relatively cautious policy did not initiate these revolutionary changes but, together with the emphasis on reform, helped create the conditions in which they could take place. In the end, the Soviet government was not able to reconcile the contradictory demands of sanctioning reform yet maintaining control and helping to legitimize socialist governments in Eastern Europe.

The internal and external foundations of the power of the normalized regime in Czechoslovakia underwent significant changes in the latter half of the 1980s. The use and threat of force over two decades had amply demonstrated to the majority of citizens that it was more prudent to accept what they had, as things would not improve anyway and the process of attempting betterment would in the end only make them worse off. If public fear diminished and the conviction that nothing would change disappeared, however, the government could expect major difficulties. If, as indicators in this period suggest, economic difficulties grew into a crisis requiring radical solutions, the regime would be caught in an impossible situation. The failure to satisfy people's expectations would weaken the government's grip on power, but the implementation of drastic economic changes would lead to adverse and uncontrollable consequences that were bound to spread across most social groups. The illegitimate government, unwilling to act upon Gorbachev's advice and unable to cope with the gradual evaporation of fear prompted by the example of dissident and countercultural activity and the effect of a distant perestroika, would find itself with a diminishing ability to use force to preserve itself and a declining capacity to deal with economic difficulties. The Czechoslovakian regime's troubles initially erupted in the form of social crises; these provide the focus of the next chapter.

~2~

The Czechoslovak Regime in Crisis: August 1988 to October 1989

The relationship between the CPC and Czechoslovakian society was under some strain by the early months of 1988. As described in the previous chapter, the social contract between the Communist rulers and the ruled involved an implicit bargain wherein the government provided reasonable standards of living and security in exchange for refraining from activities threatening the stability of the regime. For instance, price levels of basic products had not changed significantly for twenty years or more, and the government saw to continuity of employment with a guaranteed income, for which no great performance was generally required. The regime also tolerated varying degrees of pilfering and turned a blind eye to those doing private work on company time. In return, the people on the whole acquiesced in the "normalization," not only by not engaging in activities expressing direct opposition to the regime but also by abstaining from activities expressing or generating attitudes that tended to undermine social conformity. In addition, periodic participation in acts of ritualized yet empty support for the regime was de rigueur. This state of affairs allowed the regime to continue to function according to Article 4 of the republic's constitution, which guaranteed the leading role of the party, and to remain a highly inflexible political organization opposing any demands for radical reform. In practice, this led on the one hand to the people's retreat into the private sphere of relatively isolated family units and on the other to the party's strict control of all public activity. Such control was vital to the maintenance of a regime lacking any basic legitimacy.

The sources of threat to this arrangement and to the stability of the regime arose from three major internal and external developments: the growth of public criticism, economic difficulties, and the changes in Eastern Europe. The mushrooming of dissident groups and the appearance for the first time since 1968 of public demonstrations weakened the notion that the regime was beyond criticism. Further, the power of the state to deal with public criticism and opposition by the exclusive use of repressive measures was limited, as in at least one area of popular concern—namely, ecology—the government itself was forced to recognize the existence of a severe problem. Air, water, and soil pollution derived from the outmoded general structure of the economy, with its emphasis on archaic heavy industry requiring enormous energy consumption and its lack of incentives and capital for dealing with the problem. The complications for the party hence involved restructuring the economy while limiting the social and political impact of such reform and solving the dilemmas associated with a shortage of capital. The external sources of trouble were related to the development of economic and political reforms in the Soviet Union and with the accelerating drive for political pluralism and a market economy in some of the neighboring socialist countries. These changes produced direct and indirect pressures. In the former case, the relations between Czechoslovakia and its partners in the Council for Mutual Economic Assistance (Comecon) and the Warsaw Pact were complicated by the growing divergence of policies within the individual countries, which on occasion threatened to undermine cooperation. In the latter case, the changes in the Soviet Union, which could not be kept from influencing Czechoslovakian society, altered the previous sense of resignation and provided a stimulus for the contemplation of the possibility of change. In 1989 this belief was strengthened enormously by the far-reaching reforms taking place in Hungary, Poland, and, eventually, East Germany.

Growth of Public Criticism

The year 1988 represented a point of departure in terms of the emergence of the novel phenomenon of public demonstrations that went ahead without government approval. They were significant for a number of reasons. First, as noted in the previous chapter, such protest was a fundamental challenge to the system in which the pretense of complete public agreement was accepted as the sole form of apparent legitimation. A dangerous precedent was created when people visibly demonstrated that it was no longer necessary to abide by the requirements of public loyalty. As early as 1986, public opinion polls indicated that a large proportion of the population did not agree with either the ideology or the policies of the party, though there were as yet few public signs of this dissatisfaction.[1] As already noted, however, the regime did not demand that people actually believe in the official propaganda, rather that they behave publicly as if they did. The unauthorized demonstrations of 1988 brought out the unambiguously repressive nature of the regime and generated a great deal of adverse publicity at home and especially abroad.

Repression affected different generations in different ways. The younger generation, who not seldom formed a majority at demonstrations, were not vulnerable to the same types of indirect oppression as their elders, insofar as they were not employed and had no dependents. Neither had they experienced as adults the trauma of 1968 and the repressive normalization that followed. Their elders, by contrast, had more or less reconciled themselves to a situation marked by resignation and conformity to ensure that they would survive "in comfort." Explicit social sanctions therefore had a much weaker impact on the young in 1988, and the state had little or no option but to use force to attempt to keep them under control. Arguably, the central difficulty confronting the state was that the younger generation, having been brought up entirely under the conditions of the normalized socialist regime and with no long history of involvement in organized dissent, was impossible to marginalize and isolate in the same way as the explicitly dissident groups. The manner in which the security forces dealt with the demonstrators—the use of armored transporters, water cannon, and trained dogs—brought out the quasi-terroristic character of the regime and its ham-fisted way of dealing with any overt opposition. The cumulative effect of these demonstrations and violent acts of repression affected public consciousness. It is reasonable to assume that increasing numbers of people, starting with relatives and friends of the demonstrators, were forced to take a view on the rights and wrongs of the demonstrators' case and the government's response. In these conditions, resignation and apathy became more difficult to sustain.

Despite police brutality, the number of demonstrations increased from mid-1988, indicating that the policy of repression had not proved an effective deterrent. The first major public demonstration took place in Prague on August 21, 1988, and commemorated the twentieth anniversary of the invasion of Czechoslovakia. Some 10,000 demonstrators, mainly young people, marched through the center of Prague chanting slogans in favor of freedom. Others expressed support for Gorbachev. Near the site of Jan Palach's self-immolation of January 1969, Tomáš Dvořák and Hana Marvanová, two leading members of the Independent Peace Association (IPA), read out a petition denouncing the invasion as a crime and demanding its public reassessment. Democratic elections, the abolition of censorship, and the rehabilitation of the victims of political persecution figured among the other demands. The procession to Old Town Square was swollen by numerous passersby and was applauded by residents along the route. Toward the end of the demonstration, when numbers had declined to about 1,000, the police dispersed the crowd with tear gas and batons in the vicinity of the National Theater. Although several arrests were made, members of Charter 77 were not much in evidence, as most had left Prague to preempt arrest, the standard practice of the government in dealing with dissidents before an important anniversary or other public event. The authorities were nonplussed to discover that the source of protest was outside the expected dissident quarter, which helps to explain the hesitation of the security forces. The cause and course of the demonstration, the nature of popular participation in and public response to it, together with the publicly made demands raised fundamental questions about a government that had come into existence as a result of the Soviet invasion and that had been both architect and executor of the repressive normalization that followed it.

On October 28, 1988, an unofficial demonstration went ahead in spite of a vituperative press campaign indicating unambiguously that demonstrators would be subject to the full force of the law. In addition to making the preparations of the security forces highly visible, the government had taken other preemptive steps, such as the house arrest and detention of some leading activists. Among those detained were not only the established Charter 77 dissidents but also the young members of the Independent Peace Association who had been involved in the August demonstration. The government also attempted to minimize the chances of a high turnout by declaring October 28 a public holiday for the first time since 1968. The twofold purpose behind this declaration was to appropriate the anniversary of the founding of the republic and, because the day fell on a Friday, to give most people an opportunity to go to their country cottages for a long weekend. Nevertheless, some 5,000 gathered in Wenceslas Square chanting "Freedom! Freedom!" and "Masaryk" (the name of the founder of the republic and its first president). Police intervention this time was swift and brutal, involving truncheons, water cannon, and tear gas. A number of people, including bystanders, were beaten, and scores were detained. The general significance of this event, apart from the obvious willingness of the state to use force and of people to take to the streets, lay in its questioning of national identity and in the political use and significance of national symbols. This was as important for the regime as for the opposition. For the latter, the First Republic involved democracy and national independence, a stark contrast to the nature of the normalized regime. Popular association of national identity with the First Republic provided for the possibility of treating the regime as ultimately alien to what the nation was or ought to be. The government, well aware of the public's esteem for Tomáš Masaryk's republic, attempted to appropriate its heritage. In the government's organization of a meeting the day before the demonstration, Miroslav Štěpán, head of Prague's Communist party organization, referred positively to some aspects of the First Republic, in particular its guarantee of democratic rights, yet added that only the CPC at the time had understood the republic's weaknesses, thereby implying that the CPC had inherited all that was best (but not what was worst) of the republic.[2]

The fortieth anniversary of the Universal Declaration of Human Rights on December 10, 1988, saw the next public demonstration organized by the independent dissident groups in Prague. It was unique in that it was the only such demonstration that was officially sanctioned. Approval was due at least partly to the official visit of President François Mitterrand of France, the main object of which was his stated intention to address the issue of human rights. All independent groups, including Charter 77, the IPA, and the Committee for the Defense of the Unjustly Prosecuted (known locally as VONS), were represented in the crowd of roughly 5,000. Particularly striking was the appearance of slogans and leaflets, which had not been seen for decades. A petition demanding the release of political prisoners was circulated. Some of the best-known dissidents, including Havel, appeared on a public forum. This action alarmed the government, as it showed that the emollient approach had its own difficulties. Protests were raised by the People's Militia, and the Central Committee by all accounts reached the conclusion that a repetition of such an event could not be permitted. The issue of human rights provided the basis for disparate political groups to come together on a common platform. Further, such protest made it difficult for the government to suppress human rights, as it was a signatory to human rights agreements and was, at the same time, under pressure from both West and East to ensure that those rights were not violated.

The government's shift toward a harder-line approach to the problem of containing public demonstrations is well illustrated by the police interventions during the so-called Palach Week beginning January 15, 1989, to commemorate a young student who had committed suicide to protest the Soviet occupation. All demonstrations associated with this anniversary had been banned by the government ten days beforehand. Yet several thousand people met at various places in Prague on the first day. The police responded with indiscriminate force, including the use of water cannon in freezing temperatures, tear gas, and arrests. The most significant of these occurred on the second day, with the detention of some of the leading dissidents, among them Havel, who was subsequently charged and sentenced to nine months in jail. The nature of the intervention and the government's stance caused it great embarrassment, not

least as its representatives were at that time present at a meeting of the
Conference on Security and Cooperation in Europe (CSCE) in Vienna to
finalize new commitments to human rights. The U.S. delegate condemned the Czechoslovak government for violations of the Helsinki
agreement.[3] Even the Soviet government, which was publicly committed
to the idea of the Common European Home, with its emphasis on
peaceful and cooperative relations and on human rights, seemed disturbed by the situation. The Soviets had little interest in seeing the
further destabilization of the situation in Czechoslovakia, which perhaps
explains why the Soviet Communist party newspaper *Pravda* published
an article on January 20 roundly criticizing the organization of the
demonstration in Prague.

The government's use of force and the imprisonment of leading dissidents produced strong reactions at home and abroad. About 400 people
signed a public petition demanding the release of Havel. In an open
letter, a relatively large number of artists, among others, likewise demanded Havel's release and further appealed for an end to police violence
and for the opening of a dialogue between party and opposition. A
second open letter addressed to the prime minister came from 670
members of the academic and scientific community. Later endorsed by
2,000 other intellectuals, it pressed the need for an open dialogue, free
access to information, and democratization leading to a pluralist democracy. These letters eventually paved the way to the most important
petition; entitled "Several Sentences," it began to circulate at the end of
June and by September had collected 40,000 signatures. Its limited list
of demands included the release of all political prisoners and the implementation of basic freedoms and human rights and a reevaluation of the
events of 1968.[4]

The government's robust approach was again manifested at an alternative May Day demonstration held in the afternoon after the ceremonies
had been concluded. The predominantly young people gathered at
Wenceslas Square repeated demands expressed at previous actions, with
the important difference that they also showed support for Gorbachev.
(The security forces did their work in the customary way, and in the
process Gorbachev's portrait was demolished.) The pattern of confrontation established in this and previous demonstrations held, too, for the
protest actions later in the year, in August and October. There was even
evidence of solidarity among protestors from other Eastern European
countries: At the August demonstration, nine Hungarians and three Poles
were among those arrested.

Apart from these expressions of direct opposition to the government,
there were other examples of protest activities linked to the state's policy
toward religious freedom and in particular the Catholic church. For

instance, 2,000 mainly elderly women demonstrated in Bratislava on March 25, 1988, and in early December 1988, in Olomouc an unreported demonstration took place that involved 1,000 Moravian Catholics. This was part of the steady revival of religion from the late 1970s, associated above all with the Catholic church, that whittled away at the core of the totalitarian structure of the regime. The higher clergy, in particular Cardinal Tomášek, the archbishop of Prague, were active in this process. Tomášek's petition, "Suggestions of Catholics for the Solution of the Position of the Faithful," written in March 1988 to protest the state's treatment of believers, was signed by 600,000 people. Further, his Easter message appealing for "The Spiritual Renewal of the Nation" as a preparation for the millennial celebrations of Saint Vojtěch, an early Czech émigré who had fled from religious persecution, also found a resonance, especially with the many families who had lost someone to the West.

This period was characterized by the emergence of numerous dissident and independent opposition groups in addition to the old, established ones. Though they did not involve large numbers of people, they represented a range of interests from human rights to the environment; the Social Defense Initiative Group founded in 1988 and the ecology group Brontosaurus were typical examples. Most were formed as independent citizens' initiatives and had no intention of mounting a direct challenge to the state, though the government ultimately thought otherwise. For instance, those concerned with peace issues, such as the Independent Peace Association, embarrassed the officially sponsored peace organizations. Although the regime supported independent peace initiatives in the West, it was anxious to maintain control of peace as an issue in its own backyard. Of particular concern to the government was that the peace movements linked peace to justice, democracy, and human rights.

Another problem the government faced was the issue of ecology. In an area of great and growing public concern, independent green organizations frequently raised damning criticisms of the government. Even official organizations were increasingly and publicly critical of national policy toward the environment. This concern had also begun to permeate the highest organs of the state. As a result, the government was unsure how to deal with independent green organizations: Though it was theoretically possible to restrict their channels of communication to the public, the government was unable to do so in conditions when their message was being more or less repeated through official ecological organizations, such as the Czechoslovak Union of Environmentalists. Neither was the regime willing to confront the difficulties inherent in a cleanup, as this would force it to address the problem of the structural deficiencies of the economy.

Economic Difficulties

By the late 1980s, the government was facing certain economic woes linked to the structure of industry. Though Czechoslovak industry produced a wide range of products, it was relatively uncompetitive and therefore unable to find a place in Western markets that would allow it to satisfy the essential need for capital for reinvestment. Trade within the Comecon area was becoming an increasingly difficult problem given the likelihood of basic changes in the trading relations of the countries involved. The Soviet Union, in particular, presented the largest area of uncertainty.

Questions concerning the economy were related to the pressing need to reduce high-energy input into industries such as steel, fertilizers, and petrochemicals so as to liberate capital for modernization and investment in areas of low-energy high technology. Comparison with the structure of Western economies indicated that industry in Czechoslovakia was outmoded and reflected the need for sectoral change. Traditional industries, principally heavy industry and metallurgy, formed the core of Czechoslovak industry and produced at high cost as a result of spiraling energy costs and low worker productivity. The difficulties were thus twofold: how to reduce the costs of production and how to achieve far-reaching structural change without introducing the concept of the market or accepting the major social costs involved. A number of influential economists in the official institutes, such as the Institute of Economic Forecasting, regarded that as impossible. Karel Dyba, for example, argued that a radical change in the engineering and metallurgical industries might involve laying off 2 million workers. He noted that a real market was necessary to prove that Czechoslovakia could not, for example, continue to produce one ton of steel for each of its 15 million inhabitants.[5] The regime was unwilling to contemplate the introduction of the market, and even if it had been so inclined, it could not have afforded to introduce radical changes resulting in large-scale unemployment; only a genuinely politically legitimate government could possibly attempt to do that. A regime based on an absolute rejection of the 1968 reforms could not even deal with less radical solutions.

Changes in Eastern Europe

This developing crisis took place in the context of changes in the whole of the region that had a powerful impact on both the population and the government in Czechoslovakia. These changes were most apparent in Poland and Hungary, where the regimes most openly expressed their support for perestroika and Gorbachev. In Poland, the acceleration of the process toward radical changes dated to the end of August 1988, when the government responded to the largest wave of industrial strikes since 1981 by expressing its willingness to enter discussions on the country's future with Lech Walesa, the leader of the banned trade union, Solidarity. Though this did not entail the legalization of Solidarity, it clearly implied an official recognition of the importance of Solidarity's role in the process of resolving the deep-rooted crisis in Poland. Roundtable talks beginning in mid-September 1988 led first to an agreement on the legalization of Solidarity. A package of reforms was subsequently accepted and later passed by the Polish Parliament on April 7, 1989. This followed the announcement of a fresh constitutional arrangement of March 9 creating a second chamber, the senate, and an executive presidency. Elections to this body were planned for June, and the new electoral law gave every Polish citizen the right to run provided the candidate had the backing of a political party or social group or was supported by a petition with 5,000 signatures. Both provisions reflected a significant move toward genuine pluralism and a major step away from the doctrine and practice of the party's leading role. These agreements were reached after protracted and often acrimonious negotiations in which internal sources of dispute, including the Catholic church, were as conspicuous as the external. The Polish government was then faced with a deep financial crisis connected with an inability to meet its interest payments and accordingly sought the aid of the French, West German, and British governments for the rescheduling of its debts. These governments, which had cut economic links with Poland in 1981 following the declaration of martial law, thereafter insisted on the legalization of Solidarity and a move toward pluralism as a precondition for any such help.

Elections were held on June 5 and 19; though the turnout was only 60 percent, Solidarity won a spectacular victory: 99 seats out of 100 in the senate and all 161 in the lower house in the second round of voting. Of the 65 percent of seats Solidarity was not allowed to contest in the lower house, the Polish Communist party was allocated 38 percent, and the rest went to the allied parties and independent Catholics. The outcome demonstrated that if there had been genuinely free elections, the Communist party would have been swept out of office; it was clear that the party had little legitimacy. The complicated arrangement arrived at in April ensured that whatever the popular will, the Communist party would retain power, a setup designed to provide reassurance to the Soviet government. This expedient, however, started unraveling soon after the elections. Even though it still gave the presidency to General Jaruzelski—if by the narrowest margin—it failed to deliver the installation of a Communist-led government under General Czeslaw Kiszczak. The reason for this was that the subservient and reliable minor parties previously allied to the Communist party deserted it at the critical juncture and went over to the anti-Communist camp. This switch in support was instrumental in bringing about the first non-Communist government in Eastern Europe since 1947 as Tadeusz Mazowiecki, the Solidarity representative, was named prime minister on August 19. His government was committed to achieving full political pluralism and rapid economic change. Within weeks, under the guidance of Leszek Balcerowicz, the economics minister, plans were laid to transform the Polish centrally planned economy into a market economy.

Hungary had a history of reform under the Kadar regime. Kadar's support for perestroika was reciprocated by the esteem in which the Soviet government held Hungary. One of the strongest limitations on the development of reform in Hungary, however, was the unquestioned leadership of the Communist party. When it came, the fall of Kadar was important not only for its symbolic significance but also for accompanying personnel changes, which weakened the grip of the more conservative party leaders. Under the new leadership of Karoly Grosz, the party on the one hand expressed a commitment to the maintenance of the principle of democratic centralism. On the other, however, it inaugurated a policy of socialist pluralism, with guaranteed rights for citizens to create new institutions representing their own views and interests even if different from those of the party. Legislation was planned allowing voluntary association and religious freedom. Various opposition groups began to organize themselves thereafter, and in January 1989 legislation was enacted that approved in principle the right to form not merely voluntary organizations and associations but also political parties. This marked the formal advent of political pluralism in Hungary.

Growing public concern for the state of the economy and the environment obliged the Hungarian government on occasion to change its policy, for instance, on the ecological effects of the Gabčikovo dam project. Though this switch reflected a growing responsiveness to the public, it brought the Hungarian regime into conflict with the Czechoslovak government, which had almost completed its part of the project. Sensitivity to public feelings was also visible in the increasing stratification in the party. The balance of power was gradually shifting to the more popular, radical wing led by Imre Pozsgay. At the end of January 1989, Pozsgay was able to state on Budapest radio that a draft report of the special party committee to reassess the country's history had concluded that the Hungarian uprising of 1956 had not been a counterrevolution but a popular insurrection. Despite resistance from the diehards, Grosz confirmed this interpretation in a speech at a crucial Central Committee meeting on February 12. This new interpretation of 1956 was dramatically affirmed by the solemn public reburial of Imre Nagy and his comrades, the leaders of the uprising, on June 16.

The emergence of political pluralism was further exemplified by the appearance of new groups, the transformation of older dissident groups into political parties, and the revival of those parties (for instance, the Smallholders party) abolished after 1948. The outright victory of the Hungarian Democratic Forum, with the support of the other non-Communist groups, in the August by-elections demonstrated the shift of public opinion against even the reform Communists. The transformation of the party was completed at the congress beginning on October 7, when it was renamed the Hungarian Socialist party. By the end of the year, however, the old guard had reemerged under its former name, still loyal to Grosz. Even though the party was not formally voted out of office until March 1990, to all intents and purposes October 1989 marked the end of the Communist regime in Hungary.

Throughout the 1980s, the German Democratic Republic had one of the most conservative regimes in Eastern Europe. Unlike the Czechoslovak leadership, it did not even pay lip service to perestroika, claiming that as its system was working satisfactorily, such reforms were unnecessary. The inertia of the East German government can be gauged by Honecker's refusal in early October 1989 to heed Gorbachev's warning that governments failing to respond to popular wishes put themselves in grave danger. At the same time, the East German regime provided some comfort for the Czechoslovak government, which, with Romania, formed a kind of conservative axis within the Warsaw Pact and Comecon. Yet major economic and environmental difficulties gave rise to public dissatisfaction with living conditions within the GDR. The danger for the regime lay in that this discontent was expressed in people's desire and efforts to emigrate to West Germany—long the issue on which the state was most vulnerable. It is not therefore surprising that the crisis that ultimately led to the demise of the state was sparked off by a significant number of vacationing East Germans who attempted to leave for the West from Hungary in the summer of 1989. As a country bordering the West and with a reformist regime, Hungary was identified as offering the best opportunity for escape, as well as an accessible meeting place for divided German families. Throughout the summer, relatively large numbers of East Germans tried to escape, whereas others sought refuge in the West German embassy in Budapest.

Already experiencing difficulties with the flood of refugees from Romania, Hungary eventually decided to resolve the problems posed by the East Germans by letting them leave through the open border with Austria. This was in contravention of the 1969 treaty with East Germany, which committed both countries to preventing each other's citizens from leaving for third countries without permission. Within thirty-six hours of the opening up of the borders to the East Germans on September 10, 10,000 of them had left in packed trains and decrepit cars. Vivid pictures of this jubilant exodus flashed across television screens in both Eastern and Western Europe. Combined with the legal emigration of 50,000 citizens from the beginning of the year, the mass departure helped to create significant labor shortages in some East German industries. The émigrés were generally young and skilled, people the regime could least afford to lose. News of the exodus provided the spark for massive demonstrations centered in Leipzig. Citizens were soon calling not only for freedom of travel but even for free elections, freedom of the press, and the legalization of New Forum, the largest opposition group. These demonstrations escalated from a few thousand in Leipzig in the last week of September to 70,000 in East Berlin on October 9. The Leipzig demonstrations held every Monday evening grew thereafter from 70,000 to almost half a million by mid-November.

With the support of Moscow, the reformist elements within the East German Communist party responded by replacing Honecker with Egon Krenz on October 18. The new government attempted to stem the tide of popular discontent by making various concessions, opening roundtable talks and, on November 9, making the crucial decision to allow freedom of travel. Neither these concessions nor even the appointment of Hans Modrow—the most prominent reformer in the East German Communist party—as prime minister satisfied the public; by mid-November their demands went far beyond the call for the introduction of democracy in East Germany to the demand for full-blown reunification—in effect, the dismantling of the East German state. After the East German government had announced the right of all citizens to travel, West Germany received some 4 million East Germans over the weekend of November 10 and 11. Sections of the Berlin Wall, the most visible symbol of the division of Europe, were torn down, making an enormous and immediate impression on the millions who watched on television in both East and West.

These changes in Eastern Europe were significant to Czechoslovakia in at least three separate but related ways: in their direct impact on the government, in the effects on the population, and in the regime's response to the people's reaction. In the first case, the government became increasingly isolated within Comecon and the Warsaw Pact. This complicated its economic difficulties in such a way that there were unambiguously negative consequences for trade relations and economic integration. In addition, mounting conflict with reformist regimes was apparent—for instance, with Hungary over the Gabčikovo project. The Czechoslovak government's anxiety over popular opposition to the scheme was apparent in its condemnation of the Hungarian television interview with Dubček in May 1989. Given the changes in Bulgaria in the second week in November, in which reformists had replaced Todor Zhivkov and his associates, and leaving aside Romania, the Jakeš regime had become the last bastion of conservatism in Central and Eastern Europe. The collapse of Communist regimes, particularly in Hungary and Poland, provided a great fillip for the opposition in Czechoslovakia. Their former dissident colleagues in Poland, for instance (namely, Jacek Kuron and Adam Michnik), were now either in government or Parliament. Not only the opposition but the whole population was faced with the thought that if radical change was possible not simply in Hungary and Poland but even in East Germany, then it had a realistic chance in Czechoslovkia. This question was made more tangible because these changes had occurred without provoking any direct Soviet intervention. In effect, a crucial barrier to change in Czechoslovkia was removed by dispelling any lingering apprehension of a repetition of the 1968 invasion.

Given the way in which the government and party leaders responded to the development of the crisis in 1988 and 1989, certain things became clear. Though there were indications that problems, especially of an economic character, were being discussed at various levels within the party and people had become aware of the need for reform, the entire upper stratum proved itself to be recalcitrant and, in the event, incapable of reacting adequately. The personnel changes, for example, beginning with Jakeš's succession to the leadership of the party in December 1987, did not produce any increase in the number of reformists in the party. Even the least radical of economic reformers—Lubomír Štrougal, the federal prime minister; Bohuslav Chňoupek, the foreign minister; and Peter Colotka, the Slovak prime minister—were replaced. Their successors were either more conservative or, like Ladislav Adamec, the Czechoslovak prime minister, incapable of confronting the government consistently with the need for radical change, though he is credited with having warned Jakeš that "if we do not resolve it ourselves within two years, then the street will decide."

The regime's failure to respond showed that the government was a prisoner of the legacy of the invasion of 1968 not only as regards policy but also respecting the selection of personnel: There was no significant group of reformers close to the party leadership and capable of influencing it who were ready to take over during a crisis. Under such circumstances, rumors—never substantiated—pointed to a desperate conspiracy to radically overhaul the Communist system. The plot allegedly involved the StB (the Czechoslovak secret police), the KGB, and a leading ex–reform Communist of 1968 vintage, Zdeněk Mlynář, a friend of Gorbachev from their student days and a prominent Euro-Communist. These rumors went so far as to suggest the utilization of student demonstrations as a prelude to a takeover that, given conditions, could not be achieved peacefully. Though this was not beyond the bounds of possibility, the parliamentary committee later set up to investigate the whole matter failed to come up with any conclusive evidence of conspiracy.

PART TWO

The November Revolution

~c 3 ~

Black Friday

Young people, as we have noted, were prominent in the public demonstrations of late 1988 and early 1989, though only a few were identified with the dissident opposition, principally the student sections of the Democratic Initiative and the Independent Peace Associations. There were casual links through student friends—often the sons and daughters of dissidents, who were not always excluded from higher education. These small, informal groups were more or less isolated from one another by the conditions of the normalized regime, and this isolation was reinforced by the unwanted though fitful police attention some students attracted by signing petitions for the release of Havel and Jan Ruml, cofounder of an underground newspaper. It was therefore essential to find a nonpolitical issue that would draw students together without being directed into harmless channels by the party-sponsored Socialists Union of Youth (SUY). An innocent-looking and relatively politically neutral educational issue was raised in spring 1989 after a meeting in Vienna of the Conference on Security and Cooperation in Europe, to which the Czechoslovak government was a signatory. Paragraph 53 of the higher education law guaranteeing the SUY an administrative monopoly was in clear breach of the CSCE agreement.

In March the students of the mathematics and physics faculty reacted by organizing a petition demanding an end to the monopoly and the formation of a system of self-administration. Despite the fear of persecution, about 12 percent of the student body signed, and a similar petition had equal success at the engineering and electronics faculty. Contrary to expectations, the dean was not opposed, and a committee of eight students formed the Working Party for the Preparation of Student Self-Administration, which held open meetings of students and worked with faculty. Elections to the organs of the self-governing student body were scheduled for November 20. Other faculties attempted something similar;

their limited success suggests that their academic leaders were less rigid than the Stalinist dean of the pedagogy faculty of the university, Sykora. The rudimentary cooperation and exchange of information between faculties this process fostered grew into an alternative student organization later known as STUHA,[1] though they referred to themselves as the independent students. It had no stated program other than to "awaken the sleeping universities to a struggle against communism,"[2] but few, if any, of the students believed they would win. Nevertheless, they organized several public protests, for instance, against the introduction of the hundred-crown banknote carrying the image of Klement Gottwald, the first Communist president and coauthor of the 1948 Communist revolution. Their system of networking also enabled them to mobilize 200 students in protest against the operation of a disciplinary commission convened by Sykora to examine the cases of two students said by the secret police to be active in the Democratic Initiative. A protest inside and outside the building, which provoked a favorable reaction among passersby, caused the affair to be dropped.

The students regarded the public demonstration of October 28, 1989, as a landmark in the radicalization of society, helped by the publication in *Mladá fronta,* the youth movement's daily, of a censored version of the antistate demonstration and the police attack. The Prague City University Students Council (CUSC) of the SUY was not immune from this process. Indeed, radical reformists among them had already been giving STUHA access to the publishing facilities of the Student Press and Information Center (SPIC) run by the CUSC. Alternative student magazines, such as *Kavárna, Emko, Proto,* and *Situace,* circulated, though in small numbers, and SPIC produced handbills and even petitions (one destined for the Ministry of Education demanded the removal of Marxism-Leninism from the curriculum; it was swallowed by events, though it surfaced in another form). Some of those in the CUSC, without the knowledge of the leadership, offered to cooperate further with STUHA, which by then had representatives from eight university faculties, in organizing a demonstration for November 17. The CUSC would ensure the action was legal, and the independent students would ensure a high turnout.

There is little reason to doubt that the highest party circles already knew what was afoot. Discussion in the Central Committee centered on dialogue with the opposition, a matter that became more pressing with the fall of the Berlin Wall on November 9 and the removal of Zhivkov in Bulgaria a few days later. Optimists considered December 10—Human Rights Day—as the likely date for the outbreak of mass demonstrations. Reformers within the CPC believed the December plenum would bring radical change. Pessimists within the dissident opposition thought it would take until spring 1990 to achieve a legalization of the opposition. A transitional period would then lead to free elections, after which the party would hand over the government. General Alojz Lorenc, head of the security forces and arguably the best informed of all party leaders, believed the party incapable of either a radical turnabout or of suppressing the process of change. The best the secret police could do, in his view, was to block the final act for a time.

The March Begins

November 17, 1989, was the fiftieth anniversary of the death of Jan Opletal, a date with special historical significance in Bohemia and Moravia. On this day in 1939, Adolf Hitler, angered by Czech resistance to the German occupation of rump Czechoslovakia, unleashed his Special Action Prague, during which nine student leaders were executed and a further 1,200 university students transported to the Sachsenhausen concentration camp. All Czech universities were closed down and more than 1,200 teaching staff thrown out of work. The terrorizing of Czech youth and the softening up of a significant part of the intelligentsia is remembered as another first step in the attempted denationalization and ultimate annihilation of Czech culture. These events are retained in the national consciousness by the annual act of homage to the memory of a young medical student, Jan Opletal, who was fatally shot during an anti-German demonstration. His struggle embodied young people's resistance to foreign occupation in general and to acts of Nazi persecution in particular. The CPC had to some extent diluted this celebration of nation by stressing Opletal's resistance to fascism and combining the ceremonies with those marking International Students Day.

Plans for the organization of the demonstration went ahead at a meeting on November 9. Representatives of the CUSC and seventeen faculties finalized the roster of speakers and the content of the invitation issued jointly by the CUSC and STUHA. They arranged for handbills to be printed at SPIC with the names of twenty students and their contact addresses, which later provided the focus of faculty strike committees. There was, however, discord about the destination of the procession. The CUSC hinted darkly that Wenceslas Square, a stone's throw from Opletal's monument, was out of the question. Vyšehrad, the site of the grave of the Czech poet Karel Hynek Mácha was finally chosen, though by a margin of only nine to seven—the latter urging a march to the square—with one abstention. Two days after the meeting, the Prague reform wing of the SUY, made up mainly of unpaid and part-time student officials in the CUSC and faculty representatives of the SUY, was defeated at the youth union's national conference. The reformists decided that the youth organization could provide no solutions and that they would throw in their lot with the independent students in the crucial first week of the strike.

Some 2,000 to 4,000 people were expected to assemble on November 17, 1989, in front of the Institute of Pathology on Albertov from where Opletal's funeral procession had led off fifty years before to the day. By 4 p.m., 15,000 had gathered, wearing the tricolor and carrying candles and white carnations. A large proportion were people who had not dared to demonstrate in January and October. Banners were prominently displayed bearing slogans of a general political nature, for instance, "Academic Freedom," "Democracy and Law," "Dialogue cannot be conducted on the street," and "You can't do anything without us." Many supported "Genuine Perestroika" and "Free Elections," others were more prosaic: "We want to live in a normal way." Still others wanted action: "Who if not us? When if not now?" A nod in recognition of International Students Day came from the independent students carrying a banner reading, "Students of all faculties, unite!" A humorous touch, which became a characteristic of the whole revolution, was visible, too: A sign with the wrong case ending was a mocking tribute to Jakeš's level of literacy, which had made him the laughingstock of the nation, particularly after the baffling public circulation of a professional-quality video recording of Jakeš addressing a meeting of party secretaries in western Bohemia. Not only his grammatical errors but the crudity of his thought showed him to be extremely dense.

The crowd was addressed first by one of Opletal's colleagues, who unsentimentally noted: "In Mauthausen concentration camp, we had one good slogan: Be hard against the hard, and that's what I advise you now." Miroslav Katětov, a mathematician disgraced after 1968 and a member of the Club of the Independent Intelligentsia, invited the gathering to remember the example of the Prague Spring. Both speakers were enthusiastically applauded. The short speech made by the representative of the CUSC was taken as an appeal to allow perestroika time to bring about change and was given short shrift. Martin Klima for the independent students harked back to 1939 in an impassioned speech: "Our forerunners well knew that oppression was worse than death, that freedom must be fought for and that it is not possible to live without it." The crowd responded by chanting for Jakeš's resignation. Klima went on: "The defense of freedom—the fundamental yardstick of human existence—is the message of the student demonstrations from the beginning of the Nazi occupation." These sentiments stirred powerful feelings of anger and sadness in his listeners. This and the mood of pathos evoked by the spectacle of flowers, flags, the singing of the national anthem, and the flickering light of the candles by which the students and citizens in a "living altar" made their way up the hill to the Slavín, the burial place of Czech national heroes, forged a bond that made them reluctant to disperse afterwards.

Instead of breaking up at this point, as the SUY organizers had agreed with the authorities, the demonstrators animatedly discussed the next step. A speaker for the Independent Peace Association made an impromptu speech appealing for support for political prisoners. Representatives of the Movement for Civil Freedoms and some independent students continued to urge people to march to Opletal's monument via the statue of Saint Václav in Wenceslas Square, which, unknown to them, had already been ringed by the police. Students debated, often bitterly, with members of the political opposition from the post-1968 generation, enumerating the rights and wrongs of perestroika and stressing the futility of waiting for change. Among the chanting and shouting of slogans came a rumor that the police had cut off the Gottwald Bridge, blocking the shortest route to the city center. A majority, though not all, were determined at that moment to march to Wenceslas Square. Those at the head of the procession, intent on the shortest route, led the marchers toward Charles Square; as they came down the hill, they were greeted by train whistles and the V-for-victory signs from drivers crossing the railway bridge. The procession halted at the end of Vyšehrad Street. The direct route to the center was barred by helmeted policemen carrying Plexiglas shields and truncheons. The first blows fell and the first arrests were made.

Evidence suggests that the police intended to lead those arrested to National Avenue, where units of the antiterrorist squad were waiting. In anticipation of a frontal attack, the first rows of students sat on the ground. Despite the threat of a one-sided confrontation, the procession did not break up. Instead, it turned down toward the river. Drivers honked encouragement. Trams and buses were stopped by the several-kilometer-long column as it moved along the embankment. Their passengers, many shoppers, and chance passersby joined the demonstrators, as did local residents. By the time they had reached the First of May Bridge, their numbers had grown to between 50,000 and 55,000. A sense of their own strength gave the protesters a feeling of security that thrust any awareness of physical danger to the back of their minds. They reasoned, too, that the government could not explain away such a gathering by reference to "rioters" or manipulation by "Western centers," as had been customary in the past.

The chanting and slogans grew and expressed more explicit demands: "REAL Dialogue," "Free Elections," "Abolish the monopoly of the Communist party." But they did not lose their good humor. The marchers boisterously greeted the first enemy of socialism as they passed under the unlit windows of Václav Havel's flat. "It's terrible," somebody ob-

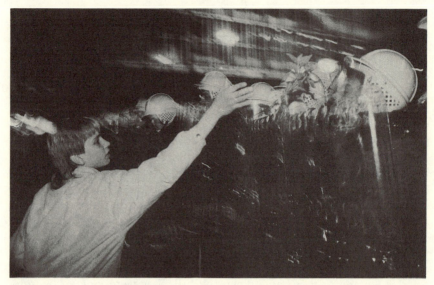

Flower-power and armed force: Members of the Socialist Union of Youth confront each other on National Avenue, November 17, 1989 (photo by Tomki Němec).

served laconically, "that history is passing under his windows and he's out in the country writing his plays." Yet it was clear that the marchers identified themselves with what Havel represented and, likely, that the time had come to stand up in his support. The column turned right past the National Theater into National Avenue to the cries of "A nation for itself," echoing the maxim that had been emblazoned on the National Theater at its inception in the late nineteenth century as a response to German-Austrian domination. Much of the significance of this and other national symbols returned when people stopped to consider in these circumstances how the Communist state had done much to deprive them of their national identity. The commotion brought the actors and staff of the National Theater to the windows, applauding "this performance for democracy with a cast of thousands."

Empty Hands—and Violence

Led by students carrying the national flag and a large banner proclaiming "We don't want violence," the leitmotif of the revolution, the procession went on for a further half kilometer, as far as a department store, where the road was cordoned off by a phalanx of civil police in full riot gear. There was a bizarre quality to the ensuing standoff in that the average

age of the security forces was more or less the same as those in the leading ranks of the demonstrators. The latter raised their arms and chanted, "Our hands are empty," though, as they later said themselves, their hearts were in their mouths. They called further for a free passage to Wenceslas Square and an open dialogue with their representatives. The distance between the two sides shrank to about three meters, the tension of the youthful security forces was becoming as visibly great as that of the students. Inaudible warnings broadcast through the public address system of a police car were answered by cries of: "Wenceslas Square and then home!" A police cameraman erected a set of aluminum stairs behind the police ranks and started filming the demonstrators. No doubt in preparation for this action, the security forces had been checking their files for noted dissidents and information on student activists supplied by their so-called documentation groups. Each unit was made up of three officers in civilian clothes, pensioners formerly employed in the Ministry of the Interior and local government, and student function-aries in the SUY, all of whom reported to a uniformed member of the security forces. It is known, for example, that ninety-seven civilian members were at work in various units during the October 28 demon-stration attempting to discover the intentions of students who could not otherwise be traced because they had no contact with dissident groups.

On November 17, however, the police were confronted by thousands of unknown, young faces who had started to come to terms with their fear. This realization also removed any possibility of invoking the standard explanation for protest actions, namely, "manipulation by Western agen-cies." The appearance of a drunk waving the national flag and insisting on the students' right to continue on their way nevertheless gave them an opportunity to discredit the affair by referring the next day to "drunk-en elements at the head of an allegedly student demonstration." After some students had led the man away, others lit candles around the flag draped on the ground separating them from the security forces. Two students offered carnations to the stony faces behind the Plexiglas shields, and others placed lighted candles at the feet of the police, who were not only indifferent to these gestures but also to any action that they previ-ously would have taken as provocation and reason to attack. The more or less good-natured calls of the police to disperse were repeatedly drowned out by chanting for access to Wenceslas Square and the statue of Saint Václav. In between, a tipsy woman picked up a flag and waved it in such a way under the noses of the police as to come close to assault, all the while addressing them as her sons. They did not react, perhaps partly because of the presence of the Western media, who eagerly recorded images of the forest of flickering candles, flags, trampled flowers, and the sounds of the demonstrators seated on the ground and singing "Where

Is My Home"—the national anthem—"We Shall Overcome," and former president Masaryks' favorite song, "Oh, my Son, my Son." Camera crews from the local studio, Krátký, were at work, too.

After about two hours, the police, visibly irritated by the failure of their authority and especially nettled by the demonstrators' jangling keys at their "jailers," began to lose patience and read the riot act. Warnings were repeatedly broadcast to return to the embankment—an impossibility because the police had cut off the head of the demonstrations and blocked every escape route. About 5,000 people were isolated from the mass behind and completely encircled by more than 1,500 police. Two policemen set off across the scaffolding on the corner of National and Mikulandská streets in pursuit of a man with a video camera. The security forces began a slow and remorseless advance on the seated demonstrators, beating them about the heads with their truncheons as they tried to rise and kicking them as they fell. The sight of bloodied heads and the evident ruthlessness of the police sent a shock wave through the demonstrators, who rose in unison and tried to flee. An armored Black Maria with barbed wire mounted on its front fender began circling within the confines of the area cordoned off by the police, causing panic as people attempted to get out of range. The police continued to set about the crowd with their truncheons and boots, and not even those already lying injured on the ground were spared. The students raised their hands above their heads and chanted "Empty hands," "No violence," and "The world is watching you" to no avail. Brutal treatment was meted our indiscriminately; as depositions later showed, the police did not hesitate to attack the elderly, professional people, and even parents with children.[3] Indeed, the youngest casualty was thirteen and the oldest eighty-three.

The security forces relaxed their encirclement in only one place, opening a narrow alleyway through which the students were invited to pass to escape being crushed against the walls of an arcade. As they went through in single file, they were beaten across the head and shoulders. The police were reinforced by units of the Red Berets, a parachute regiment trained in antiterrorist methods; unseen at previous demonstrations, they were by all accounts more experienced and more proficient in their use of manual force, including martial arts. Even after the demonstrators had run the gauntlet into Mikulandská Street (causing injury to 593 persons, a commission of medical officers of Citizens Forum later discovered), they were still not safe. Red Berets in pairs picked out individuals at random and worked them over. Others prowled around dishing out arbitrary punishment to the knots of people on the concourses of the local Metro stations who were listening with dismay and disbelief to the accounts of those who had been beaten up. Meanwhile, rumors were flying that tanks had been seen protecting Prague Castle, the seat of government. There was the whisper of the death of a student. Telephoning into and out of Prague was difficult.[4]

The Staging of the Attack

It is now known that one of those who fell in the first rows of demonstrators was a lieutenant in the secret police named Zifčák. He had entered the student movement under the pseudonym Růžička. In his deposition at an inquiry conducted by the military prosecutor in early 1990, he stated that he and his superior, Colonel Bytčánek, were involved in a plan in which agents of the secret police led the student demonstration from the medical faculty on Albertov to National Avenue to an eventual clash with the police. During the confrontation, Zifčák was isolated by the Red Berets at a prearranged signal from a Major Šípek and apparently beaten to the ground, where he lay as if dead. At the same time, he was protected until an Interior Ministry ambulance took him away. This was said to be part of a wider plan—sanctioned by Lorenc, the deputy minister of the interior; Vykypěl, the deputy commander of the second executive of the secret police; and Hegenbart, the leader of the Thirteenth Section of the CPC—by which it was intended to discredit Jakeš and Štěpán.

Lorenc was privy to other matters that hinted at the imminent demise of the old-guard Communists. He knew, for instance, that against all diplomatic protocol, Gorbachev had snubbed Jan Fojtík, the Politburo member in charge of ideology, by not meeting him during his visit to Moscow, principally because of the embarrassment CPC leaders had caused him and Soviet policy in Europe, as we have seen in the previous chapter. Fojtík admitted as much during an interview immediately after his return in the early evening of November 17, saying the time had come for the party to revise its attitude toward the Prague Spring and to critically evaluate the role played in it by the then leaders of the CPC. In effect, this amounted to the undoing of the old regime. It may be the case that Lorenc had been kept informed of these developments in Moscow by a KGB general, Grushko, who appeared in Prague on November 14.

Other snippets of evidence indicate that something was in the wind. After consulting Jakeš and Štěpán on the morning of the seventeenth, František Kincl, the federal minister of the interior, had also given the police instructions to prevent student access to the city center, but nothing more. As far as is known, Jakeš stuck to this policy. Lorenc, who entertained Grushko at police headquarters for the entire period of the demonstration, confirmed they had been in permanent telephone contact with both Jakeš and Štěpán and the order to refrain from attack had not been countermanded or reversed. The army, too, was involved, for on

November 15 the general staff gave orders to certain regiments to prepare for an attack on "antisocialist forces" (the conventional phrase for dissidents), though most if not all were outside Prague during that weekend. Curiously, university graduate members of the forces were explicitly excluded from these units.

The question remains whether someone outside the Central Committee gave the order to attack. The first parliamentary commission to look into the affair concluded that "the attack was planned beforehand and carried out according to it. . . . Certain signs indicate that the attack was organized by two command centers that were differently instructed." It added, "the KGB was informed of the situation, although the degree of influence it had on the preparation and execution of the attack has not been proved." It concluded, "It is also possible to infer from several depositions that the attack was designed to lead to the removal of the then political leadership of the CPC." Shortly after the report appeared in spring 1990, students found that six of the commission were StB agents. This effectively discredited its conclusions, though the public had in any case been disinclined to accept that the secret police had effectively toppled their masters before handing over power to their friends in dissident circles. We consider this and other theories in the next chapter.

~c 4 ~

The Toppling of the Stalinists

The powerlessness of the student demonstrators against the machinery of state security was underlined by the unprecedented escalation in its use of force. The protesters took this to have been not merely an act of deterrence but also a form of punishment, that, if left unchallenged, would be repeated. Resistance developed to meet two needs. First, the public had to be awakened from its deep-seated apathy, which required the formation of alternative means of communication, given that the official media was likely to remain under government control for a time. Second, the majority of students who had nothing to do with STUHA or the reform wing of the SUY, and probably no interest in either, had to be mobilized on a mass basis and won over to a form of action ultimately involving society as a whole. Such widespread action could neither be ignored by the state nor dealt with by violent means. Eventually, the idea originated of a student-led general strike.

Immediately after the police attack, audiences and actors in the Vinohrady and other theaters were informed of the night's events by some of the shocked and injured victims. Prominent among those who recounted the beatings were students from the Theater Academy of Musical Arts (TAMA), who through their teaching staff had strong contacts with the theatrical community in Prague. At the same time, small groups of students from many other faculties were gathering in homes, at halls of residence, and at student clubs to debate their response. Most students and citizens, however, were ignorant of what had happened until the next day, when foreign radio and television stations provided them with a rough outline of events that their own media referred to as a demonstration "disturbing peace and public order."[1] There was some doubt as to the next step. Most of the leading dissidents were out of Prague, as were most members of the CPC Central Committee. In student circles a mood of despondency was punctuated with outbursts of defiance reflected in the various proclamations of a strike and appeals for public support written by the independent students and others at different faculties.[2] At the outset, there were few grounds for believing that they could influence their student colleagues to overcome the indifference they had shown to previous protest demonstrations. They had further to confront the difficulty of reaching and rousing members of the public, who, if they were not away at their country cottages, were reluctant to respond to allegations of police brutality when information was incomplete and unverifiable. The death of Martin Šmíd, a student at the mathematics faculty, for example, was reported erroneously but in good faith on Radio Free Europe by Petr Uhl, a leading dissident and radical socialist lawyer active in the Committee for the Defense of the Unjustly Prosecuted.[3] This and the report of the French Press Agency stating that four students had died were the result of disinformation planted by the StB to cast doubt on the students' stated commitment to nonviolence and thereby discredit them in the eyes of the public. It also gave the state a pretext to arrest Uhl on a charge of "defaming the republic by spreading slanderous information," at the same time suggesting that the dissident opposition, prompted by Western press agencies, had annexed the leadership of the demonstration.

The independent students' fears of expulsion from university, social persecution, and imprisonment were intensified by the distribution of their contact addresses at the demonstration. One way or another they also felt responsible for the death of a fellow student. This, however, did not keep them out of circulation, as the StB had hoped it would, partly because they were unconvinced by the source of information, Šmíd's alleged girlfriend. Her subsequent disappearance and the knowledge that Šmíd had no girlfriend of that name pointed to a stratagem of the police. Nevertheless, their apprehensions were increased over the weekend by the arrest of groups of students making preparations for the student strike. Some accounts suggest the police were half-hearted and lacked direction in their conduct of the interrogations, which, in conjunction with the students' release from prison the same day, may indicate that they had been given no precise instructions. It is unusual that the police did not seem to quibble with the students' claim that the demonstration had been spontaneous; given the efficiency of their surveillance techniques, they must have been aware of plans for the march.

It is unclear to what extent the CPC was reliably informed of the extent of the injuries during the demonstration. Some, like Adamec, had merely been told that a threat to public order had been successfully dealt with. The party's monopoly of the means of information, as in the past, was used to limit any damage. *Rudé právo,* the party paper, referred to a "breach of public order" but studiously avoided any mention of victims.[4] The appearance on the walls throughout the Metro system of posters claiming 500 injured helped to extract an official response from Prokopec, the minister of health, who insisted that only 10 students had been hospitalized and another 26 treated as outpatients.[5] The trade union paper *Práce* spoke of injuries to 17 students and 10 policemen.[6] It added that 143 students had been taken to the police station, of whom 9 were charged, 21 paid fines for disturbing the peace and were thereafter released, and the remainder were held pending investigation. Many of the injured had preferred not to go to hospitals for fear of arrest. The presence of plainclothes agents on the streets ripping down all protest posters but conspicuously leaving the Šmíd cult intact provoked much comment suggesting that the demonstration had involved greater numbers than the authorities cared to admit. In addition, the police had leaflets printed and distributed using the initial student declaration but adding a sentence about Šmíd, which was designed to keep the news of his death uppermost in the minds of the public.

The state of student opinion was by and large still unknown, even though the demonstration was the talk of student and artistic circles. For many, the nagging worry induced by the knowledge that the state was able to apply sanctions at almost any time in their school or professional careers was, in conditions of relative isolation, wound up into outright fear by the thought that next time they could be shot at. Many were preoccupied with the notion that if the news blackout in the official media could be maintained, then they could never break out of their isolation. Even if uncensored news filtered out to industrial and commercial Prague, students were skeptical about the reaction their demands would elicit from workers and employees. They had no faith in the SUY and no means of coordinating students from different faculties. That most students lived at home also played its part in enhancing a sense of insularity. The exchanges of the students at the faculty of journalism reflected their doubts and were not untypical of the debates young people were conducting throughout the city: They considered going on strike. They were neither revolutionaries nor tragic heroes but simply young, fairly average people, many of whom had been traumatized by the police attack. Yet even at that early stage, about a third of their faculty and similar sections of the film and theater academies and the philosophical faculty supported the idea of a strike. Bearing in mind the aftermath of the failed demonstrations of previous years, others suggested that a minute's silence and the posting of handbills would be protest enough. In the end, they postponed a decision until the following day.

The Growing Cast

The students of the theater academy had fewer misgivings partly because of their close involvement with STUHA and the efforts of Martin Mejstřík, a founding member of the independent students who had a seat in the CUSC. They arrived at a decision to strike on Saturday morning, the day after the march. One of their leaders, Pavel Chalupa read their strike proclamation in the early afternoon at the Realistic Theater of Zdeněk Nejedlý, where most of the Prague theater world, including the general managers of the individual theaters, had gathered. The proclamation demanded a government inquiry into the circumstances surrounding the Friday events; announced the cancellation of the opening performance at Disk, the students' own theater-club; and appealed to the students and teachers of all other faculties to join them in a week-long protest strike. The tumultuous reception the strike announcement received reflected as much a general distaste for the party's control of their art as disapproval of the regime's violent methods.

Subsequent debate showed the demonstrators were divided on the form the protest should take. The actor Tomáš Töpfer urged his listeners to accept the suggestion of his Vinohrady Theater to link up with the student strike and, to press home the point, call a two-hour general strike on Monday, November 27. Others were more cautious, pessimistic about the sympathy actors and students could expect from the public. A one-day strike "but not now" was another view. A few favored delaying the strike until Monday to give the demonstrators time to overcome their organizational difficulties and sabotage a live television transmission from the National Theater that evening. Jiří Kodet, an actor-manager, spoke for many when he observed, "We've been messing about like fools for the last forty years—every evening—and that's why we've only got where we are now. If we want to do anything more than we've done so far, there's nothing left for us but not to go on stage."

The debate repeatedly came to the brink of a strike decision and fell back. All agreed it was the only way to express their protest not only about the demonstration but also about the petty and grave humiliations they had had to put up with respecting censorship and artistic freedom. But there were two main sticking points: the old bogey of police and inquisitional repression and the fear that a strike would be met with public indifference. With time pressing and some theater companies half-way through the door on their way to matinee performances, Arnošt Goldflan, director of the Brno Ha Theater helped those gathered to make up their minds:

The National Theater in the service of the revolution (photo by Pavel Wellner).

Sitting here, we have no power whatever to direct anybody. We cannot decide for our colleagues from those theaters who couldn't get here. And we all know how things are done: They begin with a negotiation and end in isolation. The inescapable fact is that every one of us will have to decide for himself. Take a risk and believe that everything will work out, and if it doesn't, then reconcile yourself to the fact that you are in for it. I want to tell you that we've just come to an agreement with Petr Oslzlý [a playwright]—the authors and we are going off to the Juniorklub theater to read our audience the "Protest of the Students" we've heard here and let them know that that's why we're going on strike.

His listeners rallied to him, and within a few hours matinee audiences across Prague had discovered that they were getting more than they had paid for. Instead of an afternoon's entertainment, they were in effect offered an opportunity to raise their voices against the party and state. The actors read the students' proclamation and informed their audiences that they were going on an immediate week-long strike. Far from asking for their money back, which some faint hearts expected, the public greeted the action with wild applause, a spontaneous rendering of the national anthem, and a minute's silence.

This turn of events established connections that were later to be of critical importance. The acting community had taken the first step in forging a direct link with the people at the critical early stage of the revolution, becoming one of the principal conduits for uncensored and reliable information, helping to bypass the official media. The theater became a center for the transmission of news, public debate, and, when the actors chose to exercise their talents, the performance of excerpts from banned plays and prose readings, all of which did much to strengthen the sense of common cause against the state. The public had also been asked in effect to face the issue of censorship, which it had repeatedly suppressed in the interest of survival, though faced with it on a daily basis for more than twenty years. People were shocked at the betrayal of the heart of a system of arbitrary power even more violent than they had assumed it to be. The actors, moreover, were able to communicate directly with part of the core social groups on which the Communist party depended. Writers and actors had been bound up with the struggle for national survival in Czechoslovakia since at least 1848, when actors helped man the barricades during the uprising in Prague against the oppressive authorities of the Austrian Empire who controlled the Czech Lands. Theater exerted a traditional pull on the affections of the people and, in contrast to the situation in the Anglo-Saxon world, often formed part of the leisure activity of the working class. In practice, this helped open a channel directly onto the factory floor, which, as we shall see, exerted pressure on the factory committees and the Communist trade union organizations (known collectively as the Revolutionary Trade Union Movement, or RTUM) at first in the capital and thereafter in the industrial towns of northern Bohemia.

The protest action at the same time gathered pace in student circles. On Saturday afternoon, Mejsktřík announced the theater academy and actors' strike to a large crowd waiting at the statue of Saint Wenceslas. A few hours later, the students at the medical faculty running the critical and Catholic-oriented student newspaper *EM* joined them. They contacted two young lecturers in the pathophysiology department. One of them got to work and wrote the declaration of the Academic Forum, which appeared on Sunday morning, November 19, preceding the declaration of Citizens Forum. This combined a protest of the academic staff with proposals on how to set up a democratic, collective system of self-government throughout the university system. The medical students elected a strike committee and then set about establishing a network based upon "circles." Those they chose to represent them were mostly radicals, which put the usual student representatives, the SUY moderates, at a disadvantage. Nevertheless, though the chairman of the strike committee assumed full dictatorial powers over meetings, he was fully supported by the SUY. The cracks in the nominally Communist establishment continued with the decision of the dean of medicine, Pacovský, to support the strike. Referring to his own experience, he reminded the students that strikes had failed in 1968–1969, though he gave an assurance that as long as he remained dean, no sanctions would be taken against anyone choosing to participate. Similar meetings were held in all faculties over the next few days. Only one dean, Sykora of the pedagogy faculty, refused his support and indeed threatened a violent clearing of the faculty buildings. He was, however, overruled by the faculty workers' council of the Communist party, who helped the students lock themselves in.

Although there was no sign of mass protest throughout Saturday, encouraging news was coming in from the provinces that theaters in Gottwaldov (now Zlín), Uherské Hradiště, Hradec Králové, Most, Kladno, and Brno had joined the strike. The evening performances in Prague had shown, too, that support from the public was growing. Reports of the death of Martin Šmíd, however, put a different complexion on matters for a time, leaving many people confused until a live television interview with him was transmitted on Sunday evening. That morning a section of youth had proved that they already had lost their fear by marching along National Avenue and placing hundreds of lighted candles in the places where dried blood was still visible, notably in and around the arcade on the corner of Mikulandská and National streets. Across its entrance, they draped a large black banner bearing the inscription, "Jan Opletal 17.11.1939—Martin Šmíd 17.11.1989." The occupants of a police patrol car parked at the crossing of National and Spálená less than one hundred meters away made no move to intervene. The scornful applause of passersby also failed to rouse them as they stared fixedly at the car floor. Yet the inactivity of the security forces contributed to a heightening of tension, and the complete lack of reliable information racked it up another notch.

Late in the afternoon, a crowd gathered at the statue of Saint Wenceslas, mainly people who had assembled in the adjacent Charles Square to commemorate Šmíd and visitors leaving the local hospital. There was much talk of support from the north Bohemian miners. In the growing gloom, young people lit candles, formed themselves into a giant cross, and, bearing aloft the state flag inscribed "17.11.1939–17.11.1989," set off down the square followed by more than 20,000 people. This ad hoc demonstration reflected all the features that characterized those on subsequent days: a myriad of state flags, tricolors on every lapel, banners, lighted candles, and chanted slogans. The marchers intended to continue their protest under the windows of Prague Castle, the seat of the president, across the river Vltava. As the head of the column stepped onto the First of May Bridge, a convoy of police cars sped across the parallel Jirásek Bridge and cut them off. Not only was the exit from the bridge sealed and likewise Old Town Square, but a wall of police roughly two kilometers long guarded every access to the castle. The security forces preventing egress from the bridge adopted a defensive posture, and though the crowd returned to the center of the city, it was clear that it had become aware of its strength and visibly grew in confidence as a result.

After the demonstration, students from all faculties made their way to the Star hall of residence. Some came on their own initiative. Others, however, came as elected representatives of the strike committees that, with the help of STUHA and the contact addresses, had come into existence on all faculties within the previous twenty-four hours. The outcome was the founding of a coordinating committee of Prague students made up of two delegates from each faculty who hammered out the first program of the students, the Proclamation of the University Students to the Workers and Peasants of Czechoslovakia.[7] The theater academy became the organizing center of the student strike. But not all the delegates to the committee were radicals. Some urged caution and were indirectly supported by students who were returning from the provinces after a weekend at home and, having no inkling whatever of the state of affairs, saw no reason to join the strike.

A significant step in broadening the basis of opposition to the regime was made on Saturday, November 18, with the formation of Citizens Forum (CF), an umbrella organization of disparate groups, including the Student Strike Coordinating Committee, that became the basis for a mass, national movement of unprecedented proportions.[8] As the name suggests, this was not a political party but an organization devoted to uniting all members of society as a preliminary to an open discussion on the future of Czechoslovakia and as a prelude to dialogue with the CPC and the government.[9] Its demands were relatively modest: the removal of the architects of the post-1968 normalization, likewise those responsible for ordering the breakup of peaceful demonstrations; an inquiry into the police attack; and the release of all prisoners of conscience. Most of those represented were members of the old dissident groups or citizens' initiatives, with an emphasis on those seeking civil, legal, and human rights; others were organized in the so-called revival wing of political parties that had been cooperating with the Communist party in the National Front Parliament, namely, the Czech Socialist and People's parties. Members of Obroda—a reform group started by Communists who had been purged during the normalization yet retained Marxist beliefs—stood on the same platform with Catholic priests and writers from the Pen Club and Artforum. Though motley in its social and political ideas, the forum

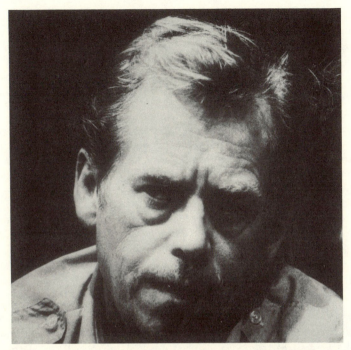

Václav Havel—one of the founding members of Citizens Forum.

was based in a relatively narrow social group of Prague intellectuals. This had important ramifications. For one, the absence of any working people in the early days did not help to dissipate public suspicion of an organization where dissidents were prominent. This attitude was not confined to the provinces. Accordingly, a high profile was attached to the slogan "A member of Citizens Forum is any freely thinking person—Citizens Forum is not a nickname for Charter 77." The subsequent co-optation of Petr Miller, a Kolben-Daněk worker, and Milan Hruška, a miner, to Havel's negotiating circle helped fill out the social profile of CF, but it still could not then legitimately claim to represent all classes of citizens nor all nations. Many Slovaks, particularly on the Catholic clerical right, looked askance at this urban, intellectual movement in which Czech humanist influence predominated, seeing it as an encumbrance to the later realization of Slovak national aspirations.

The radio and television news blackout ended on Sunday evening, when the usual television scheduling was interrupted to accommodate an appeal to the nation by František Pitra, chairman of the Czech government and member of the Central Committee. His broadcast produced cynical laughter in Prague and head scratching in the countryside.

He placed the blame for the outcome of November 17 squarely on dissident shoulders and effectively exonerated the students. The students, however, did not react as he wished and perceived condescension in his attitude, which only increased their determination. Pitra noted:

> This Czechoslovak way of perestroika is only two years old. It respects our history and is a thorn in the side of members of certain circles at home and abroad. Every chance of an organized destabilization and a sweeping away of incoming reforms is welcome. For that reason, they misused the action of November 17 and everyone must be shocked by the recklessness of the disinformation that one student died after the intervention. . . . This shows nothing is sacred to these organizers. It shows who is who, who is after power and why, who misused the students, artists, and young people. I declare that nothing in these reports is true. No armed units took part in the police action. The spread of mendacious and untruthful rumors of dead and injured have impressed many and influenced their attitudes.[10]

The Role of the SUY

With a strong student presence in CF and the occupied faculties under the control of the Student Strike Coordinating Committee, the writing was on the wall for the SUY. Nevertheless, the opposition of the party youth organization, too, was decisive in the first days of the revolution. Indeed, it amounted to an ad hoc coalition with the two other centers of resistance and played its part in toppling Jakeš and Štěpán and the other Stalinists. Though officials of the SUY had also taken a beating during the demonstration, many students doubted the union would protest, as it was widely regarded as an essentially supine and formal organization entirely subordinated to the CPC. Its attitude to the 1988 demonstrations had won little public credit. Yet its low-key efforts to open a dialogue with young people by founding two discussion clubs in February 1988—promptly stepped on by the Central Committee—were overlooked. At the outbreak of the student revolt, however, the SUY was well placed to influence the course of events. Its chairman, Vasil Mohorita, had a seat in the presidium of the CPC Central Committee. The union, too, had its own newspaper, *Mladá fronta,* which was one of two newspapers to break the censorship after November 19. Further, it had a direct line of access to working youth, a majority of whom were organized in the youth movement's basic organizations at their place of work. In the critical early stage, this became an important contributory factor in the dissemination of information and the growth of resistance, especially within larger factories, whose gates were firmly shut in the faces of striking students and actors alike.

The declaration of the Central Committee of the SUY[11] issued on Sunday evening fully supported the student demand for an inquiry into the demonstration and urged the speeding up of new laws on assembly and association. It was careful to support the decisions of the seventh and ninth CPC congresses, which outlined the policies leading to the introduction of perestroika, but chided the Central Committee for its failure to act. Most important was its support for the principle of dialogue as the way out of the crisis, which gave it common ground with the students and CF. Arguably, the leadership of the youth union adopted this relatively radical stance early, not least from reasons of self-interest. They calculated that if their nominal members, the students, were able to launch an alternative organization, which with the emergence of the faculty strike committees they in effect already had, then the SUY would be swept away. It is of course not at all clear to what extent professional functionaries in their middle years had any appetite for change, except perhaps where it was whetted by the prospect of the older generation's making way for them.

Whether Mohorita saw the writing on the wall from those members of the CUSC who were actively involved in STUHA or was privy to information gleaned in his position in the Central Committee, in the short run his response earned him great popularity, which was reflected in slogans such as, "There is no Vasil like Vasil; everybody reaps what he has sown" and "Mohorita has left the trough." The declaration was important for a number of reasons: It was the first public rejection of the party line from a party organization, and it showed that the SUY had in effect taken a stand on the question of censorship. Fojtík's efforts on behalf of the Central Committee to bury the youth union's declaration were wrecked by its appearance in the union's own newspaper on Monday, helping to prize open the floodgates of censorship and demonstrating a commitment to dialogue. Mohorita's call for "personnel changes" and for the reform of the legal code was strongly supported by the leaders of the SUY (not a few of whom were members of Obroda) and at that stage coincided with CF's demand for a legal state, a precondition of which was the removal of the party leadership.

The SUY made itself useful in other ways. On Monday morning, its faculty committee formally handed over authority to the strike committees organizing the occupations of the faculties. It thereby dissipated the confusion among the large, uncommitted section of the student body who were not at all sure who represented the students. Its influence was not removed from the faculties. Youth union representatives were elected to the strike committees at the mass meetings of the students at the faculties of medicine, economics, law, and physical education. Though the radicals never quite overcame their distrust of the SUY members, they quickly came to recognize their value, not least in conducting negotiations with the dean and faculty members, an area in which most of the radicals were devoid of experience. Further, the union turned over its office accommodation on each faculty, complete with telephone and simple copying facilities, to the strike committees, giving them significant help in the struggle to communicate directly with the people. Within a day or two, this process was repeated in secondary schools throughout Prague.

The CUSC played a broader role. In conditions in which the Student Strike Coordinating Committee was exclusively engaged in pulling together the faculty committees into something resembling a coherent whole, the council took over the coordination of the strike committees for all the faculties in sixth district of Prague, namely, agriculture, technology, and applied chemistry. Given the danger of StB officers' intervening at TAMA, some argued for the transfer of the strike center to the council building, but events overtook them. The council operated rather as an important, temporary link between the students and the public. SUY officials gathered information from the faculties and passed it on for publication in its newspaper, *Mladá fronta*. In addition, it acted as a springboard for public opinion in that social organizations and individuals responded to its declaration of protest by telephone or letter before CF had established itself as the operating center of the revolution. Many resolutions came from SUY branch meetings, not only in educational institutions and factories but—more ominous for the party—in the basic organizations of the Communist-sponsored trade union movement and of the CPC itself. Having been so long associated with a party dominated by Stalinists, however, the youth union found it impossible to recover the ground it had lost among the students. Confusion and inertia also played a part, and SUY functionaries made little attempt to lead. As they knew, the strike was a clear expression of public opinion, yet they were still unable to abandon their mentor entirely. For instance, the SUY faculty representative at the Academy of Applied Art concluded his speech at a meeting by saying, "A strike is an extreme solution, but when you consider it essential, we are not against."[12] The SUY was chary about organizing the afternoon march from the law faculty to the demonstration in Wenceslas Square. The SUY officials at the engineering faculty made no response whatsoever to the situation, whereas their counterparts at the philosophy faculty played a restraining role: Although landslides favoring an occupation strike were recorded at other faculties, students in the philosophy department supporting strike action won the day by a margin of only 393 votes to 342.

The Party and the People Respond

The Central Committee had few options in its response to the challenge posed by the students and CF, and it is doubtful if anything, even mass repression, could have saved the regime (except in the short run) after Tuesday, when the citizens of Prague took to the streets in the hundreds of thousands. But there was the question of who could be trusted to carry out such repression. The old solution, Soviet troops, was not available. As Gennadi Gerasimov, Gorbachev's spokesman, observed, "The crisis is an internal matter, part of the process of democratization and it is not for the Soviet Union to interfere."[13] Some in the Central Committee toyed with the idea of a "Chinese solution" (as used at Tiananmen Square in June 1989), but not since Anton Gajda's bungled and feeble attempt at a military coup in the early 1920s had the army involved itself in politics. Evidence suggests that the other wing of state repression, the security police, had already grown tired of papering over the cracks;[14] after Tuesday, they were conspicuous by their absence.

The only hope for the Stalinists in the party was to fall back on their traditional bulwark, the industrial working class, and attempt to restrict the movement to Prague by cutting it off from the rest of the country. They counted on at least neutralizing sections of the population whose welfare was tied up with party patronage, especially in the SUY, the RTUM, and, to a degree, the reforming wing of the party, by promising to accelerate the introduction of perestroika and deepening its structure.[15] The democratization of political and social life, too, was promised and in particular a relaxation of centralized rule by delegating power from Parliament to the local administrations, known as the national committees. Yet any good this might have done was immediately negated by the open support the old guard gave the police attack, the tone of its statement showing it to be very far from either democracy or decentralization. It ran:

> Since the 1988 proclamation, dozens of laws have been introduced . . . that have speeded up perestroika by a whole year. . . . For us perestroika means dialogue. . . . We welcome all views but not in this atmosphere of emotion. We do not wish to follow this road of confrontation along which certain antisocial elements are trying to force us. However, no government in a legal state can suffer the abrogation of the constitution and the laws of the land. Accordingly, the governments of Czechoslovakia, the Czech Lands, and Slovakia agree with the measures that aimed at the restoration of order, the protection of property, and the lives of the citizens. . . . We cannot idly look on at the activities of these groups that operate in conflict with the Czechoslovak legal order and are incited from abroad.[16]

Some, however, mainly among the chairmen of the party factory committees and basic organizations, were impressed by this statement, and agreed to organize the factories in defense of the party.[17] Yet the nationwide meetings of the members of the basic organizations of the RTUM held on Saturday, November 18, offered quite a different picture. All their complaints—from the failure of concerns to pay piece rates, to the breaking of collective agreements, to the absence of factory directors to answer their grievances—made them disinclined to believe any promises about the New Economic Mechanism.[18] They refused to accept CF as a proscribed organization and opened the possibility of access to the factory floor. In this respect, however, the CPC was confident that their factory directors and the People's Milita would prevent this. They also expected that, as parents, workers would exert pressure on their student offspring to avoid any active participation in the revolt. In the event, this was a factor in the immobilization of about one-third of all students, mainly, however, in the countryside.

The pressure from the street for dialogue grew daily in intensity. The protest quickly spread from the university faculties to secondary schools—seventeen in Prague were out in support by noon on Monday, November 20—and from the initiative groups in and around CF to the professions. For instance, most of the university rectors tacitly supported the students' strike on the condition of nonviolence, and they recognized the strike committees as partners in negotiations. Some 380 journalists met to address the question of open dialogue in the press. The backbone of the Communist judicial system was similarly stirred by events, 142 judges in Prague signing a petition in support of a legal state and dialogue. The actors, who had taken on dual roles as both newsreaders and moderators for the nightly discussions with the public, recruited graphic and plastic artists to the cause; with the help of the Federation they secured the closure of all galleries and exhibitions. The Gallery of the Young and the Mánes and Špála galleries became the printing, distribution, and organizational centers of CF. Cinemas, too, became centers of dialogue, abandoning their movie programs and inviting the public to participate in meetings with artists and other prominent personalities. The citizens of Prague gained information in other ways, mainly from handbills and posters. News gathered at the CUSC was delivered through the theater academy to all faculties for reproduction by whatever means were available. In the first week, this involved the laborious typing out of protests and proclamations, making copies with carbon paper. Where facilities were relatively sophisticated, they were cyclostyled. Photocopiers became available only after the Communist regime had collapsed. The apparently trivial but relentless grind of typing for eight to ten hours a day and more, undertaken more often than not by the women students, had the

The flowering of slogans on the statue of St. Wenceslas in Prague (photo by Jaromír Bárta).

important effect of educating and radicalizing. Previously passive students became acquainted with issues and individuals of which they had had only a blurred idea even a few days before. It helped develop a powerful sense of community and purpose, though the grueling routine these methods of communication imposed gradually caused enthusiasm to wane. It was not surprising when the students began to reduce their input or drop out of the struggle entirely, a process that became marked in early December.

Handbills, posters, and slogans became a feature of the revolution. They provided an alternative to the mass media, still largely under government control, and strengthened the breach in the system of censorship initiated by *Mladá fronta* and *Svobodné slovo* (the organ of the Czech Socialist party, or CSP). The flood of posters, proclamations, and broadsheets that appeared at every station on the Metro and every public building in the city center was swollen by official letters of protest made by shop and office managers, who displayed them inside their windows, making it difficult for the police to get at them. Under these conditions, it was impossible to limit the flow of information. In some cases, especially where banners and posters had been hung on the walls of university faculties, the security forces asked students to remove them. When students refused, the police did not press the point. They did, however, attempt in a half-hearted way to counter the tide by producing their own copies of student proclamations with the central demands missing, passing them off as the voice of concerned citizens. The technology used, however, gave the pseudo proclamations away, as it was far superior to that available to the students. In addition, these flyers were not posted on walls during the honest daylight hours but thrown out in sheaves late at night from unmarked cars whose registration numbers betrayed the presence of the secret police. Some of these pieces of propaganda, from a shadowy organization calling itself the Left Front, demanded "death to the Communists." Their distribution coincided with a widespread rumor that the CPC was preparing a "Jaruzelski solution" to the crisis. This apparent attempt to provoke the students into violence was wildly un- realistic. Nevertheless, for safety's sake, students avoided carrying any- thing that could have been construed as a weapon; discussing publica- tions of dubious origin, especially dissident literature; and even wearing the tricolor, except in Wenceslas Square and on National Avenue.

On November 20, an antigovernment demonstration took place involv- ing about 150,000 people who gathered in Wenceslas Square to support the student demands. Adults were vastly outnumbered by young people of school or university age, who by most accounts amounted to 90 percent of the assembly. Communication was hampered by the lack of a public address system, and there was little evidence of a clear and practical program. The students were heartened, however, by Mohorita's promise to resign as chairman of the SUY if the authorities again intervened, which they understood as the first definite switch from a significant member of the party apparat. Though the students intended a march of protest on Prague Castle, they contributed more to the struggle for the ending of censorship. As they passed down the square, they halted in front of the adjoining editorial offices of the trade union newspaper *Práce* and of *Svobodné slovo*. Students showed their appreciation for the latter paper's honest reporting, chanting "We are with you," "Come and join us," "Write the truth," and "We want genuine information." They were less charitable to the union paper, chiding it with shouts of "Don't lie to us," "Shame on you," "*Práce* lies" and "*Práce* talks drivel." Though the journalists had a mounting sense of physical danger, half expecting an attack, they later had cause to reflect on the moral example youth were setting for their elders and betters. A feeling of shame that began gnawing at the journalists spread to many sections of adult society and indeed ultimately became a factor in the mobilization of the nation.

The students continued as far as the embankment, where they were joined by reinforcements from the adjacent philosophy faculty. Their path to the castle was barred by security police, who had sealed off both ends of the Mánes Bridge to prevent any linkup with an equally large group of protesters from the mathematics faculty in Little Town Square. Trams had become caught on the narrow bridge, which conveniently prevented the deployment of armored transporters. Yet despite the press photographs, which suggest the imminence of a violent confrontation, there was only the occasional flash of tension. The students' sitdown demonstration passed peacefully, not least because of the display of wit, which even amused some of the police (among whom, incidentally, were a high proportion of Slovaks who had been drafted into the force on the assumption that they could be relied upon to repress the Czechs because of historical friction). Many students jangled their keys and called out, "Time, ladies and gentlemen, please," in imitation of calls to drink up before closing time in the pubs. They rang hand bells and sleigh bells and sang: "Ring out the old; ring in the new! Merry Christmas!"

Jakeš responded to Mohorita's "desertion" by making the idle threat to crush the existing youth organization and replace it with another, further missing the point that the SUY, despite its usefulness to the course of the revolution, was in the process of being marginalized. Despite the show of force they were able to summon up, the police were also in a predicament. They knew that more and more citizens were protesting against police violence and that these complaints—which were not limited to the events of November 17 and provided many examples of earlier misdemeanors—were publicized daily in the broadsheet of CF, *Informační servis*.[19] This awareness, in conjunction with flagging police morale, helps to explain their adoption of a defensive stance. Anything else would simply have further inflamed public sentiment against them. They were visibly uneasy, too, when they heard the students chanting: "The public wants protection" and "You should serve the people." The police quickly saw that they were in a situation not of their own making. This manifestation of a police presence in great numbers was in fact their last show of strength; within twenty-four hours the basic organizations of the RTUM and the CPC within a major section of the security forces promised not to intervene on a large scale unless the highest party officials accepted prior responsibility. At the same time, they expressed a lack of confidence in the leadership and demanded cadre changes at the top.[20] These combined actions were an attempt among the rank and file of the police to limit the damage to their public image and were likely to justify their powerlessness in the face of demonstrations that had reached uncontrollable proportions.

The CPC, nevertheless, had one or two shots left in its locker. Prague clearly was lost to it and could never be fully recovered after Tuesday. But the provinces were a different matter, and the party made every possible effort to keep them in the dark. None of the non-Communist newspapers arrived at their destinations outside Prague: The post office

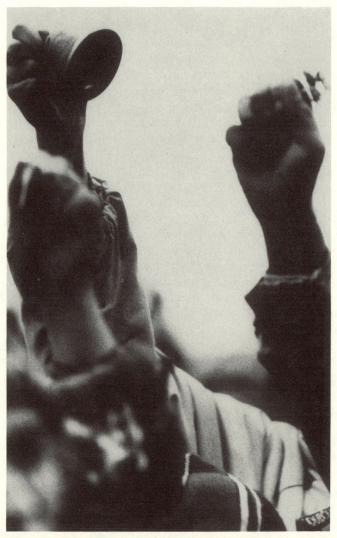

The sounds of liberty in the streets of Prague.

failed to deliver to subscribers, and the Postal Newspaper Service kiosks in every town outside the capital stocked only the party organ, *Rudé právo*. All newspapers had been printed as usual, but every consignment was intercepted before it reached the railway station for onward transmission. Workers at cooperative farms along the Prague-Ostrava route were often puzzled to find bales of newspapers scattered beside the railway track adjacent to their fields, evidently tossed out of the night train.

Because television and radio still did the party's bidding, its grip on the provinces remained firm. The declaration of the SUY had not been broadcast in either medium, though both had recorded it, and the protests of the students and CF had not been aired, keeping adult citizens in a state of uncertainty, particularly as some gave credence to rumors of martial law and an impending military coup.[21] Two different sets of television news programs were broadcast in the first days of the revolution, one for Prague and the other for the rest of the country. An attempt had to be made to alter the complexion of the official media, so long a focus of resentment (crystallized into the student slogan, "Television is lying through its teeth, just like *Rudé právo*").

While the students provided the source of external pressure in the struggle for Czechoslovak Television, a movement led from within by the basic organizations of the RTUM and SUY pressed for greater honesty and freedom in reporting events. Though the Central Committee of Czechoslovak Television expressed itself against the police attack, it did not broadcast its view, largely because of the efforts of the general director, Batrla. His veto was, in the short term, enough to prevent the protest of television employees, including those at higher levels in the hierarchy, from feeding into the growing and open public discourse on issues such as censorship and centralism. This phenomenon was characteristic of the struggle in most larger corporations throughout the republic. Batrla, like other directors of important public and industrial institutions, was eventually unable to ignore the pressure for change: Organized by the RTUM, 700 of his 1,500 employees signed a petition, and mass meetings of his entire staff drew strength from 15,000 demonstrators ably marshaled at the gates of the television complex by students of the faculty of journalism. In these circumstances, Batrla's threats of instant dismissal were empty, and he was forced to address his employees' demands. These included the nationwide broadcasting on television of the videotapes of the police attack made by Krátký film studios and the students of TAMA, coverage of the daily demonstrations in the city center and of the opinions of the most important "unofficial structures" in the form of a discussion studio, publication of the petitions and resolutions of the people, and reports of the reactions of foreign media to events in Czechoslovakia.

In varying degrees, institutions in other areas of the official media also experienced a movement from below against the old conventions, notably in the party newspaper, *Rudé právo*. Omissions (for example, of Mohorita's threat to resign) and falsehoods (for instance, that young people passing themselves off as students had forced pupils and teachers in secondary schools to join the strike) continued unabated.[22] But the old forms of discipline imposed on journalists were being eaten away by the mass demonstrations. On Tuesday, November 21, more than 200,000 took part, citizens outnumbering students; with pointed symbolism, they were addressed by the opposition from the balcony of the newspaper offices of *Svobodné slovo*. The slogans littering the city spoke volumes: "*Rudé právo* [literally, Red justice] is turning white," "You can't even believe the date on *Rudé právo;* carry a calendar with you," and "*Rudé právo*— Today in the world: Archduke Ferdinand in all likelihood shot at Sarajevo." The medical community spoke of the party newspaper's "terrible decline in ideas and moral role."[23] Zdeněk Hoření the paper's director, remained unmoved by these barbs or by the protest of fifty-seven members of the SUY in the flagship of Communist censorship, the Czechoslovak Press Agency, which brought out the basic organizations of the RTUM against him in his own newspaper. The Communists' monopoly of information seemed near an end when 300 staff members of the basic organization of the CPC in Czech Radio met and condemned the Central Committee's stance and expressed support for CF. Picking up a proposal of the Prague City Theaters' strike committee, they challenged the CPC to make two hours of air time per day available for open and public discussion "as a reflection of the pluralistic thinking of the different sections of the population . . . and above all [to allow] the participation of Citizens Forum."[24]

Students of the film academy played an important role in organizing the campaign, which vividly brought the harsh reality of the police attack to the provinces. Within two days, 5,000 still-photo documentaries had been distributed nationwide with the help of all university faculties except those at Plzeň, Hradec Králové, and Ostrava, which were not then on strike. Barrandov film studios and the Film Academy of Musical Arts put together multiple copies of Hamerník's and others' film of November 17 in a collage format, which made a greater impact than the cyclostyled accounts of eyewitnesses. In Prague these were played on a continuous loop system for the crowds gathering in front of the Mánes Gallery complex, the Špála, and the Laterna Magika Theater.

Student doubts about working-class support, which they knew would ensure the success of their cause, were allayed to a point by a small but growing body of evidence that there was proletarian opposition to the CPC. During the first two days of the revolution, *Mladá fronta* received protest resolutions from members of the public identifying themselves with the student stance on the police attack and calling for a renewal of socialist society but making no mention of CF, which was at that stage not widely known. Although these represented only a portion of protests dispatched on November 22 and 23, more of which were addressed to the SUY, they give at least a rough idea of the profile of the protesters. On November 22, 203 protest letters were received, of which 97 were supported by 9,689 individual signatures, the others sent in by organizations of all kinds. Of all the resolutions, 30 percent were from basic organizations of the SUY and 20 percent from the trade unions. Five originated from the basic organizations of the CPC. About 80 percent (161) emanated from Prague. By November 23, the picture shows a slight change, 193 resolutions arriving and 111 of these showing 9,720 signatures. Those from SUY organizations numbered 54 (about 28 percent), from RTUM 33 (17 percent), and protests from Prague showed a slight decline to 133 (68 percent), suggesting a growing interest from the provinces. Conspicuous were those from Brno, Plzeň, and the northern Bohemian triangle. Taken as a whole, of 396 resolutions, the SUY and RTUM together accounted for nearly half (47 percent). The remainder were sent in by groups of individuals at their place of work not organized into or not wanting to be identified with official, political, union, or social associations. A total of 19,409 people, of which 4,267 are definitely described as "workers," signed 208 resolutions. The number of workers may be higher, as some signatories referred to themselves ambiguously as *pracující,* which could mean either white- or blue-collar workers. The breakdown of these resolutions by economic activity is also revealing. About 25 percent came from industry and commerce, 15 percent from science and research institutes, 9 percent from the building trade, 6 percent from medicine, 5 percent from education (other than students), and 5 percent from cultural fields. It is, of course, impossible to establish the social composition of the protesters from this rudimentary and incomplete data. It does at least show the strength of opinion in support of Mohorita's stand against the CPC and for the reform of society; it also suggests that the students were not justified in assuming that all industrial workers were in these conditions the natural allies of the party.[25]

Evidence exists, too, that workers, mostly of the younger generation, actively strengthened the students' alternative information campaign. Even before the students had gone out into the factories of Prague, workers brought money and material aid to them at their faculties. Some had come to harangue them, resentful that the planned strike could destabilize the economy; they left convinced that the students' cause was just. Others were enraged by the assertion in *Rudé právo* that the workers had agreed with the police intervention. For instance, print workers from the Prague paper mills, furious at being treated like children, supplied students with paper, printing inks, and all the paraphernalia needed to produce posters and handbills. At the philosophy faculty, they arrived with ink for cyclostyling stencils hardly obtainable anywhere, enabling the students to run off copies for distribution of more than eighty items ranging from petitions to political pamphlets.

The Central Committee's threat, after its meeting early Tuesday morning, to restore order "by all possible means," was a clear indication that the party was alarmed by the challenge the students posed, particularly as 80,000 of them were then on strike across the nation. Though the party had made it difficult for them to make much headway against the censorship in the provinces, it was only a matter of time and organization. Further, the Central Committee had been inundated with criticisms from diehard party members who were confused by the conflicting accounts of the crisis in the official media and demanded a clear line. Rising discontent from the basic organizations of the party, whose primary interest was socialist reform, also threatened to undermine support for the leadership of the Central Committee. They were quite blunt: "For the last forty years, the Soviet Union has been our model and our slogan was: 'With the Soviet Union for all time!' But now that Gorbachev has opened up their society, this has ceased to be and no further reference is made to it."[26] The question was whether this section, located in the lower and middle ranks of the party, was prepared to abandon the leadership in its search for the reinstatement of civil and democratic rights in a reformed socialist system. Its interest as regards the former coincided to a large degree with CF. Though their economic values differed markedly, this was not then an issue. The Stalinist leaders hence could not fail to be squeezed by their fusion into a popular, mass democratic movement.

Štěpán, the leader of Prague City Council, invited "the workers of Prague, members of the People's Militia, and other armed units to deal with the antisocialist circles."[27] But the workers showed themselves unwilling to do the party's dirty work, and the militia proved unreliable. It is true that the fear of armed intervention from these party irregulars was at its most acute late Tuesday morning, when the appearance of 600 armed members of the People's Militia in Old Town Square within spitting distance of the law and philosophy faculties seemed to give substance to Štěpán's threats. Indeed, the atmosphere of mild panic is reflected in the response of the Student Strike Coordinating Committee, which issued a declaration "To All the Governments of the World and the United Nations."[28] The militia in both Prague and Brno, however, ignored Jakeš's orders for their mobilization and eventual intervention against the students. This was a severe and unexpected setback for the party leadership, and some delay ensued before troops were bused in from border towns in northern and southern Bohemia, with orders to attack and clear the student-occupied faculties on the night of November 21 to 22.

A further snippet of evidence suggests that members of the Central Committee were unprepared or at loggerheads with one another, for the concierge in the Ministry of the Interior building, where the soldiers were to be accommodated, had not been warned of their coming and refused them entry. They spent the night in their buses in subfreezing temperatures and were grateful for the constant supplies of soup and hot drinks delivered by students. Other units had appeared at factory gates in the suburbs but had been given no further orders.

The Tuesday afternoon demonstration involving more than 200,000 people also gave the Central Committee reason to doubt the viability of a violent solution. Within a few days, members of the militia in the giant Kolben-Daněk plant in Prague, inspired by the example of the police, demanded an end to censorship, a transfer of power to the basic organizations, and personnel changes at the apex of the party.[29] This mood spread rapidly to factories throughout Prague and outside. As far as the CPC was concerned, the People's Militia was a dead letter, a fact confirmed two days later, when the militia units in the Olomouc railway yards in central Moravia, the first of hundreds, voted themselves out of existence.[30] The age structure of the militia was a factor in weakening loyalty to the party leadership. The younger members, though given certain minor career and financial advantages, evidently decided it was not worth becoming involved in the party's struggle for power as a previous generation of militiamen had done in the late 1940s, though under very different historical circumstances.

The failure to mobilize the People's Militia shifted the attention of the Central Committee to the army as a possible means of preserving the party's power. The involvement of the military in politics was not entirely without precedent in postwar Czechoslovakia. For instance, in January 1968 Miroslav Mamula had conspired with generals in the army, two of whom subsequently committed suicide, to keep President Antonín Novotný in office and halt the rise of Dubček and the Communist reformers. In late 1989 there was less clear evidence how the army would react. It was known that an action code-named "Intervention," involving over 13,000 trained conscripts led by 790 officers and 155 tanks, had been prepared to deal with the demonstrations expected for the anniversary of the Soviet invasion in August.[31] Numerous reports of columns of tanks lined up in a hamlet outside Beroun, thirty kilometers southwest of Prague, encouraged some to believe that the action had been revived. Conscript infantrymen in two regiments, kept on standby in Plzeň and Pardubice, were denied access to television and newspapers, received no visits, and were confined to barracks. The attempt to insulate these soldiers from the outside world betrayed the high command's fear that they might have developed a sense of common cause with students, not

A civic sense reborn, Prague, November 23, 1989.

least on the more prosaic question of conscription. Branches of Military
Forum, modeled on CF, even then supported one of the students' demands calling for a reduction in the length of military service. The
consequences of this implied threat to discipline disconcerted the minister of defense, Milan Václavík, who proposed a military solution at the
CPC plenum on Friday, November 24. Doubtless, armed force was seriously contemplated in the first week, partly as a last refuge of the
desperate members of the Central Committee. This is borne out by a
recently published report.[32] Havel subsequently expressed his and the
nation's gratitude to General Miroslav Vacek, the outgoing chief of staff,
for not resorting to force during the crisis. At all events, the military
option was narrowly defeated in the Central Committee, and Jakeš's
resignation followed shortly after. Curiously, many important people
ended up in the hospital, including Václavík and Hegenbart, who had
evidently found the burden of security matters too great a strain on his
heart.

The demonstration on Tuesday afternoon represented a watershed for
the opposition. At 4 p.m., Wenceslas Square was thronged with more
than 200,000 people chanting slogans and carrying banners egged on by
squadrons of honking taxi drivers and, at the top of the square in front
of the slogan-bedecked façade of the National Museum, convoys of truck
drivers. In contrast to the Monday demonstration, there was organization
and amplification. Students and actors thrown into a leading role by the

Two faces—revolution and reform. Václav Havel and Alexander Dubček on Wenceslas Square, November 23, 1989.

strike movement announced a new seven-point program;[33] representatives of sections of society marginalized, not to say criminalized, by the "restoration of order" after 1968 also addressed the crowd. The dissident priest Václav Malý read a message from Archbishop Tomášek appealing for a transformation of church-state relations and a continued adherence to nonviolent means of change. Jan Ruml, cofounder of the underground newspaper *Lidové noviny* spoke of the necessity for a free press. The citizens of Prague saw Václav Havel for the first time, and he introduced CF and explained its aims. He also referred to the morning meeting between student and citizens' initiatives and Adamec—Havel himself was not present—arranged by an organization founded to seek out a means of dialogue between government and citizens. Petr Burian emphasized the actors' determination to stay on strike in solidarity with the students' demands and appealed to the public to support the general strike on November 27. The speakers made it clear throughout that they were not intent on the destruction of socialism but rather its renewal on democratic, humanist principles. In conclusion, Marta Kubišová, banned from performing since the late 1960s, sang "Song for Marta," which, like the songs of Karel Kryl, had been an anthem of opposition for nearly a generation.

Tuesday also saw the beginning of an abrupt change in people's attitudes toward one another, which is possible to describe but difficult to convey. A good-natured patience replaced the habitual public, and very often private, surliness, and a kind of simple, low-key gallantry appeared. People gave up their seats on public transportation; shop assistants apologized politely for not being able to satisfy customers' wishes instead of brusquely refusing to assist them. Strangers made eye contact and were not afraid to let minor confidences slip. People were generous with their money. More than 20,000 crowns[34] was collected from individuals for the students' fighting fund on the first day, when their strike had hardly gotten off the ground, and substantial donations continued thereafter. They also gave freely of their time and effort. Workers, pensioners, and housewives made regular visits to faculties with food and encouragement. The editorial offices of non–party newspapers, with the exception of *Mladá fronta,* received hundreds of offers to help to deal with routine tasks of typing, telephoning, receiving and recording protests, and simply running errands. A 75 percent drop in recorded crime from mid-November to mid-December reflected the newfound, if temporary, sense of community.[35] This was exemplified in a general way by a novel tolerance of subcultural youth groups that was quite uncharacteristic of Central Europe as a whole. For instance, a place at demonstrations was allowed, albeit warily, to punks, so often a favorite and soft target for the police, whose violent efforts to "straighten them out" were rarely condemned by the public. The atmosphere is perhaps best summed up in contemporary slogans, which are more redolent of the medieval Bohemian mystic Petr Chelčický than of a modern-day revolution: "People, be kind to each other" and "Remember the poor and forsaken."

The meeting between the CF and Adamec was significant in a number of ways. It was not, however, the opening of dialogue with the CPC, for its leaders had parted company with their erstwhile colleague, whom they described privately as "the liquidator of socialism." Adamec's assurances that the state would not use force to "restore order" nor impose martial law helped to remove public fear of a violent outcome and likely helped bring the marginally committed onto the streets to protest. The stress on the reform of socialism within the speeches of many speakers at the afternoon demonstration was arguably derived, for tactical reasons, from a statement of the chairman of the government, who had observed: "We shall protect socialism. That is not under discussion."[36] His belief that the events represented a great step on the road to the achievement of perestroika coupled with the promise of the New Economic Mechanism impressed the basic organizations of the youth union and the CPC more than the students and CF. But the latter supported him on the need for new laws safeguarding civil and democratic rights.[37]

The threat of violence fed by the apparent solidity of Communist institutional power acted upon the student community in a number of ways. It provided a compelling reason to cooperate closely with all opponents of the regime. This practical necessity helped quiet the doubts many students expressed about operating jointly with dissidents in CF. There was a belief, too, that the student demands, though they were significantly more radical than those of CF, would be obscured in the emerging mass movement. The Student Strike Coordinating Committee was propelled toward an acceptance of a coalition with the dissidents and in the process became reconciled to the fact that there was no way back. This awareness helped develop a win-or-die mentality that became a source of inspiration to the inhabitants of Prague as a whole. The third arm of the alliance was the SUY, which in the first days of the movement was vital in gaining student access to factories and places of work. In the interest of unity, the Strike Committee stopped the distribution of their own more radical Ten-Point Declaration and accepted that of the Central Committee of the youth union as a joint proclamation.[38] A majority of students, however, believed the SUY declaration was too vague. This and their misgivings about the role of Mohorita–who some thought was using his newfound popularity among young people to lay the ground before making his claim for the leadership of a new and reformed Communist party—produced a plebiscite securing a return to their original declaration.

The sense of vulnerability to armed force encouraged them to accelerate the movement of student "missionaries" into the great industrial complexes in Prague and in the countryside before the student strike centers could, as they thought, be crushed. Informing the industrial backbone of Prague was no easy task, as the experience of the students of the school of economics suggests. As early as Tuesday, November 22, delegations, often made up of one student, one actor, and one teacher, were sent out. At Tatra-Smichov, the senior managers in the factory administration ensured that the delegates got no further than the factory gates. But they were able to address the workers the following day, off the premises. At another heavy machinery factory, TOS Hostivař, the workers were in sympathy with their aims yet unwilling to support their strike. The director of Kolben-Daněk Traction permitted students access to the plant on terms set by the factory committee of the SUY. He refused, however, to allow discussion during working hours. This policy was replicated in many factories throughout Prague. In Pragotron, for instance, the student delegation waited hours for the shift to end before they were able to address the shop-floor workers. The director, too, was present and when invited to take part in the dialogue, laced his response with "an invincible wall of phrases on the imminence of perestroika," as one student later reported. The SUY was also indispensable in gaining entry to other large industrial complexes, such as the Prague Bakeries and Flour Mills concern. There they were reminded that the People's Militia had not completely abandoned their strong-arm methods: They were thrown into the street, though they managed to distribute copies of their demands and agitation materials. Although these early trips were not always successful, the evident commitment of the students to their cause began to act on the industrial workers in such a way that only the most prejudiced continued to believe that their strike was simply a pretext for loafing about.

This was not the view in the countryside, where matters looked bleaker. In many places, the reaction to the appearance of these student "missionaries" was more effective in blocking access to industrial and other workers than the activity of the police. Delegations arrived in relatively large numbers—about four hundred expeditions were organized by the medical faculty alone in the first two weeks—and many were arrested by the police and held incommunicado, most for a couple of hours, a few for up to twelve. Their leaflets and proclamations were confiscated, but there were no reports of brutal treatment. The students, however, were more concerned by the attitude of the working population. Indications of the gulf between the provinces and Prague were reflected in their counterslogans: "It's our work that feeds you, you brats!" and "We pay for you to study, you urchins, and now you're even cutting school." The nation's wage earners were not averse to roughing up the students on occasion, though in general this amounted to little more than scuffles. Some of the responsibility for this hostility fell on the secretaries of the factory committees of the youth union, who, in contrast to their colleagues in the capital, showed no interest in opening a dialogue in their own territory. This rebounded on Mohorita in Prague; he was bitterly criticized for failing to compel them to follow the official SUY line, one factor coinciding with a gradual but accelerating decline in his popularity.

The students' insistence on a general strike complicated the attitude of a large proportion of the population, particularly outside the capital. On the one hand, the people feared economic destabilization and were lukewarm toward the strike. On the other, there was much support for the students' call for the resignation of eight leaders of the CPC and the abolition of the leading role of the party, demands the university authorities thought too radical. The students, however, were resolute, and they led opinion in CF where opinion was not then solid. But they easily destroyed the party's notion that they were economic saboteurs. Not only did they suggest a strike lasting a mere couple of hours, but they also made up for any expected loss of production in advance. Beginning on November 23, they worked one complete eight-hour shift without payment for anyone who would have them. Their activities were models of "the honest work" Jakeš had recommended as the way out of the crisis. They operated a watchdog scheme in groups of five to keep order and tidiness at national monuments where they maintained permanent twenty-four hour vigils. They posted stewards to help organize and police the daily demonstrations in Wenceslas Square. They baked bread to discredit Štěpán's allegation that their strike was causing supply problems. They cleaned up public parks and gardens, not to mention the environs of their own faculties; swept streets; and, in a small way, made a strong practical commitment to improving the urban environment. They gave blood, and the medical students among them helped out on a regular basis in the understaffed hospitals and clinics. Their example won widespread public admiration and belied the official depiction of the students as scroungers and layabouts, though of course some did take the opportunity to put their feet up. The powerful impression they made caused the public to wonder ruefully how children born and raised in a society where moral devastation was the norm had been able to rise above it. This experience was reflected in the words of a worker: "It is a terrible dishonor when it is the children who have to strive for the reform of our society." This shaming personal experience, as much emotional as political, was pivotal in coaxing people out of their apathy, at least enough to speak their mind, offer moral and often financial support, and, when they could, to organize in their places of work free of the trammels imposed by the old-guard RTUM functionaries.

Hitherto, the students had had a higher public profile than CF, partly because the latter was based upon a tight-knit group of artists and intellectuals, who were to a large degree cut off from the general public. The disinformation pumped out during the normalized regime had had some effect, such that the public had a fuzzy perception of the organization as everything from a group representing the interests of political prisoners to an embryonic party seeking a revival of capitalism. The people first became directly acquainted with CF through Havel's speeches in Wenceslas Square on Tuesday. The first newspaper article to print CF's own self-description appeared on Wednesday, November 23. The public as a whole was able to identify more easily with CF than with the students as it was "not a political party but an open association of citizens."[39] This respected the people's resistance to all forms of political organization developed over the years and lessened the fears of those who saw a greater potential for the use of state violence in the formation of a political party. The Student Strike Coordinating Committee came out unambiguously in support the same day, and its outlets of information began to publicize the CF's activities and distribute its proclamations. Prominent among them was their proclamation on the general strike.[40] CF invited citizens to form strike committees in their place of work, offering to coordinate them though specifically excluding any directive function. The committees were intended to have wide autonomy in recognition of the democratic need for responsible adults to operate as they themselves thought fit. By the end of the week, both strike committees and separate local branches of CF had sprung up all over Prague.

Events in Slovakia provided added problems for the CPC. The founding of Public Against Violence by the actor Milan Kňažko helped spread the opposition movement to Slovakia. A great crowd of about 80,000 gathered in the Slovak capital, Bratislava, on Wednesday morning to hear and applaud their demands and listen to Dubček. The protest meeting gained piquancy with the news that Ján Čarnogurský, arraigned for publishing an alternative newspaper, had suddenly been released and all charges dropped, suggesting that on this question the Slovak Communist party was more responsive to public pressure than its Czech counterpart. This was visible, too, in the early meetings party members sought with Slovak students striking in Bratislava, Košice, and Prešov. The rapturous reception accorded Dubček, the classic victim of the normalized regime, and the organized presence of significant numbers of workers from the giant petrol refinery Slovnaft suggested that Slovak Communists were in the same predicament as were their Czech comrades.

Leaders in Prague found it difficult to accept the new conditions in which it was impossible to lock up or otherwise intimidate the opposition. There were signs that they were giving ground to the public demand for dialogue, though they persisted in their dictatorial attitudes, displayed in the way they debated with the public, whether face-to-face or in the press, and in their stubborn refusal to countenance change. For instance, Štěpán praised Archbishop Tomášek for his part in the canonization in Rome of a fourteenth-century Bohemian princess, Anežka, which he called "an act of great patriotic and cultural significance." Štěpán's real purpose was to persuade the archbishop to use his influence with the prominent group of Catholics in CF and with the students to end their strike. The party's choice of emissary could not have been worse. Reports in the party press distorted the substance of their meeting, drawing a sharp rebuke from the archbishop, who stated that his commitment to truth obliged him to give his full support to CF. Another example involved the meeting of Minister of Education Jana Synková, the Student Strike Coordinating Committee, delegates of strike committees from all the faculties in Bohemia and Moravia, and all university rectors. The upshot of their discussion was, according to the party press, an agreement to end the strike on Sunday, November 26, and to resume classes on the morning of the day scheduled for the general strike. These and other instances of deliberately falsified reporting hardened the students' resolve.

Students' suspicions were not allayed by maneuverings on the part of the Central Committee of the National Front, which hinted strongly that political change was in the air. This formal coalition of the CPC, Czech Socialist party, and People's party in the National Assembly[41] planned a parliamentary commission to prepare a new constitution strengthening the legal basis of the socialist state. Citizens were to have the right to take any disputes concerning their civil, political, or legal rights to a new constitutional court. Krupauer, the general procurator, was ordered to speed up the framing of new laws on the press, association, and assembly and work out proposals for the independence of the judiciary. This cut no ice, largely because the demand for an inquiry into November 17 had been blatantly ignored. When pressed, Krupauer relented, adding that the commission of investigation would be made up of a "special group." Apart from the sense of injustice this included, Blahož, the director of the Institute of State and Laws, commented publicly that it was all a sham, as the forces of the Ministry of the Interior were beyond the reach of the civil code and could only be investigated by a military tribunal. The students accordingly prepared for any submergence of the issue by filing 150 depositions of eyewitnesses in their own archives.

It was evident that the CPC had no coherent plan to deal with the new situation. Křeček, the secretary of the National Front, officially withdrew the party's condemnation of students and demonstrators as "criminal elements," whereas Ladislav Toman, first vice-president of the Czech Socialist Republic, displayed the real face of opinion in the Central Committee. In a speech to the students of the faculty of agriculture, he said dialogue with demonstrators was impossible because they had not sought nor received permission to assemble; apparently unaware of events, he also maintained that the government could not meet CF, which was an illegal organization. He added that although the question of the leading role of the party would be addressed in the new constitution, personnel changes were the sole preserve of the Central Committee.

In Prague support for the party had shrunk to such a point that only the echelons of the union bureaucracies of the RTUM and the Central Council of Trade Unions (CCTU) could be counted on. Yet they were unable to commit their members in the same way. Indeed, they alienated them completely by presuming to speak in their name in their messages of support to the Central Committee. As a result, support for the general strike hardened in the factories, and for the first time workers appeared in great numbers and on an organized basis at the Thursday demonstration in Wenceslas Square. Particularly encouraging to CF was the presence of the industrial workers from the ČKD group. The party's supposed backing from the industrial workers was proved to be a dead letter with the reception accorded Štěpán at the ČKD Locomotive Works. Attempting to marshal support there, he observed that the party would not be dictated to by children, referring to the striking students. The workers' response was swift and damning: He was howled down with shouts of "We are not children."

Most if not all opposition groups were united in their demand for cadre changes in the Central Committee as a prelude to the restoration of political, legal, and civil rights. Some thought it the essential first step in the cleansing and renewal of socialism, others in the evolution of a multiparty system and eventually the revival of a liberal, parliamentary democracy based on a market economy. The publication of CF's policy document "What We Want" on Thursday, November 23, gave a powerful push to all these groups.[42] Support for the demands spread across all age levels and social spheres. It ranged from the footballers of Slavia and Sparta to the virtuoso violinist Josef Suk (grandnephew of the doyen of Czech national composers, Antonín Dvořák), from pensioners to the legal establishment, from the medical profession to the media. The list grew after Thursday, when Czechoslovak Television broadcast reports of the demonstrations in Prague to the provinces, which signaled the beginning of the end of the party's ability to manipulate opinion in the countryside. It is true that Jakeš received a few genuine offers of support from party and union organizations in Most and Plzeň, but these were quickly swamped by the founding of local CFs or ecological initiatives. At that point, the workers in the heavy industries of Ostrava were an unknown quantity. In the event, geography dictated that their interest developed only after Jakeš had fallen.

The presidium of the CPC could no longer ignore the pressure from the street nor from within. Adamec had gone to Moscow to consult Gorbachev. The Prague district committees of the party and the SUY blamed leaders for their failure to respond to the demands of their basic organizations. As a result, these organizations had abandoned the party and RTUM and come out in support of the student demands, and political associations in the factories had simply collapsed.[43] Opinion polls conducted from November 22 to 24 suggested that 88 percent of the population favored cadre changes.[44] The youth union, too, was adamant that Jakeš had to go but unsure about the general strike and CF. It believed that if it did not take command of the strike committees in the factories and faculties, they would be lost to Havel. The SUY left the decision on the strike until Saturday and agreed to talk to CF without preconditions and to push for cadre changes in the presidium. At this time, there appeared to be close cooperation among Mohorita, Adamec, and Jindřich Poledník, the new head of Czechoslovak Television. The extraordinary meeting of the Central Committee finally took place after two postponements on Friday, November 24. It repeated all the reforms promised by

Close to the end—the general secretary of the CPC, Miloš Jakeš, on the evening of his resignation, November 24, 1989.

the National Front and granted some of the student demands by shortening military service and giving the right to travel freely abroad. A new press law was promised giving the media more autonomy and likewise a new election law giving a variety of political parties and independents the chance to enter Parliament. The major overhaul of the Communist system was to be completed by quickening the economic reforms and delegating power from the center to the local government administrations, the national committees. But the failure to address the problem of the leadership made all such concessions moot. Jakeš finally resigned along with the entire presidium, though not before trying to squirm out of it by suggesting that only Karel Hoffman, Alois Indra, and Husák should go. With an indifference to public sentiment that amounted to contempt, the last two named kept their functions of state. Hegenbart was nominated to take over in place of Jakeš, but in the end Karel Urbánek, the safe candidate, became the new general secretary. Only three of the "collaborators of the normalization" did not find their way back into the newly elected Central Committee. Miroslav Zavadil, the union leader, was not dropped; neither was Jozef Lenárt. Perhaps most inflammatory of all was the continued presence of Štěpán, the villain of November 17.

~c 5 ~

The Collapse of the Old Regime

The party's strategy of removing only the most discredited members of the Central Committee and replacing them with relatively youthful candidates not identified with the normalization was inadequate as a means of appeasing the public. The situation outside had gone so far that the ruse simply could not work. This was evident in particular from the public reaction to Urbánek's election. His provincial origins and his former profession of railway stationmaster made him the butt of jokes embodied in popular slogans reflecting an aversion as much to a lack of professional competence in government as to a lack of education and accomplishment in the individual. People remarked, "We want a government of technocrats" and "Masaryk spoke seven languages. Can anybody be found here who can at least speak good Czech or Slovak?" Yet the public reaction to Urbánek's appointment was minor compared with the outcry raised by the retention of odious figures in the Central Committee. Even before the daily demonstration—which had outgrown Prague's main square and been moved to Letná, a large, open space in the city center once used mainly for military parades—public protests were flooding into the Czechoslovak Press Agency. But dissonant and more influential voices were also raised closer to home.

The Prague Communist party structure rested on the so-called basic organizations that existed in factories, offices, and educational institutions. These were subordinated to territorially based district committees and city committees. Early on Saturday the chairmen of the basic organizations of the CPC secured Štěpán's resignation as leader of the Prague City Council. Their support for some of the basic demands of the students and CF indicated the sea change in grassroots party opinion against the Central Committee. For instance, they asked the procurator to investigate the moving spirit behind the police attack, accepted the principle of dialogue, and expressly asked their representatives to negotiate with CF. They urged the formation of public discussion groups to ventilate the question of the events of 1968 and the role played during and after by leading members of the party still in their functions. They left the principle of democratic centralism in ruins with their directions to the party presidium to inform them to what extent the student demands had been met. Though they supported Urbánek's election as the first step in the renewal of the party, they refused to accept the views of the Central Committee as binding without the assent of the basic organizations. Their demand for a cleanup of the editorship of *Rudé právo* also reflected a novel interest in ending censorship. Yet their support for the student demands and for a call to return to grassroots input into the affairs of the party was not backed up by any commitment to the general strike or explicit sanctioning of CF.

The CPC's refusal to make any significant changes in the leadership did nothing to alter the balance of opinion in its favor and against the general strike. The concessions the party made, principally the release of eight important political prisoners, including Petr Uhl, Jiří Ruml, Miroslav Kusý, and Ján Čarnogurský, all of whom subsequently played important parts in CF, were minor and suggested the CPC had no clear idea how to meet the challenge posed by the mass mobilization of the people. In general, the party relied on the industrial and agrarian working class to ignore the appeals of the students and CF to support the strike scheduled for November 27. They counted, too, on the fact that because the right to strike was not part of the constitution of the republic, social conformity would work in the party's favor. Party leaders further argued that a strike was not necessary when the New Economic Mechanism was in place and socialist democracy was guaranteed by dialogue with all parties and the "imminent" decentralization of power to the local administrations. The conference of CPC basic organizations on Saturday, November 25, showed no great enthusiasm for a strike, though not from any great sense of loyalty to the party. Rather, the organizations saw that their legitimate grievances were being reflected in the resolutions of both party and union factory committees and had reached the Central Committee. Their reluctance also hinged to a significant degree on the definition and associations of the word *strike,* which most people, workers or not, knew only from folk memories of the First Republic or from the wide coverage Czechoslovak Television habitually gave to strikes in Western European countries. The images of police violence during the British miners' strike of 1984 were not easy to dislodge. Yet it was not clear to what extent the Central Committee could maintain sufficient authority over its 1.7 million members to at least neutralize them when all the signs indicated an incipient three-way split among the leading cadres, the younger middle-ranking members of a pro-Gorbachev disposition, and a radicalized grassroots.

The Central Committee's arguments were based on a conventional notion of strike entirely different from that of Havel, which in the end proved decisive. Though the original idea for a general strike belonged to the students,[1] its character was determined to a large extent by Havel and his associates, who well understood the reservations of the industrial workers, especially outside Prague. Havel considered it a political protest strike, and the proclamation of Citizens Forum on the general strike indicated economic damage was not part of its agenda.[2] In an effort to stave off an event that was in effect an informal referendum on Communist power, the CPC nevertheless condemned it as a form of economic sabotage. CF responded by making it plain that the planned strike had none of the qualities normally associated with strikes, either as regards aims, timing, or organization: It was an opportunity for the public to register protest and an informal referendum on the leading role of the party, which had that very day been abolished in East Germany. It was timed for 12 noon, which for industrial workers and a majority of administrative staff alike meant the last two hours of the working day. For others, it involved a slightly postponed and extended lunch hour. More significant, people were invited to form strike committees themselves in their place of work. For the first time, people were offered an opportunity to elect a strike committee, initiate, run, and conclude the strike in their own way beyond the maw of the union and party bureaucracies. The role of the National Strike Coordinating Committee of Citizens Forum was nondirective; it functioned as an information center, gathering, collating, and passing on information on the preparations and course of the strike.[3] There was no intention of attacking the flow of production in the economy as a way of bringing the party to its senses, nor of interrupting the essential flow of services to the community. For this reason, the strike in service industries and public transportation was intended to be only symbolic. Its essentially benign character was underlined by students' standing in where required, helping allay public concern, particularly about health care.

The growth in support for the strike in Prague coincided with the fall of Jakeš—seventy-seven industrial companies had expressed themselves for the strike by November 24.[4] Regionally, it developed in accordance with the ending of the information blockade. Students finally won access to the factories on November 23 after the protest movement in Czech Television was able to broadcast Štěpán's embarrassing confrontation with the ČKD workers. The growing independence and differentiation of views in the Czech media were reflected in the mounting public interest in the

Miloš Jakeš listens to criticism in Parliament.

media and in the issues they opened up to public discourse. For instance, interest in Western media sources of information fell by almost 60 percent, whereas 95 percent of the television-watching public turned to Czech news.[5] The media in effect played an important, indirect role in mobilizing opinion—though its newfound duty to inform also fueled the doubts of those who gave greater weight to their reports of imminent swinging rises in food prices.

This issue occupied center stage at the largest demonstration of the revolution, when roughly three-quarters of a million people gathered on Letná on the afternoon of November 25. Distinguished economists and workers alike dismissed Urbánek's view that a strike would cause economic collapse. Petr Miller, a ganger from ČKD Elektrotechnika, spoke for many when he referred to workers' attendance at the numerous Communist festivals. "How many times did we spend hours and hours in obligatory jubilation at pointless demonstrations and nobody was bothered. And now?" Others poked fun at the party's double standards. The claim that the strike would cause a devastating loss of production when other workers in the shape of the People's Militia had left their own factories, traveled en masse to Prague, and spent three days in the capital "strengthening the ranks of the exhausted police in their defense of public buildings," as a party communiqué had put it, cut little ice. Although economic performance in Czechoslovakia was better than that in neighboring Communist countries, national feeling on the standard of living was very largely summed up in the simple slogan, "What is two hours compared with forty years?" An observer of work methods might add wryly that at least as far as white-collar staff were concerned, two hours represented one or perhaps two of the morning shopping trips many people inveterately took during working hours.

The Catholic church, as we have already noted, played its part in the social process undermining Communist power in at least three distinct ways. As a general, cultural institution, it was the most specific embodiment of the national past and as such was ideally placed to return national identity to the people. An important step in this process was taken even before the revolution. The canonization of Princess Aněžka on November 12 in Rome opened a window onto Europe for the Czechoslovak millions who watched the live television broadcast. The temporary slackening of travel restrictions enabling tens of thousands of Czechoslovak Catholics to travel to Saint Peter's and the presence of official representatives of the CPC also indicated that this was a significant national event even for the Communist state. This affirmation of the national past had a no less direct impact on nonbelievers.

Second, representatives of the church had a high public profile in Citizens Forum, as the Letná demonstration showed, not least in the shape of its spokesman, the dissident and temperamental priest Václav Malý. Other men of the cloth, such as Tomáš Halík, doctor, secret priest, and adviser to Tomášek, worked more discreetly and effectively, counseling students on strategy. Though it is stretching a point, they were popularly and romantically associated with the historical role of the Czech rural lower clergy who had resisted the denationalizing tendencies of the Habsburg state in the nineteenth century. A small section of their urban counterparts were acclaimed for their efforts in association with underground movements, in restraining the denationalization of the people that the social and economic organization of the Communist state had involved. During the revolution, this was reflected in the slogans rejoicing in the recovery of national identity, personally and internationally; for instance: "The heart of Europe has once more started to beat" and "Citizens Forum! Citizens Forum! I feared I'd never raise my head again."

Finally, the overt participation of the church had a direct effect in mobilizing believers. As noted in Chapter 2, there was a strong current of support for religious freedom before the revolution. As events unfolded, this crystallized into the public, political activity of practicing Catholics in small and medium-sized towns and, particularly in Moravia, expressed largely in high levels of participation in local Citizens Flora. Olomouc in central Moravia is a good example. Here the concentration of Catholics who had suffered from officially inspired discrimination was striking. The draw of religious freedom and the prospect of rebuilding their professional lives pushed them to the forefront of the local CF. The religious dimension had another side that complicated matters for the CPC. Devout Catholics were to be found mainly in the countryside and were connected in some way to the land, which for all practical purposes meant agricultural cooperatives. This brought them into close proximity to the party and, indeed, many were members. There was a tension between religious commitment and allegiance to the party, and published appeals from either side, which often did not get through to many rural areas at all, simply led to muddle and indecision. This confusion, along with the constraints of rural life and the fact that the struggle between CPC and opposition was fought out largely in Prague and major conurbations, helped to neutralize Catholics.

The Catholic church in the Czech Lands is not identified with national survival as it is in Poland, yet enough of its cultural and ethical presence remained to remind people of their past as a nation. Though fewer than one-third considered religious freedom a major problem, most Czechs in these conditions attached national importance to religious festivals.[6] Tomašek's mass commemorating the canonization of Saint Anĕžka held on Sunday morning before the second Letná demonstration is a case in point. He made it clear that the church was on the side of the nation and unambiguously supported CF as an expression of national sentiment as much as for the moral basis on which it conducted its struggle. This and his public rebuke of *Rudé právo* for questioning the authenticity of his statement condemning the police attack enhanced his moral authority among nonbelievers. There was a practical bonus for CF in that a large part of the congregation in Prague cathedral were from the countryside and were quite unclear about the tide of events. After mass, they joined the demonstration at Letná and on their return home provided a conduit of reliable information reinforced by a bank of alternative news publications and agitation materials from students and CF.

The Letná Demonstration

Letná, so often the scene of contrived enthusiasm generated on International Labor Day, was transformed on Sunday, November 26, into a national celebration in which more than 5 percent of the population of the republic took part. Estimates place the figure at about three-quarters of a million. A much smaller demonstration took place in Bratislava at the same time, though its aims were almost identical: the abolition of Article 4 of the constitution guaranteeing the CPC's leading role, support for the general strike, genuine personnel changes in the leadership of party and state, and free elections. Havel reminded his listeners in Prague

Three-quarters of a million people gather to demonstrate on Letna in Prague, November 25, 1989 (photo by Karel Cudlín).

that the success of the strike depended on maintaining the normal operation of the economy and public services. He urged the strike committees to remain in a state of permanent readiness for further strikes and to simultaneously transform themselves into Citizens Fora and "self-administering and independent representatives of the common will throughout the republic." To demonstrate his commitment to dialogue, Havel had invited the chairman of the government, Adamec, to address the crowd. As might be expected at a large gathering, he was given an uneven reception. Among other factors, his refusal to accept a seat in the revised party leadership had done his popularity no harm at all. Indeed, he was at that time the most popular person in the republic.[7] His message that the government was ready to accede to all demands "in its power" was widely appreciated. People also noticed with satisfaction that he, like the Communist media, had dropped the word *comrade* as a form of address, which they took to be decisive evidence that a new era of sanity had dawned. Yet the many catcalls and cries of "Too late!" that greeted his comment welcoming the continuation of dialogue, not dissimilar to one Havel had made, reflected the widespread frustration felt at having to wait so long for a clear reaction from the party to the police attack and to the initiative of CF. Few were impressed with Adamec's view that a three-minute strike was adequate to express support for change.

Letná also showed that there was not always a congruence between the representatives of the Catholic church in CF and sections of the public. Although the latter's critical, secular, semianarchistic slant gave them no difficulty in identifying with Havel, they were not much taken with Malý's dismissive and offensive treatment of Adamec, which awoke much sympathy for the latter, not only among those present but also among the public at large; such actions, the people believed, did not serve the two central issues of democracy and dialogue. The moderator's jibes at Adamec were a poor advertisement for both and had more to do with the old authoritarianism than the new regime of dialogue. The students at the theater academy in particular were incensed with his exhibition and with the introduction in which he stated baldly: "We are the forum and we shall decide who will speak at the meeting." This high-handed behavior and the students' distaste for the barracking of Adamec created powerful tensions that almost caused them to split with CF. The students demanded an explanation, howled down a representative of the forum hurriedly sent to pacify them at a meeting of the Prague Student Strike Committee, and prepared to distance themselves publicly from Havel and his colleagues. The bitter debate that followed ended in the narrow defeat by thirteen votes to seventeen of a motion supporting a split. However, it helped to remind CF that student support was not unconditional. Many letters of complaint showed that television viewers, too, were unhappy with the situation, and Malý was thereafter persuaded to adopt a lower public profile.

A hero's welcome was reserved for a former member of the party, Alexander Dubček. His presence on the tribune with CF was important for a number of reasons. Though people had heard little enough of his activities, with the exception of his interview on Hungarian television in 1988, the courage and integrity of his struggle against Brezhnev in 1968 to preserve some remnants of national freedom had entered the annals of folklore. He, too, was the living example of the kind of rank discrimination people had suffered at the hands of the party, which had left few untouched.

Yet there was another, equally significant dimension to his role. Even at this early stage of the revolution, voices were raised in Slovakia expressing various degrees of skepticism about the intentions of the Prague CF, which some described as "a gang of rootless intellectuals from the Prague ghetto." Extreme though these were, such views put their finger on the vexed question of the nationalities, which, if it had been allowed to split the national unity that CF and Public Against Violence were cooperatively building, might have given the party an opportunity to rescue something. Dubček, as a Slovak national, helped provide a bridge between the nationalities. There were and still are many reasons for mutual suspicion between Czechs and Slovaks. Czechs of the older generation are influenced by folk memories of the First Republic. Their fathers recalled 1919, when the independence of the newborn Czechoslovak Socialist Republic was momentarily threatened by the founding in Prešov of the Slovak Soviet Republic, sponsored by the neighboring Hungarian Soviet Republic. Doubtless unaware that its leader, Antonín Janoušek, was a Czech, they easily concluded that the rural and backward character of Slovakia and the presence of sizable ethnic minorities could only hinder the process of national integration and endanger the state. Before the war Czechs complained of massive and unprofitable investment in the eastern half of the republic, whereas Slovaks spoke of exploitation.

The contrast of national stereotypes also served to point up differences. The phlegmatic, skeptical, beer-drinking, urban Bohemian was rooted in a relatively advanced industrial society and tended to dismiss the Slovaks as emotional, priest-ridden, wine-bibbing peasants unable to throw off the semifeudal survivals lingering from a thousand years of Hungarian domination. Religion also could not unite them. The supporters of the Hussite heresy in Prague and, worse, the atheist and anticlerical views of the old Czech Social Democrats were generally anathematized by the influential Slovak Catholic clergy. This sense of cultural division, though exaggerated, was aggravated by an impression of being economically hard done by and was a factor in the Slovaks' breaking away from the Czech Lands in 1940, when Monsignor Jozef Tiso founded an independent Slovak clerical republic under the patronage of Nazi Germany. The collaboration between the Slovaks and the Germans was seen as contributing to the disappearance of the Czechoslovak state.

Quite apart from the question of the Slovak language, which many Czechs regard as a dialect of Czech, these and similar attitudes were not ameliorated among a later generation in the Czech Lands after the post-1968 normalization had gotten under way. It was even popularly and falsely believed that party retribution for and after the Prague Spring was such that disproportionately more Czechs were on the receiving end, which fueled the view that Slovaks once again were evening the score. Resentment was caused too by a sense of economic discrimination. For example, two-thirds of the gross national product (GNP) was invested annually in Slovakia from the early 1970s until 1987, though its population represented only at most one-quarter.

Apart from the three main speakers, the Letná demonstration became a festival of "theater sketches brought to life and reflecting public opinion," as CF described it. Insofar as the CF did not check the credentials of the speakers (which would have been difficult, given their number) it laid itself open to the abuse of potential provocateurs. In the event, there was some dispute whether the ad hoc choice of speakers was justified. Though billed as an opportunity for common citizens to speak their minds, there was a tendency to marginalize groups, in particular political groups, that may have helped weaken or deflect support away from CF. Some, such as the vice president of the City Council of the SUY and a delegation from the Caucus of Prague Communists, were not offered a chance to address the crowd. Students of the philosophy faculty who had earlier indicated they wanted nothing to do with certain leading members of CF were similarly denied. A feeling rapidly developed that the dialogue was turning into a monologue that, until the second week of the revolution, had CF teetering on the edge of a rift.

Among the other speakers, two contributions were of unusual public interest. The first, made by economist Miloš Zeman, showed that statistics could have a powerfully emotional effect. He introduced the gathering to "several facts that *Rudé právo* will not publish," among them, that the levels of further education and economic growth put the republic on a par with the Third World. At the same time, Czechoslovakia had the highest level of pollution in Europe and the second highest mortality rate.[8] Surprise was added to indignation by the appearance of Ludvík Pinc, a lieutenant in a motorized unit of the security forces who had seen service on National Avenue on November 17. He described the dissatisfaction in the service caused by having to police peaceful demonstrations instead of fighting crime. Though he accepted responsibility for the police intervention, he pointed out that the decision had been taken elsewhere. Because the security forces were subject to military justice, it would have been impossible for them to disobey orders. Pinc expressed police support for the imminent democratizing changes and the hope that the media would discontinue their attacks, which, with the palpable hatred of the public, was having a dire effect on police morale.[9]

Štěpán's Removal

The news of a counterdemonstration in the provincial town of Litoměřice gave little comfort to the Central Committee. Even if it were not a put-up job, 2,000 people shouting slogans in support of the party was a derisory response to the protest movement that had captivated Prague. The day of the general strike showed to what extent it could claim to be an all-national concern. The party's immediate problems were mounting daily and were not helped by the leadership's inability to make concessions or take steps to quiet the social tension. The two they did take— the dispatch of the People's Militia to Prague and the cosmetic changes in the Central Committee—considerably aggravated the situation inside and outside the party.

Sheer ineptitude played its part. Some of the party notables, like Zdeněk Hoření, editor in chief of the party paper, admitted to not having even read the demands of Citizens Forum. Although Czechoslovak Television had already indicated its support for the strike, it was no longer a question of simply having lost control of the media. The party itself was split in a number of ways. The basic organizations of both the party and RTUM, which concentrated workers at the grassroots, and in some cases the factory committees as well, had parted company with the district committees made up of full-time party staff. These splits were not restricted to Prague, as is clear from the extraordinary meeting of the district chairmen of the Central Council of Trade Unions on November 26.[10] The union structure had divorced itself from its members in the same ways as the party had from its members, a point Urbánek himself had accepted in his televised speech to the nation.[11] The CCTU responded by sacking Zavadil, its chairman, and replacing him with a retired miner, Karel Haneš. Bowing to the inevitable or in the new spirit of democracy, the union left workers to make their own decision whether to joint the strike.

Urbánek also had to meet the challenge from within the upper echelons of the party. Not only was Obroda, the reform Communist movement known as Renewal, gaining influence, but a new movement, the Democratic Forum of Communists, founded by younger members, harked back to the radical socialist origins of the party.[12] Both groups drew support away from the discredited leadership in the numerically largest middle echelons of the party. The flight from the party was accelerated by the effects of the decay of the SUY and of the formation of a National Student Strike Committee (because of the emergence of strike committees at universities outside of Prague) and something similar to an independent student trade union. This had implications for the provinces. Younger workers organized in factory sections of the SUY, aware of students' resigning en masse from its student sections, also began to agitate for reform. The youth union regional secretaries responded by softening their blockade on student access to the factories in an effort to preempt the expected demand for an entirely new youth organization; this move in fact only delayed the final collapse of the SUY.

After the Central Committee had torn itself into pieces in the search for a solution at an all-night meeting, it finally had to accept that the game was up even before the strike. Early on Monday, November 26, the party acceded to the wishes of the public, and Štěpán and all the villains of the normalization disappeared from the Central Committee. Only nine of the original twenty-four members of the presidium and secretariat remained. They were joined by a relatively youthful mixture of engineers and workers with the vague and vain hope, on the one hand, of satisfying public opinion favoring a government of specialists and, on the other, of appeasing the union and party basic organizations, who demanded more worker representation at the highest level. A notable addition was Vasil Mohorita, who had left the dying SUY. The decision to leave the party congress until January 1990 showed the general lack of urgency, not to say despondency, that had afflicted the leading cadres throughout. By that time, the party had shrunk to a stump. Urbánek, aware of the looming defeat over the general strike, put a brave if comic face on it by claiming that it was the people's way of celebrating his election as party leader.

In a notable change of tack, the party generously praised the students for their "unity and discipline." Either this was a facile attempt at conciliation or, more likely, an absolute failure of insight. In Prague, they were not at all united, even less in the provinces. In reality, only about one-third of the students in the capital were full-time activists, whereas one-third appeared at demonstrations more or less frequently, and the remainder never showed at all, spending an unexpectedly long vacation at home. In other university towns, the figure for full-time, active partic- ipation was lower: In Ústí and Labem it was about 10 percent and in Olomouc roughly 15 percent. Some parents, including rabid anti-Com- munists, were so fearful of their children's involvement that they even threatened to break their legs so they would be unable to participate in the strike. Other odd cameos of life in the revolution have also emerged. For instance, on the day when an armed intervention was expected, three students at the medical faculty demanded their professor examine them for their finals. He was unwilling to cooperate, and they appealed to the Stalinist vice-dean for assistance. None of them was a Communist nor even a sympathizer; they were simply "normal traitors," as the saying went. In contrast, there were both party members and candidates for party membership among the active strikers. Some threw in their lot completely with the student demands, whereas others drew the line at signing the declaration condemning the invasion of 1968.

Winning the Public Over

One is bound to ask why the party machine made such a lamentable job of its propaganda campaign against the students. It seemed to be unaware of the students' weaknesses, such as low participation levels, internal strife, and profoundly undemocratic leadership, and preferred to retell the old chestnut about manipulation by foreign agents. In addition, *Rudé právo* printed interviews with nonexistent students that were immediately discredited, even though the newspaper could easily have reached the nonparticipating students. This was to an important degree the legacy of the old style of news management determined by leading party cadres. Still, truthful reporting would not have helped much either, as the public was convinced that the paper could not change its perspective. And given that the party was under siege from so many sides simultaneously, there is good reason to doubt that the party press was capable of doing anything else, particularly as it was in the end unable to insulate itself from the pressure for change from its own journalists.

In the week following the police attack, a survey suggested that more than half the public believed a general strike would be harmful.[13] In one way or another, however, roughly three-quarters of all citizens joined the strike. About 38 percent stopped work for the full two hours, 9 percent for a shorter period, and 24 percent showed support in ways recommended by CF and Public Against Violence. In general, participation was higher in the Czech Lands than Slovakia. Some 57 percent of all adults in Prague actively participated in the strike.[14] About half of them took to the streets. Of the remainder nationally, about 10 percent were prevented from showing support and the rest chose not to take part.[15] Interestingly, for the period of the strike, demand for electricity fell by 13 percent compared with a normal Monday.[16] Damage to the economy was kept to a minimum, and in most factories lost production was made up. Health care and other essential services were unaffected, and despite their wails of protest, primary school children were kept inside under the watchful eyes of their teachers.

These figures conceal the fact that though the strike was organized in some places, in others it was a last-minute, impromptu affair. Its success in Prague was due in no small degree to the efforts of a new organization, the Association of Strike Committees in Industry. It came into existence on the initiative of factory and workplace representatives whose needs for mutual information and action and for protection against victimization could not be met by a hard-pressed CF. Accordingly, with the aid of the Metro's computer system and the cooperation of the staff of the Institute of Economic Forecasting, they set up their own coordinating body fully in the spirit of self-administration espoused by Havel. The provinces, however, lagged behind Prague in this respect. Even in industrial conurbations, strike committees were not formed until the very morning of the strike, as, for instance, in Zbrojovka, the largest factory in Brno. In many factories, strike committees did not get off the ground at all, and the directors' threats of dismissal and persuasion had some effect. In Hradec Králové, not a single trade union or party basic organization or factory committee had addressed the question of the strike. Workers' frustration turned to anger, and they formed strike committees for them-

The dismantling of an agitprop slogan that reads "Glory to Communism" at the Kolben-Daněk works.

selves, though very late in the day. In a crass attempt to win back lost ground, the local RTUM attempted to pass off the organization of the strike in the main square as all their own work. It was not very different in Mladá Boleslav, the center of the Czech car industry. The Communist city council administration refused permission for a meeting, invoking the law for the protection of open spaces. The local SSM secretary, too, refused to involve himself, and citizens were again left to their own devices—which in the end worked out all to the good. The CPC derived scant comfort from its traditionally most loyal followers, the workers in Kladno, "the iron heart of the republic" and the home of radical socialism in the 1920s. Only days after November 17, strike committees had been formed that immediately came into conflict with the local RTUM. The previously agreed-upon five-minute token stoppage blew up into a two-hour strike. Grievances about party and union privilege were laid bare, and with the arrival of Prague students to work a night shift gratis at the blast furnaces, a bond of solidarity was formed with the protest movement that the appearance of Urbánek in Kladno at 6 a.m. on the morning of the strike did not undo.

Fears that support for the strike in Plzeň and Ostrava, the two largest centers of heavy industry, would be scanty were not justified. Workers in Plzeň came out solidly in favor, though the workers of the giant Škoda engineering complex rejected those views expressed at the Letná gathering, which they interpreted as the vanguard of a drive to destroy socialism. The miners and steelworkers of Ostrava, however, were much less enthusiastic. Though management had not adopted any particularly threatening attitudes, no strike committees were in evidence. The economic crisis a few kilometers away, across the border in Poland, was visible on a daily basis in the form of Polish profiteers who bought up goods in the shops of the north Moravian border towns; this was sufficient reason for the turnout to be limited to a few thousand. Neither were miners very prominent in the strikes that took place in the other major industrial area of the republic, north Bohemia, but for quite different reasons. In Most, for example, they represented about 10 percent of the 10,000 people who met to demonstrate. Although half of them did display a symbolic commitment to strike, the remainder, roughly 43,000, did not break off production. Instead, they continued to fuel the coal-fired power stations supplying Prague and much of northern and western Bohemia with electricity.

All sides claimed a victory from the general strike, though some looked distinctly hollow—for instance, that of the trade union paper *Práce*. Its assertion that the strike was a "decisive voice in the renewal of socialism" coincided with more divisions in the CPC.[17] A section of the reform Communists experienced another split with the foundation of the Club of the Marxist Intelligentsia around the journal *Tvorba*. The political parties in the National Front began to set out their credentials as partners in the process of political change and renewal. The Czech Socialists were among the constant companions and advisers of Adamec in the government delegation's daily negotiations with CF. The People's party, irreversibly discredited, drove out its old leaders and elected Josef Bartončík leader, though his past, too, later made him the subject of much controversy. The strike brought more immediate benefits. The head of Czech Television was replaced and the end of censorship officially recognized by the abolition of the index of banned books and films. Jakeš gave up his position as chairman of the Defense Council, and Indra resigned as chairman of the Federal Assembly. The Central Committee handed over Sanops, a state-of-the-art hospital for the exclusive use of party members (and indeed the first clinic to have been built in Prague since 1945) to the Ministry of Health for the use of the general public. This was a watershed, too, for the growth of voluntary organizations, which hitherto had been refused registration but were then coming out in droves. Strike committees in some Prague factories took the first steps in the depoliticization of the factories with the abolition of the institutions of the RTUM.

Evidence suggests that a variety of motives induced the public to join the strike. Support for CF was not the major one.[18] The primary reasons were to protest against the police attack and "negative phenomena" in society (98 percent), to show solidarity with students and actors (95 percent), to support changes in the leadership of the CPC (95 percent), and to support CF (86 percent).[19] The strike's success was due in significant part to CF's tactic of adopting an informal structure and constituting itself as an umbrella organization without any specific political inclinations beyond those associated with an effective democratic system ensuring equal political and civil rights. This accurately reflected public aversion to political parties, which lingers to this day. Further, because of its strong democratic socialist and reform Communist dimension, working people—who, as polls then suggested, preferred either a socialist road of social development or a "third way"—had no fears that the movement would jeopardize the future of socialism.[20] In the end, the strike committees took advantage of the divisions between party and union members and the CPC and RTUM functionaries to organize working people against the Communist government; such opposition found a more consistent expression after it had been transformed into local Citizens Fora.

During the week following the general strike, the three main pillars of Communist power were abolished. First to go, on November 29, were Article 4, constitutionally guaranteeing the Communist party's leading role, and the amendments to Articles 6 and 16, ensuring its domination of the political parties in the National Front. A survey suggested this reflected the wishes of 90 percent of the population.[21] Soon after, a process was initiated leading to the dissolution of party basic organizations at the level of factory, farm, and workplace. Marxism-Leninism was abolished as the official ideology of the state and as the basis for cultural and educational policy. The Article 4 abolition debate in the Federal Assembly was carried live on television and was an important part of the public's political education. It provided evidence that the students' description of it as "a parliament of political corpses" was not a polemical device. Many members were visibly ignorant of the most basic parliamentary procedures. Others could not decide to which of the two parliamentary houses they belonged, even after three years of the life of that Parliament. It strengthened popular feeling that a new, freely elected, legislative body was essential.

The students, as we have seen, played a central role along with the acting community in mobilizing opinion against Article 4 and in taking the struggle to factories and farms not only to inform but also to initiate a campaign leading to their depoliticization. Less widely known is the students' struggle to topple leading Communists by invoking their own constitution. Moves were afoot at the very outset of the revolution to pick off individual members of Parliament and local government—and not only Communists—by a constitutional right of recall operating on the basis of public petition. Jakeš and Štěpán, in particular, were among the targets of this ingenious campaign, organized and led by the students of the law faculty assisted by staff members, which contributed significantly to the buildup of public pressure and led to a demand for their resignations. In the event, they resigned their mandates on December 5 following a recommendation of the Commission of Inquiry to Parliament and not directly as a result of the signature campaign. Nevertheless, it was a useful exercise in that it furnished further proof that the constitution was a sham.

Students' knowledge of the law and the constitution was put to good use in other ways. With the distribution of thousands of pamphlets, the public was informed of its rights in relation to the security forces. This unprecedented development in effect challenged the hitherto more or less arbitrary powers of the police and pegged them back still further. The People's Militia also became a subject for close scrutiny, the public becoming indignant upon learning that the militia had neither legal nor constitutional existence and could not therefore be abolished. It was enough simply for each unit to end its own activity. Indeed, when they became aware of their legal vulnerability—when the few militiamen prepared to resist the revolution considered the possibility that with the CPC out of power, they would have to answer for their own actions as private citizens before the courts—the militias in the railway yards in Olomouc and Gottwaldov, now Zlín, performed two other valuable services whose effects further weakened the institutions on which the power of the CPC relied. The law students reminded working people organized in the RTUM (roughly 98 percent of the working population) that their union had a duty to defend the rights of all workers. For all practical purposes, a worker could not be disciplined for "unexplained absence" (for example, attendance at the general strike or other action) or sacked without the agreement of the RTUM official. If a worker was dismissed with the approval of such an official, it was enough for 50 percent of the members to call a meeting and elect a new official. In many cases, the basic organizations, as has already been shown, came out of their own accord in support of the opposition. In others, where factory directors threatened drastic action, the basic organizations temporized, the workers came out anyway, and no sanctions were applied. The law students, widening their drive for the depoliticization of society, also drew attention to the previously overlooked legal position of the armed forces. According to their oath of allegiance, they owed a duty not to the republic but to the CPC, which tied them directly into the power structure of the party.

The new Communist party leadership was patently unable to resist the tide of events. Adamec had agreed to form a federal government by December 3 with representation for the citizens' initiatives and independents; the new government was intended to guarantee free elections, civil liberties, and the removal of political influence in the workplace. Yet not only was the constitutional power of the CPC in eclipse, so too was its influence on the trade union movement. Evidence suggests that within the trade unions a process was taking place analogous to the one afflicting the party, in which rank-and-file party members had simply torn themselves away from the upper echelons of party officials. As early as November 26, the Central Council of Trade Unions recommended that all basic organizations in every factory and farm hold direct elections with a secret ballot to form new, independent union organizations and to enter a dialogue with all sides "in the interests of quickening the pace of perestroika." It supposed that, free of the burden of the CPC, it could maintain itself as an umbrella organization preserving the unity of the trade union movement. The Union of Building Workers showed the council was very much mistaken. The union removed the full-time officials and all party members, broke away from the RTUM, and, without a mention of perestroika, took steps, as reported in *Práce,* "to open a constructive dialogue with the economic leadership and Citizens Fora with the aim of achieving the justified demands of working people." The union further promised to donate 1 million crowns from the RTUM's solidarity fund to the striking students.

The old union structure also came under attack from the strike committees, which had had such conspicuous success during the general strike. In many cases, factory and office committees of the RTUM had worked closely with them during the strike. Nevertheless, it was clear that the undemocratic electoral procedure of the RTUM, based on candidates chosen by the hierarchy of paid officials and indirect elections, and its uniform structure could not survive. The loose organization of strike committees remained in existence after the strike, principally to protect the striking workers from subsequent harassment and victimization. Within days, however, the workers had formed themselves into a federation of strike committees. The federation promised, too, to organize a Congress of Independent Unionists for January 1990. The spirit of the times was clearly in favor of new movements and political configurations, and this was as visible in the decline in popularity of Charter 77 compared with CF as in the collapse of confidence in the RTUM. By December 9, surveys indicated that only 14 percent of people placed

The new general secretary of the party, Karel Urbánek, under pressure in his office (photo by Miroslav Zajíc).

their hopes in the old union structure compared with 62 percent for the new independent unions.[22]

The situation for the CPC in local government across the country was not very promising. The national and county committees, the organs of local and county administration, staffed overwhelmingly by party members, were at this stage involved in discussions with local Citizens Fora that had sprung up across the country. The response of Urbánek to the world crashing around his ears was not atypical of the kind of totalitarian thinking that had characterized the CPC for much of its tenure of power and reflected its ingrained habits. It is a great irony and comfort that, when left to themselves, totalitarian regimes often cannot see the innumerable and obvious signs that their end is fast approaching. The Central Committee, arguably the best-informed institution in the republic, was no exception and persisted in believing that there was something left to negotiate. Urbánek, for instance, noted: "It is essential to show that we Communists are still here and here we are going to stay. In the present situation, we are duty-bound to respect all demands that ensure the further development of socialism. But now we hear of demands such as the abolition of the People's Militia and of the basic organizations of the party in the factories, the resignation of comrade-directors, the selling-off of party buildings, which we regard as unacceptable."[23]

There was evidence, though in highly volatile political conditions, of a strong residual sympathy for socialism, but it is very doubtful if it involved the party in its then existing form. Some 45 percent of those questioned in a public opinion survey in the Czech Lands expressed themselves for a "socialist way"; by mid-December this figure had declined by four points and continued its slide into the new year. Support was in general restricted to former members of the party (some two-thirds) and to those over sixty (roughly half).[24] Another measure of opinion was of particular significance in that it reflected attitudes outside the large metropolitan areas in the provincial heartlands of the party. This survey, conducted just after Jakeš's resignation, indicated that a majority of those polled thought the party incapable of leading society out of the crisis, whereas about 30 percent thought the opposite.[25] Given that 45 percent of the sample were workers and 5 percent agriculturalists, the poll showed the traditional support of the party falling away at an alarming rate.

While the nation waited for Adamec to come up with his coalition definitively dissociating the party with its totalitarian past and embracing democratic institutions, sections of the party apparat were pulling in the opposite direction. In the propaganda war with CF, they were found to be up to their old tricks. It turned out that Urbánek's visit to dissuade the Kladno coal miners from participating in the general strike had been stage-managed. Press photos suggested he had achieved his purpose, though his discussions were for the most part with office staff, while the enraged miners were kept safely underground. In another propaganda move, a document carrying the official seal of the Federal Statistical office and purporting to give details of the high salaries of actors, artists, and musicians was circulated throughout towns and villages. The author of this crude attempt to discredit the group most closely associated with Havel clearly was not aware that this information was only available from the Ministry of Finance. Another forged document, too, was going the rounds at the Congress of Cooperative Farmers; apparently emanating from the influential Institute of Economic Forecasting, it predicted large-scale unemployment as the price of economic reconstruction. Both its target and its alleged provenance are interesting. The CPC had long recognized the importance of the cooperatives in preserving their power and invested accordingly. It is probably not going too far to say that this helped increase the relative efficiency of agriculture in Czechoslovakia compared with that in neighboring socialist countries, which was a factor in delaying the onset of the revolution. The cooperatives, then, were major beneficiaries of the system, and this document had some temporary success in playing on their fear of change. As to its alleged ancestry, the institute was likely chosen by the unknown provocateur as it satisfied

A hope for better times—the economist Valtr Komárek, who was shortly to become deputy prime minister.

the public's hunger for expertise. Its director, Valtr Komárek, had experienced such a meteoric rise in popularity during the general strike—far ahead of Havel—that people spoke of him as the next chairman of a government of specialists. He and his colleagues had formed an Economic Forum that had close connections with Václav Klaus of the Institute of Economic Forecasting and others in CF. It was implied that plans were well advanced in CF for the introduction of a capitalist economy. This did not affect even the agricultural cooperatives, who during their congress (held on December 1 and 2) had already decided to abandon the CPC and found their own party, the Czechoslovak Agricultural party.[26]

On December 1, two days before Adamec returned to the negotiations with Havel bearing the presidium's suggestion for a coalition government, evidence of a serious internal crisis in the student movement in Prague began to emerge. Physical and mental exhaustion had taken their toll, and fewer and fewer students were participating. The elation experienced when Parliament abolished Article 4 of the constitution weakened the resolve of many and led them to believe that their major demands had been fulfilled. Some feared that a continuation of the strike would jeopardize their gains, persuading sections of the strike committees at the various faculties to press for the strike to be called off. The daily demonstration of popular power in the center of Prague had been discontinued, and the battle seemed to have been won. But the harder-headed among the students, in particular Martin Mejstřík, were skeptical. They argued that the changes agreed to by Parliament were merely promises. Further, there was no guarantee that the "broad coalition" to be announced by Adamec on December 3 would reflect the new situation, which in the event was a justifiable suspicion. Calling off the strike in the capital at a time when the student strikes were reaching their peak in the provinces also seemed to be unwise, as many believed it would give the CPC a breathing space to reorganize. Personal differences, too, between Mejstřík and Šimon Pánek, the joint chairmen of the Student Strike Coordinating Committee, complicated matters to such an extent that the committee first voted to continue the strike, then to end it, and again to continue, all within twenty-four hours. Relations between the students and CF were frequently touchy. Quite apart from Malý's perfor-mance in Letná, the prevailing belief was that unless CF quickly broke down along party lines according to political conviction, there was the prospect of a new monopoly of political power. Some student sections were piqued that CF regarded them as having fulfilled their function as the revolutionary spark and were then attempting to shunt them off into a siding.

The difficulties between the students and CF were slight in comparison with those afflicting the CPC, racked internally by divisions and externally by mass protest. Despite opposition from the Stalinists, Adamec felt bound to respond to the social crisis. After prolonged negotiations with Havel and representatives of the non-Communist political parties, he announced a coalition government on December 3. This "Sunday govern-ment" was dismissed by the students as "a mockery of our demands," the public ridiculed it in slogans such as "1.6 million Communists are represented by fifteen ministers in the government and the remaining 14.5 million people by five," "Five new ministers, fifteen merry old men," and, in mocking imitation of Lenin, "No support for the provisional government." That the Communists were attempting to retain an absolute majority of ministerial posts, inviting only one person from the National Front parties and four with no formal political affiliation, was taken to be a de facto return to Article 4. In addition, there was grave disquiet that the ministries of the interior and armed forces were still in the hands of the CPC. Less importantly, the government did not satisfy the growing hunger of the public for a government of experts. On the same day the government was announced, the CPC gave a pledge to hand over sub-stantial amounts of party property to local administrations to provide much-needed accommodation for educational institutions. The Czecho-slovak government finally admitted that 1968 was "an abrogation of the

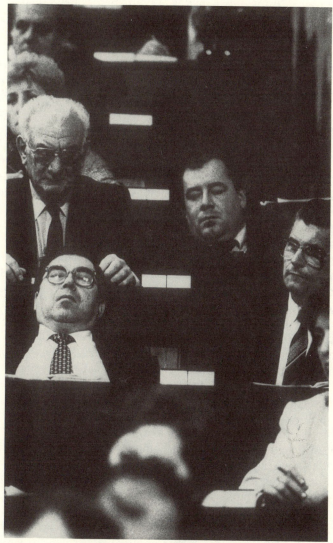

"People stay alert: Parliament is sleeping."—student slogan. Delegates slumber through a nightmare.

norms of international relations between sovereign states." Neither action helped influence public opinion in the party's favor. With the news that the state budget was financing party activities to the tune of 300 million crowns a year,[27] it was only a matter of hours before mass demonstrations started up again. CF, the National Student Strike Coordinating Committee, and the Association of Strike Committees in Industry threatened another general strike on December 11, and eleven ministers resigned the next day. Adamec followed three days later, complaining bitterly that Havel had progressively raised his demands every time they had come to an agreement. Within the next days, freedom took on visible meaning with the introduction of passport-only travel to Austria. The decision to begin dismantling sections of the barbed-wire frontier with Austria also symbolized the beginning of the end of international isolation.

The first week in December saw a palpable decline in Communist power. By December 7, 25,000 party members had resigned (though, curiously, 1,000 had joined).[28] Some 530 enterprises in Prague alone had dissolved their in-house basic organizations of the party, which was a significant proportion when compared, for instance, to the 4,182 companies that had taken part in the general strike.[29] The police were not in evidence, and Urbánek agreed that there was no longer a need for the StB. The People's Militia had started handing in their guns to army ordnance depots. The Association of Strike Committees in Industry had organized elections of nonpolitical factory committees, which amounted to the demise of the RTUM. Party members demanded direct elections to the party congress called for December 20 and the abolition of the old system of representation through regional organizations, the principal mechanism by which the Central Committee had manipulated its congresses. Further, at extraordinary regional congresses, they secured the resignations of many leading functionaries. The Slovak Communists were on the point of breaking with Prague in protest against the Central Committee's direction of their regional and county organizations. Though the CPC still had a majority in Parliament, it had stopped functioning, even in its own customarily limited way. The Czech Socialist party proposed replacing it with an executive organ to oversee the administration of the state that more or less represented the balance of opposition forces. This grew into the "government of national reconciliation." In the countryside, the movement against the party continued with the declaration of the large Union of Cooperative Farmers to support the formation of the Agricultural party.

Marian Čalfa, a Slovak Communist party member and the deputy of Adamec, was given the job of forming a coalition government that put at least half the ministries, including the interior and army portfolios, into the hands of non-Communists. The government of national reconciliation

A message from the citizens of Olomouc to Lenin, Stalin, and Gottwald: "Fly away to warmer climes" (photo by Mirka Čenková).

included seven ministers without affiliation, two Czech Socialists, two from the People's party, and ten Communists, though three of these (Čalfa, Komárek, and Vladimír Dlouhý) left the party within weeks. The inauguration of this government in effect marked the end of the revolution as an event acted out publicly in the universities, schools, factories, and, most visibly, in the streets and squares. The struggle thereafter to make free elections possible, protect the continuity of state administration, and prevent the use of state power against citizens moved behind the scenes to the lobbies of political and parliamentary institutions. The expulsion of Jakeš and Štěpán from the party did not mean that the fight to remove Stalinist influence was complete nor that the CPC had started to transform itself into a modern political party. The resignation of Husák on December 10 opened the way to a presidential election and seemed, at first sight, to offer reform communism another chance.

The Presidential Election

The breaking of the CPC's monopoly of political power and the formation of an interim coalition government roughly corresponding to the balance of political forces in the country did not yet guarantee a real democracy on the basis of political pluralism. One last major battle of the revolution still had to be won, and this involved the campaign to elect a president with prestige enough to guarantee free elections. The two characteristic features of this last stage were Havel's dramatic increase in popularity and the public's loss of its remaining vestiges of sympathy for the CPC. The election ran into difficulties because of a dispute about who was entitled to vote for the president and when the election was to be held. According to the old Communist constitution, which all agreed to abide by until the new one was fully worked out, only the members of the National Assembly were empowered to elect the president. The same constitution provided for an election within fourteen days of the resignation of the incumbent.

Havel had been suggested as a candidate by Mejstřík at the very outset of the revolution, an idea that even the radicals in the student strike committees did not take seriously until the first week of December and that the CF did not entertain until the second. His opponents were all identified publicly with communism of various vintages and convictions. The Central Committee of the National Front of the Slovak Socialist Republic nominated Dubček, whereas the SUY supported the candidature of Čestmír Císař, another reformer from 1968. The fourth nominee was Adamec.

The method of election became a cause of great debate. Although the Communists still dominated the National Assembly, they proposed a referendum, believing that in the provinces and rural areas, the name and reputation of Havel was not well enough known to secure him victory. Other political movements, for instance the Greens, demanded that the people at last be given a voice. These views were supported by opinion polls that at that time (December 12) suggested that more than four-fifths of the nation favored a referendum.[30] Some suspicion of CF and Public Against Violence was also expressed. Though they jointly had the confidence of 47 percent of the sample, about 33 percent thought they only wanted power for themselves.[31] In these circumstances, it was unlikely that an effective campaign in support of Havel could be organized within the deadline in areas that mattered. Steps were also being taken, however, to begin making a clean sweep of discredited members of Parliament and reconstructing Parliament by co-optation to guarantee the development of democracy and to reflect more closely the then current balance of political forces. With Vasil Bil'ak, one of Husák's right-hand men during the entire twenty years of the normalization, facing two charges in connection with his part in inviting Soviet forces to invade in 1968 and the certainty of his colleagues' arraignment, the CPC rid itself of all the old normalizers in the Central Committee. Their seats in Parliament were taken by co-opted non–party people. The Communists experienced a further decline in their power with the inauguration of the new Slovak government, which for the first time contained a majority of non-Communist members, and with the first nationalizations of CPC property. The party also initiated inquiries in its own ranks into the abuse of power for gain. It also agreed to end all political operations in the armed forces and other militarized citizen units by the end of the year.

The struggle for the presidency was complicated for a time by the Communists' support for a referendum. The public agreed with the idea but found it hard to accept that the Communists had suddenly become democrats and concluded that the "foxes in the Central Committee" were up to something. This confusion of opinion was reflected in Parliament, where on December 13 half the delegates favored a referendum and half were against.[32] The party's media and agitation network was still far superior to anything others could offer and was best equipped to cope with the demands of a presidential campaign within the statutory fourteen days. The National Student Strike Committee, which had still not called off its strike, demanded that the president be elected by Parliament, yet only from candidates whose "moral profile was a guarantee of the further democratic development of Czechoslovak society and who have never been members of any political party." They pressed their view by lobbying Parliament in the thousands, even busing in students from the provinces. They were also supported by Tomášek. Havel, how-

ever, with an eye on the Slovak problem, agreed to stand for the presidency
on condition that no attempt be made to drive a wedge between him
and Dubček, or, as he put it, between the Czech and Slovak voter. The
problem posed by the discrepancy between the public's wish for a voice
in the election and the constraints of the constitution was solved by a
suggestion that Parliament alone should vote in the president, but that
the ballot would be open so that the public could, if they chose, call
their parliamentary delegates to account. Further, the period of the
election campaign in the country was extended beyond the statutory
fourteen days to forty.

Havel's status internationally was a significant factor in increasing his
popularity at home. A stream of visitors beat a path to his door, including
U.S. congressmen, Italian socialists, businesspeople from East and West,
and Tomáš Bat'a, son and successor of the footwear tycoon from whom
the public expected great things.[33] Jiří Dienstbier's cutting of the barbed
wire on sections of the Czech-Austrian and Czech-German borders with
the Austrian and German foreign ministers, on December 17 and 23,
respectively, and the floods of day-trippers and weekend visitors to Vienna
and other Austrian cities were visible symbols of the collapse of the Iron
Curtain. Credit for the newfound freedom accrued almost exclusively to
CF. The challenge to Havel from the other candidates in these circumstances petered out, particularly as Čalfa in the name of the government
came out in his favor. Obroda, now in the driver's seat as regards the
reform Communists, announced that Císař had resigned, and he operated
thereafter as an independent candidate. Dubček withdrew, preferring to
run (successfully, as it turned out) for the position of chairman of the
National Assembly. Public attitudes to the CPC made Adamec a nonstarter.
He was not helped by the December 17 news of the murderous attacks
of the Communist Securitate on the people of Romania, which gave the
public cause for heartfelt thanks that their revolution had been entirely
nonviolent. It also strengthened the belief that only the election of Havel
could help ensure that conditions would never be reversed, enabling the
CPC to reimpose its dictatorship. After December 22, when all the
leading political forces in the republic agreed to accept Havel, the result
became a foregone conclusion. On December 29 he was unanimously
elected president.[34]

A week before, at its extraordinary congress, the CPC had apologized
to the people of Czechoslovakia for "the mistakes and injustices" it had
caused. It drove out the last of the old brigade, and, in a welter of insults,
accusations, and counteraccusations involving, among others, Josef
Kempný (a leading hard-liner in the old Politburo) and Urbánek, with
livid rank-and-file members hurling party cards at the podium and works
of Communist heroes raining down from the gallery, the political dicta-

torship of the party came to an end. Yet its political demise did not, as we shall see, mean the end of the economic advantages that had accrued, one way or another, to individual party members and that were to give them more than a head start in the new free-market economy. In a curious way, the economic domination of the old members of the party continued, though it took on other forms.

~6~

Reflections on the Revolution

References have been made in Chapters 2 and 3 to two conspiracy theories that suggest that the spark igniting the revolution, Black Friday, was largely the work of the Czechoslovak security forces. The one theory holds that the Czech secret police, the StB, in cooperation with the Soviet KGB was seeking to replace the Stalinists in the CPC leadership with someone closer to the Gorbachev line, in this case the reform Communist of the 1968 generation, Zdeněk Mlynář. The other favors the view that the security forces used the demonstration as a pretext for a clampdown on behalf of the Stalinists.

The Possibility of Conspiracy

Both theories raise the question of whether the revolution was an intended consequence or not. In practice, the eventual victory of the opponents of communism effectively rules out both theories, and the implication of either is that if one or the other is true, it rapidly went beyond the control of those organizing it. The notion of conspiracy is itself suspect in these circumstances in that it involves a level of complex planning predicting all or most significant developments and legislating for major eventualities affecting the main goals. Though much has been made of the mathematical expertise of the chief of the secret police, Lorenc—he is said to have constructed twenty mathematical models predicting the working out of the demonstration—it is doubtful that he took any steps at all. He did not intervene and clear the stage of CF and the faculties of the students, which anyway could only have delayed matters. This raises the question of whether, as the hub of the most extensive information network in the republic, he felt capable of containing the massive wave of resistance once it had started or whether he had no orders from the collapsing leadership.

The search for a Czech Gorbachev was also unrealistic for a number of reasons. Despite the presence of reform Communists, the whole weight of opinion in the command centers of the revolution was against communism of any variety. Though considerable support for perestroika was expressed by the basic organizations of the party and the RTUM, there was a conspicuous absence of reformist elements in the CPC and hence no one to whom such a task could have been entrusted. Mohorita enjoyed early popularity among the students in Prague, but his star quickly waned. Adamec was the most popular person in the republic until early December.[1] But his political mistakes were gross and reminiscent of the old guard, and he was written off as unable to free himself from his political heritage. Perestroika had little chance of getting off the ground without a political platform, and there was no institutional basis capable of providing it. The influence of Obroda on CF, the students, and the CPC was marginal. In any case, young people had little time for the radical socialists, mostly of the 1968 generation, with their dreams of a revival of 1968, and even less for those who had opted to emigrate. Mlynář fell into both categories.

Although evidence about the existence of a conspiracy is inconclusive, antecedents strongly suggest that change was in the cards. The course of the revolution indicated that the regime had so decayed that it was unable to rely even on the central security organs that had kept it in power for so long. The uniformed police held themselves more or less aloof from the struggle, but influential sections criticized the party to the point of demanding changes in the leadership. The People's Militia, too, refused to get involved, which, insofar as the militia was based in the factories, indicated that the bedrock of support among the industrial workers had disappeared. With the exception of a few units from the border regions, they simply left the party to its fate. The final pillar of Communist power, the army, was, however, prepared to intervene for a time. The intention to intervene was progressively modified throughout the first week of the revolution by the disintegration of the leading organs of the CPC, which in turn weakened the resolution of its leaders, and by the realization that after the general strike, the party had lost all political influence on the people. In these circumstances, the incentive to use force largely disappeared, as a successful military intervention posed all manner of difficulties concerning the subsequent running of the country. The weakness of the regime was apparent in other ways. Internally, there were severe economic and social problems; externally, it had lost the support of the Soviet Union, having even become an embarrassment to Gorbachev and his policy of perestroika.

Historical Precedents

The collapse of the regime came as a surprise to many people who, for reasons connected with the general psychological and social conditions, had never challenged it. The impact of the evaporation of fear was of critical importance, and the longer the government failed to react, the more self-strengthening the movement became. The students and CF opened a door to mass action during the revolution, enabling the people to throw off their fear and inspiring them to demonstrate on a massive scale that finally helped make them aware of the power of the collective will. This awareness had been absent in the two decades of the normalized regime, where the survival paradigm produced a general, sullen, involuntary cooperation with the party and state. Unwilling cooperation in conditions of national subjection is not a new theme in Czech history. It forms part of the national psyche and is connected in an important way with a sense of being hard done by that has tended to generate low expectations. Grumbling was endemic. But the popular discontent it expressed rarely went beyond the confines of the pub. In the end, people fell into a state of inertia by disclaiming any responsibility and acquiescing in their own fate. Under the conditions of the normalization, the regime was able to exert leverage of the crudest kind; the need to survive—and in relative comfort—became ingrained and encouraged people to withdraw from the public realm. To this was added the generational problem: Those who had reached maturity around 1968 had for the most part undergone a set of experiences that had destroyed their hopes for all time, or so they thought. The apparent impossibility of making a fight of it against such odds induced a view that lasted into the revolution and was reflected, for example, in the caution that university rectors, among many others, advised the striking students.

Similar discretion was apparent in World War II. Leaving aside the question of collaboration, there was Communist and non-Communist resistance to Nazi occupation, though it did not involve the majority. The Nazi response to the obliteration of the village of Lidice—assassination of the German head of the protectorate of Bohemia and Moravia—tended to confirm the general view that acts of resistance would only end in grief.[2] These attitudes toward the occupation are well illustrated in the novel by Josef Škvorecký, *The Cowards,* which affected the Communist authorities to the extent that they banned it when it appeared in 1958. Active organization of and participation in a rebellion was, for the most part, expressed in the Prague uprising in May 1945, when the war had only a few more months to run. The losses incurred by the Czechs in the war were relatively light compared with those of the neighboring occupied countries, and many of these were inflicted on the Jewish population.

Despite Hitler's plans for enforced Germanization involving the annihilation of those who lacked Aryan blood, the Czechs never really faced the prospect of their own extinction, unlike the Poles and, at a later period, the Israelis. The historical experiences of war and the failure of the First Republic radicalized society, and communism after the war produced a sense of history and a belief in change.

By the late 1960s, the militant younger generation of the postwar period had become middle-aged and no longer felt much sense of radicalism. The events of 1968 gave them an opportunity to put right some of the sins of their youth, particularly those committed following 1948, when they had been intoxicated by a sense of power and its reality. The old Communist cultural intelligentsia, qua Milan Kundera, had believed in the possibility of reform and change until the Soviet invasion—and, in particular, the normalization—forced them to reassess their ideals and drove them to conclude that they could not be realized, as the following quotation indicates: "If our broadly based radical front is to win, it has to grasp the fact that though it has been forced to retreat after August 1968, it has not been defeated. And so it is not necessary to adopt a risky strategy, but it should think through a rational approach about preventing the takeover of reaction and go on to realize, step by step, any opportunities for reform in the Czechoslovak situation."[3] By contrast, in a statement made fifteen years later, Kundera observed, "The Russian invasion has thrown Czechoslovakia into a 'postcultural' era and left it defenseless and naked before the Russian army and the omnipresent state television."[4] Radical but peaceful change in the context of the Prague Spring had led to disaster, which is not to imply that some reformists had not kept their radical values. However, the younger generation were not so profoundly influenced by the misfortunes of the older generation nor by the process of disillusionment affecting their parents and hence were the weak link in the chain of apathy. Though they were raised in a system of ritualized social and political activity, their will to resist was not quite blunted, and youth helped keep them immune to the disabling fear of the severe social, economic, and professional sanctions frequently applied to their parents. The ambiguity of the young is aptly reflected in an interview with three university students published in an émigré journal in 1985:

Our parents exhort us not to meddle in anything. "Finish your studies," they say, "and then we'll see." But that is not enough. I think that my generation is beginning to overcome that widely held view that nothing can be done, nothing can be improved or even made more bearable. But even we tend to deal with this problem indirectly. We tend to try to learn something and to develop our personalities and knowledge rather than to engage the issues publicly. We live as we can, and we do know how, but no one is particularly enthusiastic about it.[5]

This was symptomatic of the attitude that set students on the path to organization, albeit on a small scale and in a rudimentary way, even before the revolution. Once the students had resolved to make a stand, young people everywhere were the first to support them on a mass basis.

The Central Committee of the CPC was as surprised as the people when the revolution started. It had consistently ignored all the evidence indicating that everything was ready for a collapse, placing its trust in the fear of sanctions and the security services. Yet quite apart from the serious problems in the economy and society that were daily more visible and culminated in the emergence of public demonstrations in 1988, the committee chose to ignore indications that significant sections of party-sponsored institutions were turning against it. This is borne out, for instance, by the proceedings of the congress of the SUY one week before the police attack on November 17 and at the national conference of the basic organizations of the RTUM one day after. Once the movement started, the years of sullen discontent, disregarded as much from stupidity as policy by leading party and union functionaries, expressed itself first in the desertion of those leaders and then in the desertion of the great majority of the party rank and file.

But that was not the end of it, for most came out in support of the citizens' initiatives. The division between workers and intelligentsia so assiduously propagated by the CPC since 1948 conspicuously failed them in their hour of need. Štěpán's appeal to the factory workers was a debacle in the same way as Novotný's had been in 1968.[6] The de facto collapse of proletarian support coupled with the advent of massive public demonstrations preceded a complete failure of nerve when Jakeš and his colleagues contemplated what was at stake. It was not only a question of their losing their jobs. They had to examine their consciences, especially regarding their collaboration with the Soviets, which, technically, constituted treason. Even allowing for the disinclination of the Czechsolovak public to violence, the minds of the old Stalinist guard were no doubt concentrated on their own physical survival and on the probability that the use of force would not have advanced their case.

That the revolution was nonviolent had much to do with the character and role of the dissident movement. It had a relatively long history and, though participants were few and relatively isolated from the population, had laid down extensive networks. Considering the close attentions of the StB, it was quite outstandingly active. It is also remarkable that it survived and mobilized itself so rapidly in the first days of the revolution. The existence of networks and a more or less ready-made leadership contrasts with the situation in Romania and East Germany, where the party provided the leaders for the revolutions. Further, the Czech dissidents had contacts and sympathizers even as high as the upper echelons of the party, making them privy to inside information that enabled them to act accordingly. Linkages between dissidents and nondissidents were established without difficulty, as most activists and sympathizers were from what the Slovak clerical Right described as the "Prague intellectual ghetto." This was not large, everybody knowing or knowing of everybody else, and these connections led into most artistic and cultural institutions. The example of the students and the impressive organization of demonstrations, which never once threatened to spill over into violence, was a decisive factor in the evaporation of public fear. Though old habits die hard and the public did not come out in numbers until the day after the first—student-dominated—demonstration on November 20, the momentum the students provided built up until the entry of the workers of entire industrial complexes on November 23 confirmed the nation's rejection of the party.

The police attack, whether the result of a conspiracy or not, provided the spark for the revolution in much the same way as Sarajevo did for World War I. This explains the timing: Although few expected the revolution to break out so soon after November 17, the underlying conditions indicated that it would have come sooner or later. This is borne out by the report of a commission of inquiry, which, however, is guarded on the question of a conspiracy.

The events surrounding the revolution and their antecedents seem to be largely in character with the modern history of the Czech nation, which is better at the art of survival and, at times, at passive resistance than at open opposition and heroic acts of defiance. Revolutions do not come easily, and they tend to be nonviolent in those circumstances where victory is seen as a realistic possibility.

Hello! Josef Vissarionovich . . . Hello! . . . Hellfire and damnation!
There's no one answering any more.

AŽ PO TOBĚ, SOUDRUHU . . .

After you, comrade . . .

KONČÍME, PÁNOVÉ. KONČÍME!

We're finishing up, gentlemen. Time to go.

ZAJÍMALO BY MĚ, JESTLI SE NÁM PODAŘÍ UDĚLAT BLBCE I Z DALŠÍ GENERACE...

It would really interest me to know if we manage to make fools of even the next generation.

VŠECHNO JE JINAK, VIĎ SOUDRUHU.

Nothing is what it seems, is it comrade?

KOLIKRÁT VÁM TO MÁM OPAKOVAT, ČLOVĚČE : NE VÝCHODNÍ! STŘEDNÍ!! STŘEDNÍ EVROPA!

How many more times do I have to tell you, man—not Eastern, Central! Central Europe!

TO SE NEDIVTE, PANE REDAKTORE, ŽE VŠECHNO VÍM : JÁ VAŠE NOVINY NEČTU.

You journalists shouldn't be surprised that I know everything. I don't read the newspapers.

DÍKY NEPŘÍZNIVÉMU POČASÍ JSME SPLNILI PLÁN EMIGRACE ZA TUTO SEZÓNU NA POUHÝCH 75 PROCENT.

Thanks to the unpleasant weather, we have exceeded the plan for emigration this year by 75 percent.

JISTĚ. MŮŽETE O TOM PSÁT. ALE NESMÍTE NA TO MYSLET.

Of course you can write about it. But you mustn't think about it.

SBOHEM. A PAMATUJTE Si : ĎÁBEL - TO JE NEKONTROLOVANÁ MOC NAD LIDMI.

Au revoir and remember: The Devil is uncontrolled power over the people.

PART THREE

The Foundations of the Post-Communist State

~7~

The Establishment of Democratic Structures: January to June 1990

The Czechoslovak people greeted the new year 1990 with a sense of euphoria, optimism about the future, and a high degree of unity. The joyful mood, which we experienced during our time in Prague and the provinces, reflected, among other things, a great sense of satisfaction in having achieved liberation from the previous stultifying regime and even some surprise that the revolution had been won with such speed, orderliness, and a notable absence of violence.

Yet as we have noted, its spread had not been uniform. Provincial towns and the rural areas had lagged behind Prague and the other major cities in hailing the revolution. This was mirrored in opinion polls, which indicated that though the CPC had experienced a gradual loss of popularity, Havel and the representatives of CF had taken longer in gaining overall public acceptance. These surveys, of course, should be treated with caution, given the degree of local control exerted in totalitarian societies that tends to make people more circumspect in expressing their political convictions openly. This suggests that the old Communist authorities were able to maintain control much longer, not only by blocking the flow of information but also by exploiting the traditional rural and provincial suspicion toward Prague and other major cities. Furthermore, in the countryside, the crucial and common experience of citizens marching shoulder to shoulder on the streets and participating in the public aspect of the revolution, which helped generate the exuberance and unity felt in Prague, was largely absent. Nevertheless, by the end of December 1989, the prestige of the new president and his government had increased by leaps and bounds in the countryside and had gone far in matching his popularity rating in Prague.[1] The old regime's failure to control the media, in particular television, and the subsequent uncensored flow of information were mainly responsible for the change.

A broad public consensus undoubtedly existed at the end of the year. Yet the differences in experience and the uneven development of the revolution between town and country raise questions as to the firmness of the unity. In at least one aspect, however, there was little or no ambiguity: The old regime and the CPC had clearly been rejected, as evidenced in opinion polls showing a dramatic decline in the party's popularity.[2] Though a general consensus existed on the questions of the reconstruction of society and changes of policy, it was less clear-cut. The tenor of public discourse, visible principally through the media, private conversations, and opinion polls, pointed to agreement in four related areas. In the political sphere, this involved a return to democracy and an irrevocable breaking of the power of the party. As regards the economy, a move away from central planning to a free market was foretold. Socially, there was a widely expressed public interest in the construction of a just, ethically sound civil society and in a demand for the resolution of the most pressing social problems, of which ecology, health, and education were most frequently mentioned. There was general public concern for the position of Czechoslovakia in international affairs, which was related to the expected return of Czechoslovakia to Europe as a free and sovereign state.

This consensus was, however, subject to certain limitations. The commitment to these goals was couched in fairly general terms. The lack of any recent history of democratic public discourse, the misuse of language under the old regime, and the absence of institutions and practices to which the discourse could refer confounded the problem of establishing an adequate degree of shared public understanding of certain central terms. In practice, these words were often used and understood in an almost protean sense in the case of, for example, *democracy,* or in a contradictory sense, as for instance, with *free market,* which was demanded by a majority who at the same time wanted a guarantee of full employment. One other major qualification regarding the consensus relates to the people's perception of the difficulties facing the country and the degree to which they were willing to pay a significant personal price to achieve their goals. One opinion poll indicated that though many expected economic hardship, they also expected the position of their own families to deteriorate only slightly at worst in the year after the revolution.[3]

The new government had a wider appreciation than did the people of the scale of the problems facing Czechoslovakia. It was also conscious of the need to acquaint the population as fully as possible with the state of affairs as a preparation for the hardships to come, thereby winning and maintaining their agreement. Havel's presidential New Year's speech, for instance, painted the following picture of the state of the nation:

> Our country is not flourishing. The enormous creative and spiritual potential of our nations is not being used meaningfully. Entire branches of industry are producing goods for which there is no demand yet failing to produce for even our basic needs. A state that calls itself a workers' state humiliates and exploits workers. Our obsolete economy squanders our scarce energy resources. A country that once could be proud of the educational level of its citizens spends so little on their education today that it ranks only seventy-second in the world. We have polluted the soil, the rivers, and forests bequeathed to us by our ancestors, and today we have the most polluted environment in Europe. Life expectancy in our country is lower than in most other European countries.[4]

The government nevertheless expressed optimism in the capacity of the people to meet the challenges facing them. Havel, for example, in the same speech noted that "freedom and democracy must be based on participation and the acceptance of responsibility by everyone. If we realize this, then all the horrors that the new Czechoslovak democracy has inherited will no longer seem so terrible." He further expressed his belief that there were two main sources of hope:

> Man is never simply a product of the external world but always retains a potential to relate to something higher, however systematically the external world attempts to destroy it. Moreover, the humanistic and democratic traditions, about which there has been so much superficial talk, have continued to exist in a latent form in the consciousness of our nations and national minorities passed on from generation to generation, enabling us to discover them within ourselves at the right moment and transform them into actions.

In a more prosaic vein, the authors of the economic reform program submitted by the Ministry of Finance to the government stated:

> The fears of adverse political consequences arising from the economic reform are groundless. It is precisely today, so soon after the revolutionary political changes, that the people are prepared to accept the likely social consequences of the reform. The real extent of support for the government will only become clear after the first unpopular steps have been taken. But one thing is certain. Czechoslovak society will have to face negative social consequences in any event, and the population is more ready to face them now than later.[5]

The political problem confronting the government lay in introducing radical change but at the same time maintaining the public consensus that the necessary drastic economic measures would threaten. Its own legitimacy was derived from the revolution and the unity it had generated rather than from a consensus based upon a free, democratic vote. The government had grown out of a compromise between CF and the CPC and hence retained some members of the ancien régime. The Federal Assembly, on which the demanding legislative program depended, was also, despite expulsions and co-optations, still largely filled with the old brigade of the National Front. The principal task of this interim government was to guide the country to democratic elections—the first since 1946—which were subsequently held in June 1990. Its tenure of office and its remit were therefore seemingly limited. It had to face social and economic problems and open the way to a market economy. Yet at the same time, there was an ambiguity about its role in that the interim administration was unclear how far it could or should go in introducing reforms. The interplay among its legitimacy, public consensus, and fundamental reforms in the period up to the elections took place in four interrelated arenas of public concern: the political, the economic, the social, and the international.

The Political Sphere

The agreed complexion of the government worked out between the CPC and CF in mid-December 1989 changed in favor of the latter when some of the leading members of the government, notably Komárek and Čalfa, resigned their party membership. This was linked to the tide of opinion reflected in surveys indicating that Communist members of the government were the least popular.[6] A main task of the government was the creation of the institutional and legal conditions for the introduction of a pluralist, democratic political system. This entailed, among other actions, passing a new electoral law changing or abolishing arrangements that made the formation of new political parties difficult or impossible. This law was drafted in roundtable talks among representatives of all political trends and was passed by Parliament on March 2, 1990. The law is quite complex, especially in those areas determining the number of seats that each party gains and the number of mandates allocated to each electoral region; it is quite likely that the ordinary voter would be baffled by the procedures described. The system is based on proportional representation in which only political parties can, in practice, put up lists of candidates for general elections. In both the Czech Lands and Slovakia, parties gaining less than 5 percent of the total votes cast win no seats at all. Though the system does not involve preferential voting, the number of seats corresponding to the votes cast for those parties failing to hurdle the threshhold are reallocated to the successful parties on a pro rata basis. Voters are enabled to exert some relatively limited influence on the order of candidates on the list by expressing preferences for, at most, four candidates. One other significant element of the law is worth noting: It grants all political parties satisfying the minimum requirement for putting up lists of candidates (namely, 10,000 party members or signatures of support making up any shortfall) an equal amount of airtime on both television and radio during the forty-day election campaign. The system is clearly designed to lead to the creation of a relatively stable government based on large and popular political parties. It disproportionately favors the more successful parties and provides no space for independent candidates. It is sometimes forgotten that under the old regime, Czechoslovakia was not a one-party state, though the other parties were not particularly prominent in a largely lifeless Parliament dominated by the CPC. Popular distrust for the Communists extended in the new state to all political parties. The strong emphasis on a party political system hence seems slightly paradoxical. The principal beneficiary of public misgivings for parties in general was CF, as it had not constituted itself into a political party during the election campaign of spring 1990 and still retained its public persona as a citizens' organization, albeit in the election campaign it had to act to all intents and purposes as a political party.

CF at this stage occupied a unique position in that it was closely associated with the government and was at the same time an umbrella organization representing all citizens and covering a substantial section of the non-Communist spectrum of political opinion. Its electoral contest with political parties naturally raised the question of the kind of political role it should adopt. Havel regarded it as a temporary organization of citizens, a view challenged by others who argued for its immediate transformation into a political party. Its political complexion thereby became important, and after starting out left of center, it moved to the right. Its left-wing component became marginalized as a result. At the elections, because neither the Social Democrats nor the Czech Socialists were easily identified with a left-wing stance, there was no readily identifiable Left. This may, incidentally, help to explain the relative success of the CPC at the elections, as it arguably provided some kind of substitute. Leaving the government aside, CF became progressively less connected to the old dissident structures and rather showed unmistakable signs of providing scope for personal advancement or the construction of a political career.

Apart from CF and its Slovak equivalent, Public Against Violence, a number of new political parties had emerged such that twenty-three parties or coalitions ultimately contested the elections. These included nationalist parties and those representing ethnic minorities and peasants, the Greens, the revived Social Democratic party, and the Czech and Slovak Christian Democrats. Visitors to Prague at this time were inundated with election pamphlets from all sides but were hard put to differentiate between the respective manifestos. Most expressed a commitment to democracy, the free market, and private enterprise and a rooted opposition to communism. Concern for the environment, too, had a prominent place. A higher public profile was achieved by the nationalist parties, with their emphasis on a distinctive and narrow local or provincial patriotism. With most, if not all, parties including an environmental plank in their platforms, the Greens became net losers. Further, they, like the other smaller parties, could not offer a real challenge, the established parties deriving a clear advantage from their financial, material, and human resources, which enabled them, with their connections to major newspapers, to put their message across more effectively. The developed organizational framework and mass-circulation newspapers of the CPC and CF made it difficult to compete with either at the grassroots level.

Public awareness of the material advantages the CPC still retained (for example, its property and mass-circulation newspapers and journals) frequently raised the question of the kind of threat, if any, it posed to the new order. This followed from the experience of Communist rule and general mistrust, together with the tendency to think in terms of negations, a habit the normalized regime had inculcated by its presentation of most issues in the starkest of terms. Given that few believed what they had been told, people were inclined to take an uncomplicated opposition stance and thereby continued or developed habits of thought that could not easily be changed thereafter. An illuminating example of this problem in conditions of the emerging democracy was provided by the so-called Sokol affair.

The debate over the legal existence of the CPC in the new democratic system was sparked off by a letter sent to the Central Committee by the Prague state prosecutor, Tomáš Sokol, in mid-April 1990, a report of which appeared in the press on April 17.[7] Sokol warned the party that its affairs would be subjected to close scrutiny under Article 261 of the penal code prohibiting all activities designed to support or propagate fascism. The law, according to Sokol, banned "support and advocacy of fascism or any similar movement that aims at the suppression of the rights and liberties of the working people or that preaches national, racial, or religious hatred."[8] The main methods of such movements, Sokol argued, were terror and social demagogy. In that the ideology of the Communist movement and the party's activities over the years could be likened to those of a fascist movement, it therefore became subject to the penal code. Marxist-Leninist ideology, said Sokol, is inherently undemocratic insofar as it aims at the conquest of power, the replacement of "bourgeois" democracy by the dictatorship of the proletariat led by the Communist party. The Communist movement was thus committed to the use of violence and repression, to the destruction of the existing order, and to the construction of totalitarianism. Once in power, the party is incapable of tolerating alternative political forces and programs, and this inevitably leads to the destruction of the democratic right to choose—which, he claimed, Czechoslovak history had since 1948 repeatedly shown to be the case. The widespread use of social demagogy had also, in his view, been evident. Promises of a better society based on equality, a higher standard of living for all, and social guarantees, however utopian and unrealizable in practice, had been made to generate popular support. It was on the basis of such support that the party gained important positions in the government formed after World War II—positions that provided a springboard for the acquisition of total power in 1948.

All this, Sokol alleged, made the Communist party comparable to a fascist movement. Indeed, the differences between the party and the Nazi movement in Germany (the latter's commitment to racism, for example) are insignificant when set against the destruction of the lives of tens of millions of people for which both were responsible. Furthermore, the Nazis' ambitions of worldwide conquest were matched by the Communists' desire to export revolution. In the crucial and controversial last section of his letter, Sokol went on to argue that democracy created a defined space within which political forces could legitimately operate. A political party aiming to utilize this space with a view to abolishing it acts as a parasite on the body politic and thereby puts itself outside the legally defined framework of the political system. He did not suggest that any left-wing party with utopian ideals should be excluded from democratic life, rather that it was vital to defend democracy against those who aim to destroy it, and this meant the Communist party. In short, there was little doubt that both in terms of its ideology and practice, and despite its public protestations of commitment to the rights and liberties of the people, the party aimed at their destruction. Accordingly, a scrutiny of its activities under Article 261 was fully justified.[9]

The response to this letter was varied, if vociferous. The presidium of the Central Committee of the CPC reacted immediately and predictably. It protested that the letter was a provocation designed to discredit a legitimate political party and, through the use of lies and distortions, prevent it from carrying out its proper activities. The official line of the legal establishment was presented to Parliament by the chief state prosecutor of the Czech republic, Pavel Rychetský. He dissociated himself and his office from the letter, which he indicated merely expressed Sokol's personal opinion, and stressed that the rule of law required the state prosecutor's offices to remain unaffected by political pressure from any quarter. Moreover, he ruled that criminal proceedings could only be initiated against actual persons for specific actions and it was therefore not for the state prosecutor's office to ban voluntary organizations of citizens or their political parties. The legal evaluation of the activities of the CPC should, at best, have been addressed to the legislative assembly as a possible basis for new legislation. The chief state prosecutor's office understood the emotional reactions of many citizens to the totalitarian past but considered it inappropriate for state officials to fall victim to such sentiments when carrying out their official duties.

The general public, however, reacted more passionately. Several demonstrations took place in Prague supporting Sokol and the views he expressed, some even demanding the CPC be banned. Newspapers received numerous letters from individuals and groups strongly identifying themselves with Sokol's position. He also received backing from several political parties, and most of the press commentary was in his favor. One editorial appeared in *Lidové noviny*.[10] The author, Věra Pospíšilová, argued that in order to survive, democracy required an instinct of self-preservation and needed therefore to protect itself against those, such as the CPC, that threatened it. But she also acknowledged that persecuted former dissidents of long standing tended to take a more tolerant view, citing by way of example her own editor in chief, Jiří Ruml. This tolerance, she said, came about because the old dissidents, in contrast to those like herself who had mildly collaborated with the regime, felt more free in that they were significantly less burdened by the past and hence unfettered by any sense of humiliation.

The reaction from CF was mixed. Its coordinating center drafted a careful statement, at least partly in response to pressure from the street, upholding the right to free expression and political activity limited only by the law. It supported the city state prosecutor's right to interpret the law according to his conscience and charitably interpreted Sokol's position to be a warning of possible breaches of the law and not a call for a banning of the CPC. Various district and local committees of CF were, however, much more radical in championing Sokol's position, arguing the parallel between fascism and communism to be unquestionable.

A number of interesting points arise out of this public debate. The first concerns the difficulty of achieving the transition from a totalitarian to a democratic system when so many citizens had in varying degrees collaborated with the former regime and, as Havel would have it, with their own oppression.[11] Blaming the CPC for all the ills of the previous system obscured the degree of responsibility that ordinary citizens should accept for their own actions and their consequences and made the construction of a responsible democracy more difficult. The second point relates to the problem of how to defend democracy against its enemies. There is generally little argument among its supporters about the need to defend democracy against acts of violence and usurpation of power, though much more about protecting it from political ideas and programs. A paternalistic view at odds with the classical liberalism articulated by John Stuart Mill tends to attempt to protect citizens against the consequences of their own irrationality. This leads to citizenship's being exercised in a rather limited way. The third point concerns the role of the judiciary in defining the limits of political activity. This depends on the nature of the legislation, but it is questionable whether the judiciary can preserve its politically neutral status if legislation allows or drives the judicial system into making highly political and controversial decisions in interpreting the law.

As we have noted, breaking the power of the CPC was of crucial importance to both people and government. It required a purging of state institutions that was not at all straightforward and involved certain difficulties and ambiguities. It was not clear, for instance, whether this implied that all current or former members of the party should be relieved of their posts in these institutions. The system of *nomenklatura,* by which the party had the power to determine who held important positions in the economy and all major social organizations, meant that out of a population of 15 million, more than 1.5 million had been in the CPC. Many of them were in the party simply for career reasons, particularly in areas where expertise was required. The issue, then, was whether the government could risk the potential collapse of important institutes and enterprises by the wholesale removal of their managements in the absence of suitably qualified replacements. The question also arose to what extent a card-carrying but inactive member of the party had a greater degree of complicity in the crimes of the old regime than those who routinely collaborated. For instance, in resigning from the party, Deputy Prime Minister Komárek made a careful distinction between a member of the party and a Communist, claiming to be the former but definitely not the latter. An example of the sensitivity of the issue and its potential for creating public dissension was provided by the Cibulka case in March 1990. Jan Cibulka, a prominent member of CF in Brno, demanded a purge of party members from their positions. He organized a public petition against the local mayor, Pernica, a former manager and member of the CPC who, however, had never been directly associated with any unacceptable activities. The sole objection raised against him was his party membership, not his views or his past. This led to a split in CF in Brno and alarmed the leaders in Prague, who believed it would show the forum to be divided and have a correspondingly negative impact on voters in the forthcoming elections. They feared, too, that this would raise populist demands that they could not meet.

The purge of the Ministry of the Interior and the whole of the security apparatus presented the most sensitive and difficult aspect of the general process of national lustration. The new regime was aware of the need to purge both the institutions and their modus operandi. This involved abolishing a significant part of the secret police, the StB, and vetting its personnel. In his capacity as the new minister of the interior, Richard Sacher, a prominent member of the People's party, set about reeducating the various sections of the security apparatus. He emphasized that their new role was the protection of the lives and property of the citizens but without resorting to the methods they had used under the old regime, notably electronic and personal surveillance, unlawful house searches, threats, and harassment.[12]

The secret police was formally abolished by January 31, 1990, and part of its functions passed to new institutions. There was some difficulty, however, in identifying and locating several units of the StB and the full range of its activities. A commission led by a deputy minister of the interior was set up to vet the leading functionaries of the federal Ministry of the Interior and the general staff of the StB. This process caused great acrimony between Sacher and his deputies that eventually led to their dismissal. The purge also triggered a dispute between Sacher and CF, which criticized the minister for his slow pace and lack of thoroughness in the vetting process. One of the most damaging disclosures to emerge during this public debate was that information was being gathered within the ministry on the new MPs and even on some members of the Czech and Slovak governments. Disclaiming all personal knowledge, Sacher issued orders for the immediate cessation of these investigations; nevertheless, they continued for some time after. Though the minister confirmed that such activities were unacceptable and would not be tolerated, the whole issue raised the question about the ability of the new authorities to control the security apparatus. There were a number of people who suspected that the hopes of gaining a party political advantage was not a negligible factor in this process.

The public's hypersensitivity cannot be unrelated to its awareness that the StB could use the material it had gathered under the old regime for its own benefit and that of its former masters. The StB had only 8,000 members, but masses of paid informants had been recruited from institutions throughout the republic; even dissident organizations had been penetrated. These informants were present in the new structures and were peculiarly vulnerable to blackmail because of the records of their collaboration. Some members of the interim government, for example, were hopelessly compromised, as were some candidates in the upcoming elections; liability to the charge of penetration by the secret police was spread across the political spectrum. CF agreed to vet its own candidates, some of them quietly resigning as a result. The People's party did not deny the accusation that its leader, Bartončík, had been an agent of the police. Yet it registered strong objections to the manner and the timing of the revelation by Jan Ruml, the deputy minister of the interior who had appeared on television two days before the elections. CF, of which Ruml was a member, was accused of dirty tricks to weaken the position of the People's party, which was part of the electoral alliance with the Christian Democrats.

No party could guarantee that there were no collaborators among either its leaders or election candidates, and all were aware that any revelations of this kind would have been very damaging electorally because of the widespread public hatred for the StB and its collaborators. Indeed, we may speculate that it was in the interest of all parties, excluding the CPC, not to use information of this kind for electoral advantage and therefore it is likely that they went through the process of weeding out the collaborators gradually and out of the public eye. The whole issue raises the question to what extent the new democratic system could be an open and accountable one.

One other major problem was the national question, which Havel touched on in his presidential New Year's speech:

> My second task is to ensure that both nations approach the coming elections as truly self-governing, respecting each other's interests, national identity, religious traditions, and the fundamental symbols of nationhood. As a Czech in the office of president who swore his presidential oath to a famous Slovak and an intimate friend, I feel a particular responsibility to ensure that after the various bitter experiences the Slovaks have had, all the interests of the Slovak nation should be respected and that no offices of state be closed to its members.[13]

Havel and the government foresaw that nationalism was likely to develop into a potent political force that, if not dealt with equitably, would become a disruptive element affecting the stability of the new state. This concern was based on the awareness of the history fraught with national tensions and a knowledge of the accumulated resentments national groups felt toward one another. Particularly under the normalized regime, these problems and ill feelings had not been allowed expression at the level of explicit public discourse. As we noted earlier, the old regime could not allow an open debate on the national question and various national problems, as the control over society necessary to its survival would have come under threat. Such public discourse would have raised the question of respective national histories, power relations between the nations of Czechoslovakia in addition to relations with the Soviet Union and other neighbors. Moreover, nationalism would have posed a significant threat to the monopoly of Marxism-Leninism. It had hence to be reconstructed and subsumed in the framework of the official ideology, which involved a harmonization with proletarian internationalism and friendly relations between socialist nations. It was a form of nationalism that had little to do with the way people thought and felt.

Though the government controlled public discourse through its outright control of education, the media, culture, and so on, it could not control the existence of strongly felt nationalism at the grassroots level and its popular manifestations, such as chauvinist displays by soccer crowds and nationalist, not seldom racist, griping in pubs. This was not moderated by an open, rational, and critical discourse; though such discussion took place in dissident circles, its spread was very restricted. The danger was that once the controlling lid of the totalitarian regime and its ideology was lifted, nationalism would emerge as a potent force insofar as it was a nationalism of a negative kind based on a feeling of separateness, full of bias and resentment, and imbued with an uncritical and discontinuous sense of national history. The historical models each of the two main nations used and referred to were the First Republic and Masaryk's notion of the Czech nation, neither of which was popular with the Slovaks, and Andrej Hlinka (leader of the Slovak National Clerical party), and possibly the Slovak state of 1939–1944, which was a source of resentment for most Czechs.

The apprehension of Havel and the government was justified. Indeed, the president was the driving force in the "hyphen debate" in late March 1990. This was occasioned by the shared recognition that the term *socialist* in the official name of the republic was unacceptable. Instead of simply dropping this title, leaders discussed other appropriate changes of name, Havel taking a major part in the debate. After lengthy argument, a compromise was arrived at that may appear faintly absurd to an outsider. It was decided to hyphenate the word *Czechoslovak* in Slovakia but not in the Czech Lands. The acrimony and length of the debate showed the sensitivity of the issue and the difficulty of reaching an acceptable arrangement. It also overshadowed other important controversies, particularly that regarding legislation relating to the conditions under which private enterprise could operate, and this caused wide resentment among the budding entrepreneurial class, particularly in Prague. The growing Slovak demand for more control, not to say autonomy, was greeted with alarm by minorities there such as the Hungarians, who subsequently organized themselves into an explicitly nationalist political party. Regional "nationalism" in Moravia and Silesia was also partly sparked off by the confrontation of the Czechs and Slovaks on the question of autonomy. The national question played an important part in the elections (which we deal with later in the chapter) and had an important effect on a number of social and economic issues.

The Economic Sphere

Given the general consensus favoring a radical reform of the economy and a transition to a free-market system, the interim government found itself confronted with four tasks in the period leading up to the elections:

(1) to implement the limited reforms prepared under the previous government (see Chapter 5);
(2) to fully acquaint the public with the actual state of the economy and prepare it for the price to be paid and the harshness of the remedies;
(3) to formulate a strategy for the transformation of the economy; and
(4) to implement various measures following from the agreed-upon strategy and to provide a legislative framework for the operation of private enterprise.

The discharge of the first task was relatively uncontroversial and did not generate any difficulties. There is also little doubt that the government took the second task seriously, as it realized that its chances of seeing through measures bound to generate some economic pain would be enhanced by people's recognition of their necessity. This is clear from Havel's New Year's speech. But the authoritative account of the real state of the economy was made by Prime Minister Čalfa in a speech on February 27. He alluded to technological and economic backwardness, a consequence not of lack of investment in technology and industry but of the inefficiency of investment (primarily in big, expensive projects of uncertain profitability), the neglect of cheap forms of modernizing production, the accumulation of large and largely unsalable reserves, the excessive consumption of energy and raw materials, the low productivity of labor, and the low standards of the organization of labor in industrial enterprises.

He stressed that "the underlying cause of the poor organization of our economic management is the excessive size and hence general inflexibility of our enterprises." Compared with other industrial states, where, he asserted, one-half to two-thirds of the total work force was employed in small or medium-sized enterprises of up to 300 employees, the average Czechoslovak industrial enterprise had 3,500 employees, and small industrial enterprises were practically nonexistent. He identified inflation as a problem and related it to the existence of demand over supply, particularly in the area of consumer goods.

These problems were compounded by the worsening conditions of Czechoslovakia's foreign trade. Though some advantages accrued from economic cooperation in Comecon, these were more than outweighed by the way membership locked the economy into, as he put it, "the bureaucratic merry-go-round of mutual quotas, both imports and exports, leaving it with shortages of virtually all categories of goods. On the other hand, the share of exports for freely convertible currencies has steadily decreased, and, at the same time, the foreign debt has been increasing and had reached $7.9 billion by the end of 1989." Substantial debts had been accumulating as a result of exports covered by government credits in countries such as the Soviet Union, Libya, Cuba, and Burma, and recovery of these debts had quite often resulted in heavy financial losses.

Čalfa also highlighted the disastrous state of the environment, the severe housing shortages and the catastrophic disrepair of the housing stock, and massive problems in education and health. The costs of dealing with these problems, he confirmed, would be very high.[14] Other members of the federal and national governments made statements in a similar vein in newspaper, radio, and television interviews. The media reflected a public debate that not only raised these matters but also gave space to a discussion of possible remedies in which economic models, including the Swedish model, received attention.[15]

The third task—to devise and develop a strategy for economic transformation leading thereafter to a free market and a legislative policy to implement it—generated the liveliest debate. There was some measure of disagreement about a number of issues, notably the speed at which the various reforms, in particular price reforms and privatization, were to be carried into effect. There were also disputes about what was understood by the idea of privatization. The discussion crystallized around the contributions of the "gradualist" Komárek, on the one hand, and the radical thinking represented by Klaus, the minister of finance, and Dlouhý, the minister for planning, on the other. The former, who under the old regime had been a champion of the mixed economy understood as a combination of planning with the market, favored a slow pace of reform. His ideas reflected a concern with the social costs of radical reform, principally with the extent to which people would find them acceptable, and he unceasingly questioned their necessity and justifiability. Having regard to developments in Poland, he argued that the radical nature of privatization and the freeing of the price mechanism from state intervention involved high levels of unemployment and a recession whose depth would turn out to be much greater than expected.[16] The radicals did not dispute that something akin to the Polish model would be painful. Their starting point was that the privation involved in economic reform was unavoidable and delay would only aggravate it. They also believed the gradualists underestimated people's capacity to accept shock treatment.

The radicals opposed Komárek on at least seven points. For one, they suggested that the gradualist path could not work when the mechanisms of central planning, which Komárek presumed would continue to exist beside the emerging market, were already disintegrating. The second point related to the ineffectiveness of the banking system during the gradual process of transformation: As prices failed to reflect the scarcity of goods, services, and capital, banks would find it impossible to make decisions on, for instance, commercial credit. Third, there was the problem of realizing a noninflationary budget in conditions where unprofitable enterprises in state ownership were to be maintained during a lengthy process of high demand for state subsidies. It was, the radicals argued, difficult to follow a sound financial policy because prices, if they continued to be decided by administrative fiat, would prevent money from reaching the proper places in the economy. Fourth, they expressed their belief in the impossibility of a gradual, central reform of prices, which could only be rationally determined by the market mechanism on the basis of supply and demand. Adverse social circumstances brought about by the rational operation of the price mechanism could be adequately dealt with by a compensatory social policy protecting the most vulnerable social groups in society. Fifth, they argued that the process of transformation would be costly and could not be borne solely by the country, that the economic support of major international economic organizations that the economic support of major international economic organizations and Western capitalist states was necessary. The former had already made it clear that their support would be dependent on whole-hearted and consistent commitment to radical economic change. The sixth point stressed that a slow process of privatization was simply not feasible, principally because of the limitation of the expansion of the budding private sector this would involve but also because of the likelihood that the most efficient personnel would leave for the private sector, thereby diminishing the managerial efficiency of these enterprises. Finally, the failure to apply commercial criteria to exchange rates would mean that the benefits of foreign trade as a stimulus to competition would not work.

The radicals also suggested remedies for the then current economic difficulties. They planned to introduce monetarist measures to guarantee a noninflationary environment to help generate long-term growth, mirrored in the budget for 1990. Changes in ownership (privatization) were outlined in the complicated process based on coupons under which a part of the national property would be distributed to the population—a solution effectively forced on them, as there was insufficient capital to privatize on the basis of sale. It was not intended, however, that privatization be wholesale and immediate. Yet operating on the basis of "waves," privatization was designed to have an impact on the liberalization of the economy. The third aspect of the cure involved the radical reform of prices. This involved rationalization with the preconditions for the creation of a competitive internal environment linked to demonopolization, the commercialization and privatization of a substantial number of enterprises, liberalization of imports to create conditions of external competition, and a strong financial and monetary policy to control inflation. This liberalization of prices would involve phasing out different types of subsidies, though the authors did accept that the lack of competitiveness of the economy would require enterprises to be protected for a relatively short period of time by import tariffs and subsidies. The freeing of the economy from noneconomic considerations would require a policy dealing with the consequences of the economic changes, and the operation of the market would be supplemented by state structural policy (industrial, agricultural, energy, and so on) involving help in economic forecasting and in the process of flexible adaptation to the new economic conditions. This meant the provision of state support for those enterprises identified as having a significant degree of export potential. Finally, all the above-mentioned had an external economic dimension that went beyond trade and involved loans and investment from abroad, though during the transition to a well-functioning market, they would remain subject to state regulation to prevent any exploitation of the weak Czechoslovak market.[17]

The radicals won the day, and their program was presented to the public as the government's economic strategy in May 1990. It was subsequently endorsed by the government that came into office after the June elections. The disagreement was not as great as had been reported, and the gradualists also came out in support of, for instance, export industries with great potential. There were some differences relating in particular to the time scale and the operation of a notionally completely free market, which reflected an unambiguously ideological stance. The rhetoric often exaggerated the divide that was expressed in the resentment of the gradualists when they were characterized as opponents of the idea of the market.[18] But the acceptance of the program did not give rise to any public opposition by Komárek and his colleagues, and the election manifestos of CF and the major political parties (the CPC excepted) did not differ sharply from the radical plan. Both groups were clearly concerned with social aspects of the economic reform but proposed to deal with them in different ways, as we see in the next section.

The fourth task of the government involved the creation of the legal conditions for the operation of private enterprise and the implementation of economic measures and policies expressing the move in the direction of a market economy. The work on this legislation started immediately and was accompanied by amendments to the old civil and economic legislative codes. Though it was completed relatively quickly, the passage of these laws was delayed until April, causing some frustration among would-be entrepreneurs. The two principal laws were the law on private enterprise and the law on public shareholding companies.[19] In addition, important fiscal measures were aimed at achieving a slight budget surplus, which involved some limitation on expenditure, though it provided for the relocation and retraining of the unemployed.[20]

The government also resolved to deal with the exchange rate and the problems caused by the existence of a black market for currency and the resulting significant loss of hard currency sustained by the state. Related to this were certain deleterious effects of tourism, especially in view of the price differentials between Austria and Germany on the one side and Czechoslovakia on the other and the problem of local shortages caused by foreign tourists' buying up goods wholesale. This was not as easily solved as the adjustment in exchange rates, insofar as it devalued the Czechoslovak currency and made the goods cheaper, thereby compounding the difficulty. Steps were taken even before the election to deal with the liberalization of the price mechanism. The first step was made in late May with the announcement of the raising of a range of food prices on July 1 by an average of 24.6 percent. Aware of the social impact this would cause, the government compensated each citizen with a subsidy of 140 crowns[21] per month for two years.

The Social Sphere

The range of problems the new government inherited from the previous regime all concerned the reconstruction of civil society, but there were disagreements as to whether this was to be achieved on the basis of a free market and the rule of law or whether it required a developed notion of social justice. The collectivist ideology was replaced by an individualistic outlook, though the notion of individualism held by members of the government was at variance with that of CF, for example. Those with extreme individualist views saw society as a simple aggregate of its members. The purpose of social policy was therefore to create space for the self-determining individual to succeed or fail in his or her endeavors on the basis of merit. As they recognized that there would be losers in the new competitive environment, provisions were to be made to protect them by a combination of state support and charity that was to be differentiated on the basis of personal responsibility for one's own poverty, given that the government's aim was to stimulate individuals' efforts to improve themselves or their positions in life. Others, including Havel, mediated their concern for the self-determining individual by a concern for social justice. They recognized that the fate of the individual is at least partly determined by membership in different social groups. Hence, social policy ought to be concerned with the regulation and readjustment of relations among groups. Both of these trends were present in CF and had some linkage with the debate on economic strategy.

The issue most clearly arising out of the debate on the economy was social provision for the unemployed. All welcomed the end of egalitarianism in employment, and all agreed that the free market would produce losers in the labor market for which social arrangements were necessary. There was little dispute abut the need, for example, to take care of members of vulnerable groups who were unable to find a way out of their plight. Yet concern for the jobless was also expressed in the suggestion that they should become the target of differentiated social support designed on the one hand to prevent their becoming institutionalized as unemployed and on the other to encourage them to take their own initiatives. The election manifesto of CF quite explicitly stated, "Social security and support as an expression of social sensitivity has to be differentiated according to the circumstances and must particularly stimulate the individual's own efforts to overcome his/her unfavorable situation where possible."[22]

Both the election program and the Radical Economic Reform Strategy, as it was often called, were constructed in such a way as to involve not only the state but also charity, parish, self-help, municipal, and church organizations. This raised the question to what extent the individual had a right to social support in case of need rather than simply as a beneficiary of charity. As already mentioned, the number of unemployed who could be provided for was limited. It is noteworthy that the Ministry of Labor, which was preparing a program for unemployment and retraining of those directly affected by the economic reforms, received funds based on a maximum of 30,000 unemployed.[23] CF also envisaged that the costs of care for the old would not be borne entirely by the state but partly by voluntary organizations.

One of the major social issues was education. As Havel reiterated in his New Year's speech, "A country that once could be proud of the educational level of its citizens spends so little on their education today that it ranks only seventy-second in the world."[24] Expenditure was not the only concern, however. All agreed that the quality of education had suffered greatly, not least the neglect of certain subjects, the narrowing of access, the failure to produce research in the social sciences, the conduct of research on the basis of rigid ideological principles, the suppression of religious education, and the effects of the limitations on travel, which gave students a distorted view of the outside world. Substantial reform of the whole educational sector was required. Accordingly, new laws on primary and secondary schooling and on higher education were passed by the Federal Assembly on May 4, 1990.[25] The emphasis was placed on the introduction of humanistic and democratic principles into education as a whole. The possibility of opening schools outside the state system, for instance, church or private schools, cleared the way for both pluralism in education and parental choice. This was also designed to reduce the burden of cost on the state. Moreover, it was intended to differentiate pupils on the basis of ability, thereby reflecting the underlying meritocratic approach. The organization of university qualifications closely followed the Anglo-Saxon model (B.A., M.A., and postgraduate degrees), whereas the organization of the universities was based upon democratic principles within the primacy of their academic leaders, though with a student voice. Great stress was laid on language teaching, especially English, not least to help the young gain some knowledge of the wider world. Help from abroad was sought with curriculum development. The replacement of teachers in higher and secondary education allowed scope for the rehabilitation of those purged during the years of the normalization.

Čalfa's speech indicated a clear concern for the related areas of ecology and health. The state of the environment, especially in certain areas, led to a low quality of life that had had a powerful, negative impact on the state of the nation's health, in particular decreasing life expectancy and increasing infant mortality (see Chapter 4). A general consensus on the need to clean up the environment was reflected in the election programs of nearly all the parties. This, however, was recognized as a long-term project involving great investment, the tightening of existing controls, and the closing of polluting enterprises, not to mention the necessity of international cooperation. Because the environment was a relatively bipartisan issue, the Greens were unable to make any headway against the other parties.

The health service was in a serious state of disrepair, partly as a result of great inefficiency and relative underfunding. For instance, Czechoslovakia spent $240 per capita on health annually compared with Sweden's $2,000.[26] There was also a persistent shortage of drugs.[27] The government accepted that everybody had the right to standard health care. Yet where treatment above this standard was required, people were expected to pay. In CF's election program, it was proposed that as the economy moved toward the free-market system, the financing of the health service would shift from the state to the citizen on the basis of a flexible health insurance system. Because all would have the right to their own insurance, the implication was that private insurance companies would become involved. As in other areas, the program also emphasized the importance of citizens' responsibility for their own lives, which they would exercise in respect to their own health on the basis of comprehensive health education provided by the state.[28]

Women's issues were, to a significant degree, replaced by a renewed concern for motherhood and family relationships, partly because of ignorance and also because of the reaction against the past system based on an egalitarianism that had stressed the role of the woman as an equal in the production process. For instance, in the Radical Economic Reform Strategy there was a proposal to provide mothers with a social income amounting to half that of working women under thirty to enable them to stay at home and look after their children until the age of three. This was presented as an alternative available to all mothers in contrast to the former system, which had encouraged the placing of young children in nursery schools.[29] In their election program, CF underlined the belief that the family was the cornerstone of society and that the involvement of women in employment ought not to carry the consequence of burdening them with work at home on top of their earning activity and should not be to the detriment of the proper upbringing of children.[30]

In his February speech, the prime minister also drew attention to the very high number of prisoners, which had, on the average, attained over the preceding years 195 per 100,000 of the population, or three times the rates of custody in Western Europe. He asserted that it pointed "not only to the growing crime rate in Czechoslovakia but also to the state's overestimation of the role of penal repression."[31] Concern for prisoners' rights during and after judicial proceedings and their treatment in custody was also evident in Havel's New Year's speech. The new authorities had to face an acute problem within the penal system, as there were major revolts in most prisons over the Christmas period. Negotiations with the prisoners resulted in a firm government commitment to the reorganization of the prison system and an improvement in conditions. Further, the president announced a wide-ranging amnesty and appealed to the population as a whole to accept ex-prisoners and help them reintegrate into society. Havel's assumptions were proved somewhat idealistic when something amounting to a crime wave followed.[32]

Lurid media reporting of some appalling offenses, combined with the exaggeration deriving from word-of-mouth reports, induced the public to form an impression that crime was out of control. From this arose the belief that the police were not doing their job and that the crimes were mainly committed by Gypsies. Figures tend to bear out the former assumption.[33] The purges and the low public esteem in which the police were held had effectively caused police morale to hit rock bottom. The public heaped most of the blame for crime on the Gypsies partly as a result of prejudice. In fact, they were responsible for only 7.5 percent of all reported crime, which rose to something approaching 15 percent for street crime.[34] This type of prejudice was not a new phenomenon, but it worsened as a result of the movement of Gypsies from Slovakia first to Ostrava and thereafter to western and northern Bohemia, where authorities allocated specific places for their settlements. The Gypsies responded to both the growing hostility and growing freedom by founding the Party of the Romany People. But in the new society, gangs of skinheads (who had already disturbed public order, particularly in the major cities, under the old regime) were also becoming bolder. The skinhead problem had a crucial racial element in that the gangs' favorite pastime was to beat up Gypsies and Vietnamese workers. Nonwhite foreign students came under attack as well, and the historical anti-Semitism, too, was increasingly evident.

In spite of the history of conflict between clericalism and anticlericalism, Havel and the government were anxious to achieve a normalization of relations with the church and religion in general. This went beyond a simple reinstatement of freedom of religious belief, the government throwing its whole weight behind the church. The president in particular went out of his way to demonstrate for religion and its place in modern society. Although some tensions had already appeared when the future of the old, expropriated church properties was being discussed, the government expected the church to reestablish itself in certain areas of social life it had occupied before 1945, particularly health, education, and culture; indeed, it had already become involved in these areas through its explicit links with the Christian Democrats, its presence in everyday life increasing enormously. For instance, the Catholic mass celebrating the inauguration of the president was attended by the entire government, and religious ceremonies or issues were the subject of frequent television programs. The crowning achievement of the government's policy of reinstating the place of religion in Czechoslovak society was the papal visit on April 21, 1990. Though his reception was, understandably, not as enthusiastic as it had been in Poland, Pope John Paul II nevertheless drew enormous crowds.

Europe and the International Sphere

The central plank of the new government's foreign policy was the so-called return to Europe. The president's foreign affairs adviser, Saša Vondra, claimed that the "strategy regarding the pan-European process and the reunification of Germany was formulated much earlier than

January 1990," that it was already "formulated in 1985 in an inchoate form, but nevertheless in very concrete terms, when Charter 77 issued the Prague Appeal."[35] The return to Europe did not simply involve joining the existing Western European institutions of cooperation and integration, such as the EEC and the Council of Europe, but also transforming existing institutional arrangements concerning security. This would mean the gradual phasing out of organizations of European security, that is to say, the Warsaw Pact and NATO, and their replacement by a pan-European organization arising out of the Helsinki process. The basic ideas concerning this organization and the process involved were expressed in the memorandum on the European Security Commission presented to foreign ambassadors in Prague on April 6, 1990. With the demise of the cold war, a security arrangement based on the division of Europe was thought no longer appropriate. The potential sources of conflict were to be conceived more broadly to take in, apart from military matters, environmental, humanitarian, and economic issues.

Given this much broader concept of security, it was not surprising that the government asserted that the most suitable basis on which to build a unified all-European security system was provided by the CSCE process. The pan-European process was to have three stages: In the first, a European security commission composed of the participating states of the Helsinki process would be created that would operate side by side with and independently of the two existing security blocs. The second stage would come in the establishment of an organization of European states on a treaty basis, including the United States and Canada. The third stage would culminate in "a confederated Europe of free and independent states."[36] This pan-European strategy met with little support in a number of European capitals and in Washington.

The Czechoslovak government did not exclude all existing European institutions from its plan, however; it showed unflagging enthusiasm for the EEC. During visits to EEC headquarters, leading government figures, including the prime minister and the chairman of the National Assembly, consistently expressed the aim of achieving full membership in the community as soon as possible. For example, after signing a cooperation agreement with the EEC regarding exports and technical assistance, Čalfa stated: "We believe that the agreement we have signed today will be a milestone on the road to full membership of the community. We consider we will be able to fulfill all the necessary demands placed on us to become full members."[37] Entry to the Council of Europe was seen as an important step toward achieving this goal; guest status was granted on May 7, 1990.

The European policy of the Czechoslovak government also involved support for the reunification of Germany within the European context and likewise for cooperative arrangements between states of different European regions. Czechoslovakia became involved with Italy, Austria, Hungary, and Yugoslavia in the so-called Danube-Adriatic Region, which was envisaged as primarily dealing with economic, transportation, and common environmental problems. The government was also keen to reach an agreement with Hungary and Poland on a common approach to joining the EEC. During his Warsaw visit at the end of January, Havel explicitly warned that "if we were to return to Europe individually, it would certainly take much longer and it would be much more complicated than acting together."[38] He also believed increased cooperation would have some beneficial effect on the problems of rising nationalism in Central Europe.

The return to Europe was not seen as cutting all links with the Soviet Union, but it was necessary to normalize relations with the Soviets, for which the withdrawal of Soviet troops from Czechoslovakia was a precondition. After hard bargaining, agreement was finally reached on February 27, 1990, during Havel's visit to Moscow. The international developments and the radical changes to the economy were also viewed as necessitating a radical reform of Comecon involving a dramatic reduction of its functions and limiting it to a forum facilitating mutual trade.

The Elections

The campaign leading to the first democratic elections for more than four decades got under way in late March 1990. It was distinguished by its orderly character and by the large number of political parties seeking representation in Parliament. Leaving aside CF and Public Against Violence, all but five parties out of the total of twenty-three were new organizations. Because their political manifestos were similar, it was not easy to differentiate among them, especially on such issues as the environment, external relations, and the economy (this even applied to the single, visible member of the political "levity fringe," the Party of the Friends of Beer). The one conspicuous difference was on questions of nationality policy, the nationalist parties' stance at odds with all the other political manifestos.

At the outset, CF enjoyed a slight lead over the other parties, with 21 percent of an opinion survey.[39] As the campaign progressed, there was evidence of significant change in public opinion. Immediately before the election, support for CF had risen to 40 percent, partly as a result of Havel's campaigning, which helped amplify CF as a focus of anti-Communist sentiment. This process was assisted by the work of Klaus and Dienstbier and many other famous people, especially from the arts world. The Bartončík affair raised the question of the existence of an agreement among the parties to keep the lid on the political pasts of numerous people, revelation of which would have made it more difficult to conduct the electoral campaign and achieve the transition to a functioning democracy. Though Bartončík was described as the victim of a smear campaign, it is doubtful if the disclosure of his past seriously worsened the chances of the People's party, bearing in mind its collaboration with the old regime over forty-odd years. CF won few friends among the nationalists, however, after Peter Pithart, prime minister of the Czech national government, remarked that a vote for the nationalist parties in Moravia was a vote for the CPC. His and other people's fears that the CPC constituted a real electoral threat, which were based on the assumption that its organizational and financial power would enable it to compete effectively, proved to be more or less groundless. It did, however, provoke indignation and increased support for the nationalists in the provinces.

The elections held on June 27, 1990, brought success to CF and its Slovak counterpart, Public Against Violence and, though it became the second largest party in Parliament, defeat for the CPC. Citizens Forum gained almost half the votes cast in the elections to the Czech National Council, which, given the benevolence of the electoral system to the large parties, was rounded up to 64.29 percent. A similar percentage was achieved in the Federal Assembly for votes cast to the Czech Lands section of the Chamber of the Nations: The CF won some 3,613,513, well ahead of the second-placed CPC, with 997,919, a relatively high figure that may be explained by the absence of a left-wing party. The Movement for Self-Governing Democracy—Society for Moravia and Silesia (known locally as MSGD), with 658,477, and the Christian Democratic Union, with 633,053, were the other two parties in the Czech Lands that cleared the 5 percent hurdle. Conspicuous failures were the Social Democrats, Agrarians, and Czech Socialists—all of whom had a tradition of strong representation in the parliaments of the First Republic—and the Greens. A similar picture emerged for the elections to the Chamber of the Peoples, where CF won 53.15 percent of the vote. In Slovakia, Public Against Violence did not achieve the success of its Czech counterpart, but its percentage of the vote was nevertheless more than twice as high as its nearest rival, the Christian Democratic Movement (CDM), and almost three times as great as the Slovak Communist party. The political casualties were the old parties, the Agrarians, the Slovak People's party, and the Slovak Social Democrats, whereas the new ones, the Greens and the Democratic party, were unable to make any impact at all.

Overall, the elections brought 169 representatives of CF and Public Against Violence to the National Assembly. The results, which reflected the continuing mistrust of the voters for political parties, ensured the defeat of the CPC. They enabled CF to form a coalition government, which was essential to the forum's avoiding exclusive blame for the economic and social difficulties that lay ahead. The three nationalist parties, the MSGD, the Slovak Party of National Freedom, and the Party of the Hungarian Minority (PHM) in Slovakia, won 43 seats, behind the CPC and in front of the 40 held by the Christian Democrats. Though the nationalists raised a great clamor, popular support for them, though significant, was not great. For example, even where electoral support for Citizens Forum was at its weakest, in south Moravia (34.73 percent or 494,416 votes), it was still far stronger than support for the MSGD, who polled over 120,000 fewer. At the opposite end of the scale, CF gained 62.47 percent of votes cast in Prague.[40] All in all, the results placed the nationalist parties outside the political consensus, though, as we discuss in the next chapter, this did not limit their activities.

～ 8 ～

The Process of Transition: June 1990 to March 1991

The results of the elections gave the government a mandate that enabled it to set about implementing radical reform, though there was much debate about how and to what extent the changes envisaged were to be effected. As indicated in the previous chapter, public unity was gradually weakened in the weeks leading up to the elections, but the general agreement reflected in the similarities of most parties' election manifestos began to crack once practical and detailed policies were proposed and put into effect. CF has appeared to the public to be the one organization capable of achieving the aims it set out. It was a wide movement in effect representing the consensus of the revolution. In translating general policy proposals into specific and detailed suggestions for their implementation, however, there was difficulty reconciling the interests of different groups—for instance, unions and entrepreneurs. The problem of integrating increasingly disparate sets of views and values amplified the difficulty of maintaining a broadly consensual framework. This applied as much to constitutional matters regulating relations between constituent nations as to the nature and development of political relations in CF.

One central issue was raised by CF's status as a broad movement representing differing civic initiatives and political trends. Revolutionary euphoria and optimism about the future had generated a predisposition to consensus that for a time either concealed conflicts of interest or kept them in check. Yet as the euphoria and public goodwill gradually wore off, consensus weakened to the point that disputes emerged in at least two separate areas, in the economic field and its related social consequences and in the constitutional area governing relations between the nations. The problems raised by these differences of view bring up the

153

question of the limits of tolerance in democratic systems. If tolerance is too wide, it can, in circumstances requiring radical change, lead to a degree of immobilism. If the system is constructed too narrowly, however, it may lead to a revival of authoritarianism. The Right was, on the whole, concerned with the latter problem in that it regarded views different to its own as essentially hostile and those expressing them as enemies. Its representatives emphasized the curtailment of debate, urged speedy action, and demanded obedience to authority, all of which were often interpreted as signs of potential danger to democracy. The strains that developed in CF were hence connected with the difficulties in establishing the boundaries defining interests and views between those that were deemed legitimate and therefore had a right to exist and compete publicly and those regarded as illegitimate and hence subject to social, political, and legal sanctions. These circumstances proved too much for the maintenance of a common institutional framework, as we presently demonstrate.

The Economy:
Monetarism Versus Keynesianism

In this chapter we identify the development of policies of economic transformation in the light of rising economic troubles brought on by changing internal and external economic conditions. Contrary to expectation, the impact of new conditions in external trade associated with the Soviet Union, the Persian Gulf crisis, and the price of oil, for example, or in the internal situation, where unemployment and rising prices were causing public apprehension, did not bring about any radical shift in the positions held by the main protagonists. Extensive debate on these issues continued to be conducted in public and in the media as a whole. At the same time, the debate was carried out in highly technical terms that limited participation within it and comprehension of it to a narrow sector of the population; the majority of citizens were left largely puzzled and swayed by the appeal rather than the arguments of the presenters. It should be noted, though, that in general, there was broad agreement on the basic framework and aims of the plan for economic transformation. For example, no one, not even the CPC, opposed the market economy or privatization. Rather, the spectrum of debate operated within the framework of economic liberalism in which the main arguments reflected views embodying the contrast between monetarism, represented by Klaus and Dlouhý, and a modified Keynesianism, identified with particular research institutes and groups close to the president.

The three central planks of the government economic plan put forward by Klaus and Dlouhý related to the liberalization of prices and the market, privatization, and demonopolization.[1] These principles did not in themselves generate controversy; as we have already argued in Chapter 7, the central disagreement concerned the speed and extent of privatization and the order of the measures to be adopted. The main protagonists again took up their public disputes on these issues after the election. Komárek, for instance, observed that "the immediate introduction of a market economy would cause agony. At least one-third of all enterprises would be destroyed, and there would be economic chaos. We should not try to bring about an economic earthquake and then see if we can survive it."[2] Klaus, for his part, noted: "When considering whether to liberalize prices first and afterwards to demonopolize, we decided in favor of the liberalization of prices because of changing external conditions. At a time when the whole of Europe is changing over to a market economy and to payment in hard currency, we cannot lag behind. There is no time for us to demonopolize the economy first."[3]

Komárek's main argument was that the liberalization of prices and hence the rapid introduction of the market mechanism under conditions of disequilibrium, with demand outstripping supply, would lead to high levels of inflation and have disastrous social effects. As he said, "Demand will decline given the financial position and income of the people, and unemployment will rise; there will be a downward spiral until we hit rock bottom." His plan, which he said had been worked out over a long period of time in the Institute of Economic Forecasting, envisaged a slower transformation and a prolonged role for the state in the management of the economy: "We anticipated a market motivation in conjunction with a selective economic policy of the state that would remove certain areas of the economy and support others while utilizing and continuously strengthening the market mechanism."[4]

On the radical side, almost a direct response can be found in Dlouhý's statement that "the only criterion for the selection [of industries and enterprises to be supported] is an appropriate price system that can only be achieved through the liberalization of prices and foreign competition. . . . The idea to first create competition, improve the productivity and competitiveness of our economy, and only then liberalize prices and the exchange rate is a fiction and would lead us straight back to centralized planning."[5] It is worth noting that pressure from Western institutions, especially the International Monetary Fund (IMF), was invoked to strengthen the case for speedy and radical reform. Individuals regarded as authorities on Western economics were also cited. For example, U.S. economist Milton Friedman, who visited Prague in September 1990, publicly dismissed the arguments in favor of the social market economy and expressed support for the position represented by Klaus at a time coinciding with the parliamentary debates on the government economic plan.[6] Not even the radicals assumed that the market economy could be fully implemented overnight, and they accepted that the state would have to retain a certain interventionist role. According to Dlouhý, "The state will have to formulate its priorities [which are] telecommunications, banking and financial services, and selected parts of manufacturing and service industries [to ensure] the rapid creation of development plans [that] will help to solve our worst problems: principally the energy program, including its ecological aspects and the restructuring of metallurgy and engineering."[7]

Despite his close association with monetarism, Klaus did not reject in principle a state policy of selective support for certain areas of the economy, but he made it subject to the short-term priority of dealing with the inflation problem. He emphasized the different time dimensions of economic policy: "Development policy where development is understood as an attempt to strengthen the supply side through a new investment policy" was a long-term policy from which beneficial effects would materialize over a period of years after a myriad of conditions had been met. Ostensibly, this could be overridden in the short term by the need to fight an inflationary spiral and therefore follow a restrictive macroeconomic policy.[8] The law on the liberalization of prices was introduced in January 1990. It regulated prices of certain goods in an attempt to strengthen the fight against inflation. In Parliament Klaus stated that this law was to decide on the form and method of price regulation because enterprises and entrepreneurs existed who would otherwise attempt to abuse their monopolistic position and the condition of the Czechoslovak economy. The regulation, he suggested, should not function in opposition to the spirit of the market but rather complement it.[9] As far as demonopolization was concerned, the moderates argued that it was a precondition for the liberalization of prices, whereas the radicals believed it would gradually follow as a consequence of price liberalization and privatization assisted by foreign capital and imports.

Some of the most intense debates were generated by plans for privatization, which was at the heart of the entire economic strategy. It ultimately came to involve the "small" and "large" privatizations supplemented by two restitution laws designed to reverse all the nationalization laws after the Communist takeover of 1948. It is intended to culminate in the law privatizing land, which remained under discussion in early 1992. The small privatization involved services such as restaurants, pubs, the retail trade, and small workshops but excluded land and all properties that fell under the restitution laws. The law provided for public auction as the method of privatization, and only Czech and Slovak citizens were involved in the first round. Foreign capital, however, was both permitted and hoped for in the second. The small privatization generated great public interest, particularly as it raised the question whether employees of the enterprises at stake ought to be allowed an opportunity to bid before the public auction was to take place. It caught the public eye, too, as it bore on the controversial question of "dirty money." The possibility that the old *nomenklatura* elite and the street money changers who had grown rich under the old regime should benefit and form the basis of a new elite was anathema to most people. The issue was, however, dismissed by Klaus and his ministers, at least partly, because it was impossible to tell the difference between legally and illegally acquired money. Tomáš Ježek, the minister for privatization, stated: "We cannot ask people where they got their money from. Certainly there is dirty money here, but the best way to clean it is to put it to work."[10] Klaus strongly resisted pressure from various sections of society—including some smaller political parties (notably the Christian Democrats and the People's party) and even the president—to confront the problem of something akin to money laundering. Neither did he respond to the complaints of employees from a significant number of enterprises on the verge of privatization, who struck or threatened to strike in support of their claims for preferential treatment. His opposition was categorical, and he justified it by arguing that "if we do not accept one of the old variations of socialist doctrine according to which the enterprise belongs to those who work in it, then I know of no other rational argument supporting this kind of preferential treatment."[11] In the event, he reluctantly made a small concession, and employees buying in were given the right to pay off half the price on the basis of a loan over a period of five years. The law on the small privatization was passed by Parliament in late October and took effect in early November.[12] The first auctions were held in January 1991.

The bill for the large privatization, which the government accepted in early November, proposed that every citizen from the age of eighteen would receive a share of the national wealth in the form of coupons representing 2,000 crowns (about three weeks' pay for the average worker). It was envisaged that it would be possible to buy further, though more expensive, coupons for approximately 50 crowns per point. Over a period of time, people would exchange these coupons for shares in companies of their choice, thereby denationalizing them. As a preliminary, each company to be privatized was to produce its own prospectus allowing future shareholders to make some kind of informed choice. Although the success of the large privatization depended on the individuals' knowledge of and information about companies, aspects relating to past performance and future prospects were generally known only to industry professionals and the managerial stratum, most of whom were from the old *nomenklatura*. In spite of prospectuses, which ultimately had to be approved by the minister of finance or by another responsible state organ, ordinary people could not compete with such expertise in the process of selecting their shares, and the government had to accept the difficulties posed by a form of insider dealing. Furthermore, there was a problem associated with the unequal amounts of savings held by the public. Although such savings afforded them an opportunity to buy shares and these shares were equally distributed at the outset, the shares were on offer at a higher rate as soon as the market opened. Again, the "old structures" had the money and the know-how to take advantage of the situation, and this amounted to a marginalization of individuals and groups, again bringing up the question of social justice and inequality.

The coupon system for the distribution of the national wealth was based partly on the premise that there was insufficient capital in the form of private savings to fully privatize enterprises. Some critics, such as Miloš Zeman of the Institute of Economic Forecasting, wondered if the plan for the free distribution of coupons was not contrary to the principle of establishing a free market, as it gave away something for nothing. It was also argued that giving away state assets would reduce state revenues, affecting, for example, projects to cope with the problems of the environment. Zeman and others advocated the distribution of shares on the basis of long-term loans, so that the dividend would be greater than the interest. Employees should have preferential treatment enabling them to purchase shares in the first year at a nominal price with a twenty-year payback term. Other nationals would have the opportunity to buy after two years, and after three the way would be opened to foreign capital.[13]

The economic program of the Institute of Economic Forecasting was submitted to Parliament for consideration on September 10, 1990. The institute took issue with Klaus on a number of important points, including privatization by coupon. It asserted that one of the central purposes of privatization was to encourage the emergence and development of entrepreneurs with initiative and responsibility and thus to provide the impetus for new driving forces in the economy. The coupon method, the institute argued, would result in a thin spread of ownership, which would prevent shareowners from having a voice in the administration and development of the company's activities. The free acquisition of shares then would tend to weaken the sense of ownership. Given the relatively low number of shares held and an absence of entrepreneurial spirit among the general public, this process would tend to result in the relatively quick sale of shares acquired on the basis of these coupons to finance purchases of consumer goods. This in turn would lead to the strengthening of demand and, in conditions of insufficient supply, to inflationary tendencies. As regards attracting foreign capital, the radical program, as Klaus argued, was not enough to give confidence to the foreign investor, who looked for price stability and the reduction of risk as a main incentive. To attract outside investors, the institute argued, the semimonopolistic state enterprises would first have to be transformed into independent, commercial concerns as a prelude to privatization, utilizing employee shares as the best means of harnessing ownership and motivation in the cause of good management.[14] There were other public criticisms of the coupon method, but it was nevertheless ultimately embodied in the law passed on February 26, 1991.[15]

Joint ventures were also actively encouraged by the government, and practically all restrictions were removed on foreign capital. There were no limits placed on founding subsidiary companies with 100 percent capital from abroad. Not long after the law was enacted, the Škoda Motor Company at Mladá Boleslav concluded an agreement with Volkswagen whose terms involve a 70 percent acquisition of the shares, indicating that the Czechoslovak government did not fear foreign companies' having a controlling interest in Czechoslovak firms. Negotiations over several other joint ventures began, including one involving the giant Škoda Engineering Works in Plzeň.

Additional measures dealt with the transfer of property, such as the two restitution laws, one of October 1990 and the second of January 1991. These were not overtly economic in that they were not expected to contribute to the creation of either the free market or a new entrepreneurial class. They were, rather, social and political in that they were designed to rectify past injustice and publicly reaffirm the illegitimacy of the Communist regime and its laws. The beneficiaries of these laws were not simply former owners of physical assets with a permanent abode in Czechoslovakia but also their descendants. Vigorous debate centered on returning the extensive property of the church, many of its buildings having been used as orphanages, schools, and libraries, including the Strahov Museum of National Literature.

But returning property to an institution would not rectify injustice done to an individual: These laws did not cover any of the property nationalized between the end of World War II and the Communist coup in 1948—even though this nationalization involved a much larger share of the national wealth than that from 1948 onward—because doing so would have raised the question of former German property. Public reaction to the restitution laws therefore was not always favorable, largely as the beneficiaries were relatively small in number. In addition, those gaining nothing would, through general taxation, have to meet the bill for compensatory payments.

The last major privatization issue was the question of land, still being hotly debated at the start of 1992. There are two main proposals, one from the federal government and the other from a group of MPs known as Three T (after their surnames). The former proposal does not entail full, compulsory privatization of land but attempts to create conditions for former owners to reclaim their land or receive monetary compensation; it envisages the privatization of land that belongs to the state in a way analogous to the large privatization. It further attempts to restrict the sale of land to foreigners. The Three T proposal is more radical in that it calls for the wholesale privatization of land, including the land belonging to agricultural cooperatives. Where the land and physical assets are not reclaimed by a former owner, they would be sold off at public auctions. Agricultural cooperatives would become cooperatives of owners of land only. It also allows for the possibility of foreign ownership of land.[16] Opposition voices have been raised from the eastern half of the country arguing for separate legislation in Slovakia taking into consideration the specific features of the historical development of land ownership there. The matter has not been concluded but is pressing, as the state of uncertainty surrounding the ownership of agricultural land affects the work of agricultural cooperatives, especially at the time of spring sowing. The situation has been complicated by the indications that a substantial proportion of agricultural cooperatives have no wish to see the breakup of the cooperatives and are not keen on a return to private farming.

January 1, 1991, was the crucial date when the major measures for the liberalization of the market were introduced, namely, the liberalization of prices, the inner convertibility of the currency, and, in respect of foreign trade, the shift of the Comecon countries to trading in hard currencies. This had an immediate impact on the economy, but the conditions in which it took place were significantly worse than those in which the plan had been formulated and approved. Official statistics indicate that the economy had been adversely affected by developments abroad, particularly changes in the Comecon countries, and fared worse throughout 1990 than had been predicted: GNP declined by 3.2 percent. There was a balance of trade deficit with capitalist and former Comecon countries of some 17 billion crowns and 12.9 billion, respectively.[17] Exports to the former GDR were down by 53.4 percent, to the USSR by 11.4 percent, and to Poland by 21.4 percent. Imports had also declined, principally the import of oil from the Soviet Union, which was only 13 million tons as against the 16.6 million tons contracted for. The foreign debt increased by about $200 million to $8.1 billion. In spite of efforts to control inflation, prices rose significantly. Wholesale prices, for instance, went up by 4.5 percent for the whole year, accelerating to 16.6 percent in the last quarter of 1990; the price of consumer goods rose by 10 percent for the whole year, 18.4 percent for the final quarter. The cost of living for the average household increased; in the last quarter it rose 18.9 percent for workers and employees and 18.7 percent for agricultural workers and pensioners. The level of employment declined, and the labor force contracted by 490,000 (a proportion of these, however, becoming new entrepreneurs). Registered unemployment stood at 1 percent or 77,000. Industrial and agricultural production declined overall by 3.7 percent, though in the building and transport sectors it registered falls of 6.6 percent and 14.1 percent, respectively.[18]

The forecast of the Federal Ministry of Finance for 1991, published on January 2, called for economic growth to decline by about 5 percent.[19] It predicted that this would be accompanied by strong inflationary pressures throughout 1991, most marked in the early part of the year. Further, price rises on the order of 30 percent were expected over the whole year. It struck an optimistic note, though, suggesting that after riding out the first three months, when a very rapid increase in prices was on the cards, further rises could be limited to between 5 percent and 10 percent for the remainder of the year. This forecast looked rather optimistic with inflation reaching 45 percent in March 1991. The prediction that unemployment would not exceed 300,000 to 400,000 people, about 3 to 4 percent, was challenged by a number of experts who believed it would rise to 750,000.[20] The effect of liberalization has been to cause a 100 percent increase in unemployment in the first two months. An indication of its impact on the changing situation has come from another direction. The chairman of the state bank has noted that retail turnover has declined by 25 percent.[21] All this has brought about a fundamental change of mood among the people, whose growing anxieties associated with a significant decline in living standards have been compounded by increasing fears for their jobs. Given the overall weakening of the economy, it is likely that the government will persist with a restrictive monetary policy that will further squeeze living standards. In this context, the IMF loan to help cushion the effects of the economic changes has assumed greater importance. The strict IMF conditions, however, are unlikely to soften the impact of unemployment in particular. The trade unions have expressed dissatisfaction with the IMF deal, openly lobbying for the renegotiation of the conditions and threatening to publish the agreement if the government did not itself publicly disclose the details.[22] It is not surprising that the unions were critical of government policy, which they claimed depended solely on foreign capital and privatization, and pressed for a slower rate of reform and for an active policy to deal with unemployment.

The development of policies in changing economic conditions and the debates accompanying them raised two issues, one about the debate itself and the other concerning the reasons the radical view prevailed. The debates were vigorously formulated and highlighted the differences of the protagonists rather than emphasizing what they had in common. All the solutions of the radicals on all the important questions were successful, though with the help of certain compromises that deserve some consideration.

In an interview on February 15, 1991, Klaus provided a clue to the polarization of the debating positions. He used the example of a pendulum to explain the vehemence of his presentation:

> In order to move the pendulum by a single centimeter to the right, I must first shift it in my efforts at argument by at least two kilometers. This is not clearly understood here. . . . If I want to shift the pendulum to the right, I clearly cannot use the argument of those more or less left-wing economists and politicians who support state intervention, but I use the argument appropriate to the direction required, though I am not saying anything about where the pendulum should finally stop.[23]

This helps to explain not only his opposition to the language of any reform that links it to some form of search for a third way, some synthesis of socialist and capitalist economic principles, but also to the language of the slower reform, insofar as it stresses the importance of the interventionist role of the state. It is noteworthy how often protagonists of these views were accused by Klaus and his followers of being opposed to the market. His opponents, he constantly maintained, were tarred with the brush of 1968 reformism and simply wanted its return. Dušan Třízka, Klaus's adviser, observed:

> Our economists are indeed divided. There are basically two main groups. The first consists principally of former reformist economists of the 1960s who had been excluded from their usual research work for two decades. Today, they are basically again picking up efforts at reform they had to abandon after 1968. The second group is roughly of mine and Klaus's generation. We belong among the younger economists who could not be subjected to the proscriptions operating under the normalization process. We belong to the liberal economists who never wanted to reform socialism. We have always emphasized that socialism cannot be reformed, that the only thing that can be attempted is to minimize its catastrophic consequences and to transform it into an entirely different system. . . . We fundamentally disagreed with perestroika, which we believed could only cause enormous damage.

It is not stretching a point to add that Třízka's language assumed an almost sermonizing quality when he went on to claim that

> the market economy and democracy are natural conditions of mankind, and it should be possible to return to such a natural state. Even forty years of socialism was not able to extinguish the entrepreneurial spirit in people.

. . . I do not doubt that if we give people the chance, they will take it. At the beginning, there may be only a few of them, but they will be heroes, the new pioneers who will breach the dam separating us from the natural state of things and take others along with them.[24]

Such language was in effect a rejoinder to an earlier comment of the moderates. For instance, Komárek criticized the radicals in the following way: "We discovered that everything is very simple according to the economic reform plan. I realize that this has a certain elegance that fascinates many young economists, politicians, and journalists. . . . The idea that market forces are only kind and benevolent is naive. I cannot understand how such simplistic, radical ideas can triumph in a country as highly educated as ours."[25] There is an element of truth in this insofar as the presentation of a seemingly simple solution diametrically opposed to and unwilling to compromise with the past had great public appeal, especially among the young, though impatience for change was spread across all age and social groups. It should not be forgotten that the protagonists in these debates were engaged in a struggle for power that involved mobilizing opinion and support in the population as a whole. A further incentive to the polarization of the argument was the need for a rapid solution and likewise policy implementation, which implied a termination of public debate.

Ultimately then, the radicals achieved the defeat of their opponents by a process of delegitimization. As professional economists, most of the radicals had not been involved in any dissident activity and, accordingly, tended to differentiate between debates among experts behind closed doors and public presentations of their positions, as they were inclined to regard the public as consumers of ideas rather than as initiators or participators. Dlouhý's notion in this context of the relation between economic policy and democracy is illuminating:

In the world, an economic program is usually associated with the election cycle, that is, with a political party or coalition. These parties do not usually submit such programs to the "working people" for widespread discussion. Their programs tend to be formulated by experts, and the elected government then simply implements them. The democratic control of its implementation is then guaranteed by Parliament and the plurality of political parties.[26]

The radicals were also able to refer to economic theory currently dominant in Western circles, in particular various free-market theories, which gave them an advantage with which the moderates could not contend. The radicals were thus victorious partly as a result of their simple solutions and the public reaction to the injustices of the past. The radical economic program was also incorporated into a more comprehensive policy identified with the Right.

CF: The Shift to the Right

CF, the governing political organization, was, as we have noted earlier, a "broad church." Nevertheless after the election, there was a gradual but definite polarization of positions within it. The economy provided the main point of contention, but it was by no means the only issue. It was noticeable that positions had crystallized around certain political groupings; it was also apparent that the Right had a majority among the elected MPs of CF, and its strength was further marked in regional organizations. This group was the first to organize itself into a parliamentary club, known as the Interparliamentary Group of the Democratic Right, shortly before the leadership contest in CF. In its program, the club emphasized the market, privatization, and the preservation of the federal state and advocated Czechoslovakia's entry into NATO. As it became aware that it was in the majority, it grew in confidence. By mid-October, the Democratic Right was able to ensure the election of Klaus as leader, defeating the candidate sponsored by the old leadership, Martin Palouš, whom they described as "the presidential candidate" (meaning a supporter of Havel). This was a contest not simply between Left and Right but also between two competing notions of CF. The first related to the conception of a broad movement covering a wide range of opinion and initiatives. It was in competition with the second, a tightly organized political party representing a specific ideology. The first conception can be traced back to the old Charter 77 debates, to the concept of antipolitical politics and to the idea that a well-functioning democracy requires the creation of democratic structures and institutions permeating the whole of society. Palouš, for instance, noted:

> I wouldn't say that the forum is altogether reactionary. It achieved a great deal in a few months. I do not think that the forum as a structure acted as a brake on social development and that, least of all, it protected old ways of doing things. But it did create an environment in which political culture and civic society had a chance to grow. Now things are able to start moving more quickly . . . and therefore specialists will have to have the decisive say. And that's okay. But the central issue in the transformation of society is not the contest of specialists but primarily the transformation itself, so that institutions promoting, guaranteeing, and safeguarding freedom are created. I'm a little concerned that the dynamic specialists who have now

assumed positions of leadership should not consider this to be a superfluous matter hindering progress. They should not neglect political culture.[27]

The contrasting belief in the importance of the transformation of CF into a united, well-disciplined political party is emphasized by Dlouhý, who claimed that "at the time of the implementation of the economic reform, the government will need a strong and constructive partner. The central issue is one of unity and discipline within CF and its ability to accept the government's decision."[28] This states unambiguously that CF was to become an instrument of government policy, almost, to use the parlance of the old regime, a "transmission belt." Klaus also quite openly expressed his aim to transform CF into a political party of the center-right. A revealing interview with Pavel Havlík, Klaus's press spokesman, about the forum's future organizational plans appeared in the press on October 22, 1990. Havlík ingenuously revealed that within a year it would be changed into a political party of an electoral type. The Right, which he claimed had 50 percent of the forum's MPs, was to assume control. There was to be a purge of both the leadership of CF and of the CF group in Parliament, and as a result the liberals would be deprived of their leading positions. Most interesting was his statement that the apparatus of CF would be reduced. He added that it was important to create an environment encouraging people to leave the organization and found their own parties of a leftist orientation. Though Klaus distanced himself from these statements, changes did take place in the leadership and in the parliamentary offices. Further, and crucially, the most left-oriented groups, Obroda and Left Alternative, were expelled.

The argument between the ideas of the broad church and the tightly organized political party also involved a clash of ideas about legitimacy. For proponents of the latter view, it was the MPs who, once elected, became the repositories of legitimacy. For those who believed in the former, legitimacy was the movement as a whole, as the public had voted for CF as a movement, not as a political party and not for specific MPs representing definite programs. Certain legal obstacles hindering the change from a movement into a political party also played a decisive part in the uneasy compromise the two wings arrived at in January 1991. The dominance of the Right from mid-October generated moves toward the narrowing of positions and ideas within the movement as a whole. This was not simply connected with the expulsion of groups and alterations in the leading positions of CF and its parliamentary wing but was also reflected in the growing pressure to follow the dominant line. Those who were identified with the old dissidents were increasingly marginalized as they were pigeonholed as liberals. They were put under pressure as a whole by a policy that contained more than a hint of the strategy outlined by Havlík that they should leave if they could not accept the line laid down by the Right.

The strength of the Right in CF was not based on the old dissident structures, such as Charter 77. This was particularly true in the regions outside Prague, where the new people were those who had become politically active after the revolution. Ladislav Hejdánek, one of the first spokesmen for Charter 77, put it in the following way:

> A critical analysis of our political development since 1989 shows that not simply old dissenters were among the politically active . . . but also people who had until then been either politically neutral or those who though technically competent were politically disengaged, people who wanted in this way to cover up their compromising cooperation with the old regime; finally, there were arrivistes of all kinds who tend to accompany every major social and political change and, on the whole, reduce its quality and even its legitimacy. The level of political thought and experience among these groups is very low indeed. The revolution has tended to provide opportunities for those with low qualifications and low moral qualities.[29]

It is noticeable that membership in Charter 77 was no longer considered to be an undisguised advantage for the newly dominant Right in CF. There was, too, a distinct difference in attitudes to debate: The old dissidents were used to long and wide-ranging discussion, whereas the members of the Right unquestioningly accepted the government's program and tended to use an approach closer to realpolitik. The Right was particularly vociferous in its demand that both CF and various state institutions should be cleansed of all those associated with the old state regime. This process got under way in Olomouc on November 14 and 15, 1990, at the Sněm, an official meeting of the all-state conference of the forum's members in Parliament and government, the regional organizations, and delegates representing the rank and file; all present were required to proclaim publicly that they had never cooperated with the old StB. The purge ended in March 1991 with a nonjudicial, politically motivated ouster involving about ten MPs. People who had spent decades working abroad supporting the dissident movement were tarred with the same brush as proven StB agents, and the public manner of the disclosures—live coverage on television—had some resemblance to the witch hunts associated with the McCarthy era in the United States. Though there·was a demand to apply the same criterion to the civil service, it would have led to its immobilization; as Dienstbier and Dlouhý admitted, if successful the policy would only have brought about a severe shortage of specialists.

In reaction to the growing strength of the Right and its parliamentary organization, in early November a new association was created, the Interparliamentary Citizens Association. Its founding proclamation strongly emphasized a plurality of ideas and tolerance:

> We consider it natural that there should be different sets of opinions within CF. . . . Against national, racial, and any other type of intolerance, we emphasize the idea of tolerance. As against the belief in the one, true path, we stress knowledge emerging out of the critical analysis of problems. Against populism striving for short-term electoral support, we put forward a rational, long-term conception. . . . The economic reform is not the final aim for us but only one of the means on the way to achieving prosperity. This path of prosperity must be at the same time a path of political democracy arising out of the self-administration of people from below and not through the path of political manipulation or even fanaticism leaning heavily on the leadership principle.[30]

By mid-December 1990, the polarization within CF had led to the establishment of the Liberal Club, which contained a majority of CF members in the government. However, it had fewer MPs than the club of the Democratic Right, and the major regional organizations, such as in Prague and Brno, were also firmly in the hands of the Right. Because this situation threatened to split the organization, a compromise was reached in January 1991. It was agreed that CF would remain an umbrella movement containing two de facto political organizations. They undertook to make a fair division of the assets and agreed that neither of the two groups would use the name Citizens Forum or its logo. The president consented to head the whole movement. By early March, the Right had formed itself into a Citizens Democratic party (CDP) and the liberals into the Citizens Movement (CM). According to Klaus, the CDP would "not be led by dreamers but would be characterized by realism and pragmatism. The party wishes to guarantee that Czechoslovakia will not return to socialism under any guise." This, however, was not an attempt to ensure a completely unblemished party, though applicants for membership had to fill in a rubric stating whether they had ever been members of the CPC. The CM, according to Dienstbier and Rychetský, was to be liberal, civic, and social: "At this moment in time, the representatives of this movement consider it vital to prevent a situation emerging in which citizens, out of fear of the future, would attempt to bring back some aspects of the previous regime." They drew attention to the political climate they claimed resembled to some extent the instability of the Weimar Republic, not excluding the activities of the extreme Left and extreme Right. The government should implement the economic reform rapidly but in a systematic way so as to prevent massive social upheavals. They also stated that the CM could not avoid acquiring certain characteristics of a political party. "Membership will be registered and will be incompatible with membership of any other political party. The basic feature of the movement should be tolerance."[31] A process has already begun that will result in the demise of Citizens Forum and the formation of political parties and coalitions thereof.

The fears both wings of the movement have expressed about a possible revival of the CPC were not entirely groundless, given the economic uncertainty and the absence of any major, organized, popular alternative on the left. The local elections in November 1990 bore this out to some extent. For instance, support for the CPC in the Czech Lands held up at 17.2 percent, with support for CF declining significantly to 35.6 percent.[32] This gave CF a jolt and provided an impetus to action for all those who wanted to cripple the CPC through all available means, including the confiscation of party property.

Federalism Versus Separatism

The other major issue creating dissension was the national question, especially concerning the relations between the Czechs and Slovaks and between their executive and legislative organs. Protracted and difficult negotiations took place in the aftermath of the elections regarding the nature of the federal arrangement, in particular the actual division of powers between the two governments. An uneasy compromise was reached in November 1990 under which a division of powers between the national and federal governments was worked out. This arrangement began to unravel almost immediately as further demands were generated by increasing nationalist pressures.

Among the important issues at stake was that of Slovak nationhood, whether Slovakia could be reconciled with something less than full independent statehood. Because the Slovak National party (SNP), which was the main advocate of Slovak independence, did not achieve good results in the local elections in autumn 1990, the party was not considered a substantial threat. Yet there were strong nationalist tendencies in most of the other Slovak political parties. Radical demands aimed at guaranteeing the sovereignty of the Slovak nation were raised from within the leading grouping itself, Public Against Violence, and Vladimír Mečiar, the Slovak prime minister, used extreme demands as a negotiating tactic in the expectation that he would have to make compromises during the bargaining process. Considering the difficult relations that existed, such tactics were bound to have an impact on feelings in both parts of the republic. A further complication in connection with Slovak sovereignty was the question of the official language. This caused much apprehension among the Hungarian minority on the one hand and, on the other, impatience among the Slovak nationalists for the speedy resolution of the problem. The Slovaks demanded something akin to an independent foreign policy—which indeed the Slovak government seemed to be conducting by the end of the year.

A crucial element in the nationalist problem was the economic dimension. The different political complexion of Slovakia led to demands for a "softer" economic reform, both by different political groupings, for instance the Christian Democratic Movement, and also by Public Against Violence and professional economists. Public Against Violence was not dominated by the Right, and the general public was much less enthusiastic about the reform as it stood. There was, too, the complication caused by the differential impact of the reform when productive industry was old-fashioned and obsolete. Some sectors lived under threat of closure in the emerging free-market system. Others hoped to survive by a policy of "damping down"; for example, the armaments and related industries were in line for a significant amount of restructuring. In general, the anxiety about the consequences of radical economic reform was much greater in Slovakia. When Mečiar responded sympathetically to some of these demands, the premier and others suspected him of leftist leanings. President Havel's spokesman, Michael Žantovský, falsely depicted the realignment of political forces: "It appears as if a new coalition is emerging in Slovakia consisting of reform Communists from 1968, contemporary Communists, separatists, and people who think of the [wartime] Slovak state as the golden age in the history of the Slovak nation." He suggested that this group "has different ideas about our economic development, about economic reform, and resurrects some aspects and notions connected with national socialism." Žantovský further claimed that Mečiar, in his own way, belonged to this supposed coalition as he, too, had reservations about the current implementation of the economic reform, some of his public statements showing signs of reformist socialism.[33] The reaction from the center to all this was negative. It was not simply a question of Czechs retaining control but a legitimate argument that overall control had to be maintained in areas such as monetary policy in order for the reform to be effective. The question of the unified market also demanded central decision making. In the atmosphere of nationalist tension, the issue became more complicated in that the people who were making these decisions were Czechs. The position of the federal ministers tended to be strongly supported by the Czech government. For instance, at a press conference on March 13, 1991, Pithart, the Czech prime minister, not only rejected separatist arguments in favor of dividing the Czechoslovak economy into two independent units, with the introduction of different currencies, dividing the budget, and so on, but he also pointed to the dangers of a situation in which the federal structures formally existed but were gradually deprived of all their basic functions. The final outcome, he warned, would be general chaos accompanied by uncontrollable inflation.[34]

Separatist demands became more vociferous and were accompanied by a considerable effort to rehabilitate the fascist Slovak state and its leading figures. Some nationalists, including several Slovak MPs, organized a demonstration in celebration of the fifty-second anniversary of the founding of the Slovak state and erected a consecrated cross on the grave of Tiso, its wartime prime minister. At the conclusion of the demonstration, a proclamation of the nationalists demanded sovereignty and independence for a Slovak republic, the acceptance of Slovakia into the United Nations register of nations, and a moratorium on the reforms initiated by Klaus. The situation was worsened by their reaction to the appearance of Havel on a visit to Bratislava on the same day: The presidential group was attacked and some members of his entourage manhandled by participants in the demonstration. It brought the issue to boiling point, provoking strong feelings against Slovak nationalism and Slovak separatism, and not only in the Czech Lands. It accelerated the growing divisions within Slovakia between those leaning toward greater independence from Prague and those who remained committed to the maintenance of the federal structure. In a minority political movement but with the bulk of the population behind them, Mečiar and the foreign minister, Milan Kňažko, hoped to make a bid for power by setting up a rival faction to the mainstream Public Against Violence. The debates concerning the delineation of power and competence were based from the Slovak side on an argument legitimately claiming that there was no reciprocity from the Czech side. In contrast to that of Slovakia, Czech statehood was not in question. The proposed tripartite arrangements with Moravia-Silesia, though welcomed by Moravian nationalists at demonstrations in Brno, in effect diminished the status of the Slovak nation, as Moravia had no history of nationhood. This accounts for the Slovaks' negative reaction, encapsulated in a statement of Jozef Mikloško, chairman of the Slovak Parliament. He suggested that the Czechs found it difficult to understand the problem of Slovak statehood, because "the Czechs do not feel any problem with unfulfilled statehood. The ordinary Czech citizen identifies more or less with the federal structure and feels no bitterness. We need to deal with this question very sensitively. I talked about it several times with President Havel and he grasped the fact that it is a serious existential problem for the Slovak nation."[35] Given such feelings, it is not surprising that in some people they generated emotions identified with national and race hatred expressed in anti-Semitism, anti-

Hungarian, and anti-Gypsy sentiments, placing them near neofascism in the political spectrum.

Havel's close involvement with the whole problem of the construction of the new state was visible, as we have seen in Chapter 7, from its very outset. He made strenuous efforts to preserve the republic while attempting to find viable solutions acceptable to the constituent nations. His awareness of the fundamental importance of not allowing the problem to drag on indefinitely impelled him to attempt to resolve the question once and for all. In his radio speech on March 10, Havel stated:

> By the proposed constitution, we have attempted to define something I would call a functioning, viable federation that still has some meaning. . . . Rather than have a nonfunctioning federation that is felt to be an obstacle to the development of the republic, it is better to have two independent republics. The disintegration of the state is an alternative that we have to consider seriously. I have never denied any nation self-determination. . . . I consider, however, that it would not be to their advantage for either republic or either nation to establish themselves as two independent entities. . . . If the Slovak nation prefers this solution, then it has a legitimate right to it. I insist, however, that it should follow a constitutional, civilized, and dignified way. I therefore think the Federal Assembly should accept a law on referenda at the earliest plenary session . . . enabling us to discover what the true will of the Slovak nation actually is.[36]

The proposed constitution presented to the public for discussion on March 14, 1991, emphasized that the Czechoslovak economy was based on a single market, one currency, and the free movement of labor, capital, and commodities.

The prospects for a successful solution to the national problem in Czechoslovakia, particularly concerning Czech-Slovak relations, dimmed as the situation seemed to near a crisis point.

One further complication of the national problem is the difficulty associated with race, which is closely linked in the public mind with criminality. An overt racism is directed particularly against Gypsies, who (as discussed in Chapter 7) are held responsible for the crime wave. There have been racially inspired attacks on Gypsies recently arrived from Slovakia in Prague, Plzeň, and in the industrial towns in the north. In some cases, long-distance truck drivers mistaken for Gypsies have been beaten up and killed. Other groups are not excluded, however. For instance, the slogans at the Slovak nationalist demonstration in Bratislava were conspicuously anti-Semitic as well as anti-Prague. Attacks, too, on Vietnamese employed in major industrial towns are a common occurrence. This is reflected in, among other things, the increase in the number of criminal offenses, which rose by 63.8 percent in 1990 compared with

1989. Prosecutions, though, have declined by one-third, and the solution rate for crimes stands at 30 percent.[37]

The Status of Women
and the List of Rights

As has been noted in the previous chapter, the women's issue is being dealt with through the sponsorship of the role of the woman as homemaker and mother in the family. Pressure is being maintained from traditional quarters for women to return to their role in the home, noticeable especially from the church and the political Right and also through the constriction of the female labor force. There has been little resistance to this policy, and it seems to have generated little dissatisfaction. We can understand this if we consider the following:

> Women in employment in Czechoslovakia were in a worse situation than those in other countries, as labor-saving devices are scarce and expensive and, owing to constant shortages, much time is spent queuing for goods, especially food. After forty years of "equality" under real socialism, many women yearn for the peace and quiet and the comfortable existence of bourgeois housewives. The attempt to substitute a collective upbringing for the family has also contributed to the positive acceptance of the return to the role of homemaker and mother on the part of many women.[38]

Pressure from rising prices and the economic situation, which threatens womens' jobs first, will sooner or later tend to generate dissatisfaction; an indigenous women's movement will not then be far behind.

Given their shared experience, women do take a firmer stand on abortion. They perceive an implied threat in the List of Basic Rights and Freedoms accepted on January 9, 1991, Article 6 of which proclaims that "everyone has the right to life. Human life is worthy of protection even before birth."[39] This law was the result of a compromise, as the more radical proposal from the Christian Democrats entailed the right of the unborn child to life from the moment of conception. In the debates on the abortion laws, there were clear indications that the traditionalists wanted to impose severe restrictions on the abortion law or indeed abolish it altogether.

Passage of a bill of rights is important to a post-Communist regime because it sets the state into a democratic framework based on the rule of law and stresses the importance of the individual. In Czechoslovakia it was also significant to relations with Western Europe, as the implementation of such rights was an essential first step toward entry into the EEC. The List of Basic Rights and Freedoms is comprehensive, though there is no clause outlawing discrimination on the basis of sexual preference. Compared with the rights enshrined in the constitution under the old regime, the right to work is conspicuously absent. The amendment to the labor laws confirms that the trade unions are independent and no longer part of the state. Further, it allows the right to strike, though this right is hedged about with all kinds of regulations. The law on collective bargaining, for instance, only recognizes a strike as legitimate in the circumstances of a trade dispute. Employees cannot be forced to strike against their will, nor can anyone wishing to work be so prevented. The strike decision also has to be approved by more than 50 percent of the employees in the enterprise; thereafter, it has to go to arbitration. The trade unions were not enthusiastic about the economic reform and pressed for measures to ameliorate its impact on the workers, including a law on the minimum wage. They also pressed the government for active measures to deal with unemployment.

Czechoslovakia and the World

The central aim of the new foreign policy is speedy integration into Europe, to be understood as Western Europe. Both the president and the government have been pursuing initiatives to facilitate Czechoslovakia's acceptance, among them the hosting of the European Assembly in Prague. Passage of the List of Rights was significant in gaining entry into the Council of Europe in January 1991. Efforts are being made to achieve relatively quick acceptance into the EEC, and the first step was realized with the agreement in principle of the right of entry. The aim in the first stage has been called "superassociation." Havel has constantly reiterated his wish to join the community, not least as a bulwark against the rise of right-wing, populist dictatorships and, generally, against the spread of instability rather than as a way of meeting any external threat. Under the pressure of circumstances, Czechoslovakia is now looking for an association with NATO or for an involvement in the EEC's discussions about political union, including security policies. This is a response to the threat of internal instability generated by economic difficulties and national problems, and likewise the spread of problems associated with instability from neighboring countries. The complex reaction to the Soviet intervention in Lithuania struck a chord, largely as a result of the historical memory of Soviet intervention, and brought to the fore the security implications for Czechoslovakia of major upheavals within the territories of the Soviet Union. There was certainly concern that the collapse of the Soviet Union might bring about a flood of refugees across Czechoslovakia's eastern borders. An additional influence on the security question is constituted by the dissolution of the military side of the Warsaw Pact and the withdrawal of Soviet troops.

Though the policy of a return to Europe was present as an ideal from the beginning of the revolution, it has become more pressing. It represents a way of solving internal and external problems, not least the threat of economic collapse and the impairment of the old trade structures Czechoslovakia had been involved in, given the dissolution of Comecon, the decline in trade with its old socialist colleagues, and the failure to organize a substitute body to coordinate trade. Though Europe formed the focus of Czechoslovakia's foreign policy, the government gradually extended the process of reorganizing its foreign policy priorities, to some extent normalizing its relations with other countries. Czechoslovakia was the only country in the former Communist bloc that not only supported the allied intervention in the 1991 Gulf War but also took part by dispatching a specialist military chemical decontamination unit. It was perceived as an important step manifesting Czechoslovakia's active participation in the maintenance of international order.

The process of disintegration and party political realignment within CF continued until autumn 1991 and, as we discuss in the next chapter, was accompanied by other complications. Apart from the social tensions generated by an unsettled economy, the governing parties had to contend with difficulties associated with popular skepticism about the electoral system, the political fallout from the proposed law on *lustrace* (though this did not trouble the public overmuch), and the stubbornly persistent problem of Slovak separatism.

~*9*~

Postscript:
March 1991 to January 1992

The process of political realignment and polarization continued at an accelerated pace from March through August 1991, a period that, in the Czech Republic, was mainly connected with the further disintegration of CF. The parliamentary party split into five clubs—the Citizens Democratic party, the Citizens Democratic Alliance (CDA), the Citizens Movement, the Club of Social Democratic Orientation, and the Club of Independence in CF. The first three in reality constituted political parties, with the CDP and CDA on the right and CM on the center-right. CM in Parliament also included a group called the Association of Social Democrats (ASD), which, outside Parliament, operated as an independent group. Several MPs, including Valtr Komřek, left CF to join the SDP. Paradoxically, this political splintering left the CPC as the largest party in Parliament, though the Right and the Center-Right have dominated Parliament and opinion polls, suggesting that they have the support of the larger part of the electorate. At the end of July, for instance, the polls suggested that the Right and Center-Right, including the CDP, CDA, CM, CPP, the Czech Christian Democratic party (CDP[C]), and the Moravian nationalists, commanded the support of about 40 percent of the electorate in contrast to the 20 percent for the Left and Center-Left, including the CPC, SDP, and the Farmers' party (CFP). The extreme nationalist Right represented by the Association for the Republic (AR) scored about 7 percent.[1]

In Slovakia, Public Against Violence similarly split. The populist prime minister, Mečiar, left and founded a new political party, Movement for a Democratic Slovakia (MDS), which, though it remained a minority in Parliament, commanded the greatest support among the electorate. Mečiar himself was sacked as prime minister by the Slovak National Council and replaced by the leader of the CDP, Jan Čarnogurský. The MDS, which stood for a slower and less painful transition and for a greater role for the state in the economy, had the support of about 40 percent of the electorate by the end of July, in spite of some decline. The Left, which apart from the MDS included remnants of the Slovak Communist party and some other smaller parties, had altogether the support of some 60 percent of the electorate. The right Christian Democratic Movement (CDM) and the Democratic party could at best count on the support of 30 percent of the voters.[2]

Though elections were not scheduled until June 1992, the beginning of an election campaign could be detected in the late summer and early autumn of 1991. This was marked not least by a process of political realignment and coalition. The existing electoral system involving proportional representation with a 5 percent threshhold was the main stimulus in this development, encouraged by a desire among the smaller parties to ensure their representation, as opinion polls suggested most could have little confidence of being represented on their own. However, the largest Czech party, the CDP, consistently polled more than 20 percent in the Czech Lands, whereas the Communist party of Bohemia and Moravia (CPBM) and the SDP both achieved 9 to 10 percent. In Slovakia, the MDS, the party of Mečiar, was well in front of the others.[3] Coalition agreements were struck between various parties on the right; those left of center tended to go it alone. The most significant electoral coalition appeared to be between Klaus and the CDP, a development subsequently confirmed in January 1992. The other aspects of the campaign involved the process of transition reforms and the *lustrace*. These were noticeable in public arguments over privatization, people accusing ministers of designing policies to serve the interests of their parties and not those of the public.

In summer 1991, public disillusionment with the electoral system was beginning to emerge, particularly against a background of growing unease about the economy. Signs of a gulf between the political parties and the voters were reflected in opinion polls suggesting that the concerns of the MPs and the people were divergent, and this prompted Havel to suggest a change in the electoral system. He stated that the political parties were relatively weak institutions with a rather fragile hold over the electorate and expressed misgivings about the political sphere's being made the exclusive province of political parties:

> Loyalty to the party leadership and even the party apparatus becomes more important in deciding political careers than the will of the electorate and the abilities of politicians. Party structures can create something of a shadow state within the real state. Electoral optimism and preelection

maneuvers become more important than the actual interest of society. Too much scope exists for power-hungry people whose party membership, servility toward party leaders enabling their rapid rise within the party, can thus in certain circumstances smooth their way to positions of power and influence far beyond what their abilities would justify. It could hence easily happen that the electorate is governed by people who were not really voted in by them at all.[4]

As a solution to this problem, Havel proposed a new electoral law combining a system of proportional representation with majority voting enabling the electorate to vote for well-known and trusted individuals of any party allegiance or none. He submitted this to Parliament, which not unsurprisingly rejected it on January 21, 1992, thereby reaffirming its preference for a system of proportional representation in which independent candidates would have no place whatever. Unlike Havel, the majority in the existing Parliament identified democracy in the current conditions with the plurality of political parties and their dominance in the political domain. Citizenship and civic initiatives were to be expressed mainly through political parties. It is worth noting further that the emphasis on political parties and a parliament based on them is accurately reflected in the Federal Assembly's rejection of a proposed law on the referendum, even though the initiative presented to Parliament in January 1992 was signed by 2,259,000 citizens.[5] Though originally designed to resolve the Czech-Slovak dispute, it had a wider constitutional significance insofar as it was in effect aimed at making Parliament and the parties respond to matters of overwhelming public concern. In his regular weekly radio broadcast from the president's official country retreat in Lány, Havel described the outright rejection of the citizens' initiatives and their sponsorship of the principle of the referendum as party political arrogance toward the attitude of hundreds of thousands of citizens.[6]

The Ongoing Crisis of Nationalism

The contrast between the relative dominance of the Right in the Czech republic and of the Left in Slovakia was one of the factors contributing to the deepening crisis between the two nations. The negotiations concerning the future of the republic and its constitutional arrangements continued without achieving a successful outcome. It is noticeable, however, that the nationalist rhetoric used in particular by the Slovaks had acquired its own momentum. Though at the time of the election in June 1990 only the small Slovak nationalist party stood for separatism, a year later the Slovak premier regarded independence as inevitable. In an interview in the French newspaper *Libération,* Čarnogurský stated that

Slovakia's aim was to gain full independence by the year 2000 and then enter the EEC as a sovereign state.[7] In the meantime, the premier and his party supported the idea of a loose confederation based on a contract in which practically all power was devolved to the two states. But the most popular Slovak party, the MDS, reacted impatiently to the premier's statement; in a debate that stretched nationwide, it strongly supported independent status, which the party thought should come before the end of the century. Only Public Against Violence represents a federalist standpoint at the moment. It is noteworthy, however, that this rapid move toward seeking independence among the Slovak parties was not quite matched by public opinion. Polls have suggested that only about 20 percent of the Slovak electorate is in favor of full independence. It is partly for this reason that those who support a continuation of the federation, namely, Public Against Violence and most Czech political parties, also wanted to call a referendum to let the people decide the issue once and for all. The bill proposing a referendum, though, failed to get through Parliament, largely because of the opposition of the Slovak National party (SNP), the MDS, and the CDM.

The frustration with the continuing impasse, the opposition in Slovakia to the economic reform, and the prospect of a right-wing Czech administration's having to face a left-wing Slovak government after the elections in June 1992 has provoked a backlash in the Czech republic. In reaction to Čarnogurský's claim to Slovak independence, for instance, the strongest right-wing party, CDP, suggested that "if the Slovak premier does not abandon this aim . . . then we have no choice but to recommend speedy separation."[8]

Conflicts between Czechs and Slovaks also stimulated the rise of more extreme nationalist forces in the Czech republic, for instance, those in the Association for the Republic. This populist party has been exploiting not only the nationalist issue but also the growing fear of incipient economic hardship and the overt racism that is manifesting itself in fervent anti-Gypsy feeling. These sentiments have been fueled over a period of time at least partly by the influx of large numbers of gypsies from the East. Unlike those who have been settled for some decades, these Gypsies remain unassimilated and to a large extent ghettoized. The "Gypsy problem" has been worsening considerably, with numerous incidents of violence involving Gypsies and skinheads in various towns in the Czech republic. Judging by some of the letters published in national newspapers and sentiments expressed in private, however, strong prejudice against Gypsies is common even among well-educated, middle-class people.

The complex process of negotiation over the new constitutional arrangements involved several sticking points. The principal one was whether the arrangements would be founded on a constitutional treaty between independent states, which the Slovaks advocated, or on the federal principle as rooted in the constitution, thereby basing the relations of the two nations on the respective powers of the two republics, which was the Czech position. This dispute reflected Slovak fears that the Czech superiority of electoral strength and divisions in the future could be the reason for future amendments to the constitution, which, in certain circumstances, might bring about a return to state centralization. A state treaty, in contrast, was immutable and hence had, the Slovaks insisted, primacy over the constitution. The nationalist and separatist rhetoric accompanying this dispute declined toward the end of the year largely as a result of two factors. First, external events, especially the disintegration of the Soviet Union, the emergence of the Ukraine on Czechoslovakia's eastern flank, and the civil war in Yugoslavia, contributed to the recognition that dangers existed in separatism, and this pushed the Slovaks back toward the notion of maintaining the republic. The second factor related to the federal budget for 1992, which provided for a more generous settlement for the Slovaks, giving them more reason to stay inside the federation. The rejection of the law on the referendum and the absence of an agreement on the constitution makes it appear unlikely that matters will be fully resolved before the elections. Though the danger of the dissolution of the state is receding, there is little doubt that the process of harmonization of national relations is going to be protracted and complicated and could be severely damaged if the economic situation deteriorates significantly.

Making a Clean Break: Purges

One of the most hotly debated and divisive issues has been the question of *lustrace,* the process of cleansing the body politic by vetting officials who have been connected to the secret police and other security organs. It has spread from Parliament and the federal and republican governments to the media and civil service. The decision to undertake a *lustrace* of all members of Parliament was made in January 1991; accordingly, on March 2, in a televised session of the Federal Assembly, the names of ten MPs alleged to have been agents of the secret service were read out. All of them publicly rejected the charges and refused to resign. The accusations were based on secret service files, the so-called register that the parliamentary commission originally set up to investigate the events of November 17, 1989, considered utterly reliable. Some MPs, however, did not share this conviction in the register and raised other criticisms against the whole process—for instance, that the accused MPs were not given a proper chance to defend themselves and that the principle of the presumption of innocence was not accepted. The commission subsequently investigated members of the republican governments, the state-owned media, and the staffs of national newspapers whose editors had expressly asked for this inquiry. Most of the editors in the Czech republic welcomed the process, but in Slovakia they did not.

In early summer, the Ministry of the Interior submitted a draft law on the conditions for elected posts and appointees in the political sphere and state administration. This law was aimed at excluding from such positions all agents and collaborators of the secret service for a specified time. After a number of amendments, the various committees of the Federal Assembly suggested a new version with a substantially wider scope; it was submitted for consideration to the republican governments, the federal government, and finally to the Federal Assembly between the end of August and mid-September. This new version was designed to close off certain elected and appointed positions to a number of persons seen to be crucially compromised by their activities under the totalitarian regime. Such posts included those in the federal civil service; the army and police force; the presidential chancellery; the chancellery of the Federal Assembly; the office of the federal government; Czechoslovak Radio, Czechoslovak Television, and the national press agency; and those organs and institutions of the Czech and Slovak republics to be decided by their respective governments. The target of this law included all those who at any time between February 25, 1948, and November 17, 1989, had been members of the StB, were registered in secret service files as agents or collaborators, or had knowingly collaborated with the StB. Further, it implicated others who had held positions as secretaries of an organ of the CPC from the level of district committee upward or who either as members of the ruling bodies of the party or in its apparatus had been involved in setting the political direction of the secret service. Finally, it took in those who had held any position of command in the People's Militia.

It is interesting to note that the Ministry of the Interior refused to respond to some objections raised by the general procurator, the Ministry of Labor and Social Affairs, and the Ministry of Defense. They argued that the proposed law contradicted the List of Basic Rights and Freedoms and the International Labour Organisation's Agreement 111 of 1958 on discrimination in jobs and professions, not to mention some fundamental principles of European law, such as the presumption of innocence. The latter objection arose from the process by which the onus would be on the citizens already in or aspiring to certain posts to demonstrate their innocence. The Ministry of the Interior argued that it would be impossible to preserve the intended aim of the proposed law if these objections were to be taken into account.[9]

The *lustrace* campaign was given further impetus by the failed August coup in the USSR. It sparked off a de-Bolshevization campaign in which demands were raised for the purge not simply of the exponents and supporters of the old regime but also of all reformist Communists, irrespective of their active participation in dissent during the normalization period. The right-wing parties, and particularly the Citizens Democratic party and the Christian Democratic party publicly targeted some of their opponents in government, Parliament, and the mass media, such as Dubček, Zdeněk Jičínský, and Rychetský,[10] as prime candidates for such a purge. They also demanded that the heads of radio, television, and the national press agency be replaced for their supposed unreliability—a dubious accusation as regards, for example, Petr Uhl, head of the Czechoslovak Press Agency and one of the most prominent dissidents, who had spent nine years in jail between 1960 and 1989 as the price of his struggle against the Communists.

The desire to deal with the totalitarian past and punish those responsible for the maintenance of the old regime and its excesses as well as the need to establish clear ethical criteria for the assumption of elected and appointed public posts have undoubtedly played their part in creating a momentum for *lustrace*. But other motives have also manifested themselves, often indicating significant differences of view across the political spectrum and also between the Czechs and the Slovaks. On the whole, the greatest pressure for the most wide-ranging purge possible has come from the Right and is not unconnected to the disagreements on economic policy and the onset of the election campaign. To lump together in such a purge not merely the supporters of the normalized regime but also all the reformist Communists—even those purged after 1968—would have the advantage of seemingly delegitimizing general reformist views on the left. In this context, it is worth noting that the CDP in particular blamed the relatively slow progress of economic reform on old "Communist mafias" in the various ministries. For instance, the genuine differences of view concerning the coupon privatization and the alternate approach adopted by the Ministry of Industry were described by Klaus as "sabotage."[11]

The Slovaks have been much less enthusiastic about *lustrace*. This can be explained partly by a more left-wing trend in Slovakia and partly in cultural terms. The chairman of the parliamentary commission administering the *lustrace*, Jiří Ruml, explained it in the following terms: "Slovaks have been oppressed for a long time; they are a small nation, and they are able to forgive each other, so their resulting losses [of personnel] are not great."[12] The attempt to purge Dubček could not have a positive impact on relations between Czechs and Slovaks, as his popularity, though negligible in the Czech republic, is considerable in Slovakia.

In September 1991 Parliament passed the new law on *lustrace* with a number of amendments, some of which widened its impact, although CPC functionaries elected in 1968 and purged after the Soviet invasion were exempted. The law generated some unease and criticism abroad, especially in the United States, in respect to its abrogation of the notion of the presumption of innocence and the way in which it expressed the principle of collective guilt. In one or two cases, prominent figures (for instance, Bedřich Moldan, a minister in the Czech government until his enforced resignation in 1991) were exonerated and reinstated. But recourse to the courts was problematical, partly because of the slow progress of judicial administration. As important, however, was the reluctance of the judges—themselves subject to the same vetting process— to provoke powerful political forces by finding in favor of the plaintiff. Furthermore, many judges decided to avoid the process altogether by the simple expedient of moving into private practice as legal advisers to foreign firms.

The issue of *lustrace* has certainly inspired a great deal of passion, particularly among politicians and journalists. The general public, judging by opinion polls, seems to regard it as much more marginal to its concerns. For the supporters of this process, the issue is so crucial that they have been at times willing to give it precedence over those human rights enshrined in both national and international law. This could not fail to complicate the efforts to build a state based on the rule of law. The debate has also not been conducted without some recourse to demagogy: The spokesman for the above-mentioned parliamentary commission, Petr Toman, clearly implied that those politicians who expressed doubts about and opposition to the process, such as Mečiar and the former interior minister, Sacher, had ulterior motives.[13] No doubt the issue of *lustrace* will continue to have a corrosive effect on relations between the two republics and likewise between the political parties and on the construction of the rule of law.

Unsettled Economy, Uncertain Future

Finally, on the economic front, the sharp price rises had stabilized by the middle of the year, though a 70 percent increase in the price of electricity took place on October 1, 1991.[14] The effect of the disruption of trade with the Soviet Union and its successor republics, however, is considerable and potentially threatening. The Czechoslovak government has worked hard to secure the opening of EEC markets to Czechoslovak goods from those areas of the national economy particularly affected by this downturn, such as textiles and agriculture; it has achieved some success with a December 1991 agreement granting the country such access for a limited number of years.[15] The continuing disagreements concerning coupon privatization create further difficulty, and it is not as yet certain how consistently the program will be implemented. The coupon privatization began on December 1, 1991, and though scheduled to run for three months was extended by a month as a result of administrative difficulties involving the relatively few offices set aside for registration. A number of criticisms continued to be raised about the whole process, particularly in light of the party political overtones it took on because of its close identification with the minister of finance. Others were concerned about the ease with which foreign firms were able to acquire property in Czechoslovakia given the operation of the exchange rate in favor of Western countries. The Ministry of Industry of the Czech republic, however, in contrast to Klaus, does not regard the coupon privatization as superior to other forms, such as public auction, direct sale, restitution, the founding of shareholding companies with subsequent sales of shares to employees and managers, and transfers of shares to banks and boroughs.[16] The significant decline in industrial production—estimated at 29 percent by one author and 17.8 percent by the Federal Statistical Office[17]—in the first half of the year compared with the same period in 1990 suggests that GNP will be reduced over the whole year.[18] The dispute concerning the causes and appropriateness of the economic strategy has been revived by the appeal of four leading economists, two, Pučík and Miloslav Zelený, of Michigan and Fordham universities; Matějka of the Prague Economic High School; and R. E. Simmon, a successful U.S. industrialist with Czech origins. They have argued that there is an unprecedented crisis caused by a gross mishandling of the economy, and they single Klaus out for blame.[19] Though they may be taking an overly gloomy view, it is clear that there are major difficulties with privatization, judging by the course and results of the small privatization and likewise with the restrictive monetary policy.

The situation facing Czechoslovakia and the other Eastern European countries today is unprecedented. These are unique examples of simultaneous transitions from totalitarianism to democracy and from etatist economic systems to free-market economies. Spain, which underwent a democratic transformation yet without a radical economic transition of this nature, is hence not a very helpful model, and neither are those countries in Latin America where radical free-market solutions have been attempted under very different political conditions. The installation of democracy in circumstances of radical economic change is extremely difficult. It is not only concerned with the rule of law and formal democratic structures and human rights but also with developing a political culture to encourage a democratic mind-set. This implies not simply establishing a spirit of tolerance but setting limits to legitimate disagreement, providing a framework for the expression of conflicting interests sufficiently broad to cater to all major groups in society and allow for their resolution or management by a constant process of bargaining.

It is important that the multiplicity of interests connected with the different social categories into which each individual falls should be represented through citizens' initiatives as well as political organizations, so as to ensure that no one is disenfranchised. The idea that these interests are adequately represented in the framework of the state is faulty.

Havel is aware of this. Harking back to one of the central aims of CF in the November revolution, he still refers to the need to reconstruct citizenship as the basis for the new democracy and constantly emphasizes the importance of citizens' groups to achieve this. That such movements have not yet found a place in the political system represents a weakness, particularly in view of the role of the political parties, which he suggests are characterized by "politicking, party quarrels, insults, ill-will and intrigues."[20] In this respect, the shortcomings of the political system bear some resemblance to those of the early years of the First Republic.[21] Though the institutional basis for democracy has been laid, a political culture involving tolerance and understanding is developing only haltingly, most marked by a contraction of the room for the legitimate formulation of interests. Since the late 1930s in particular, political systems in Czechoslovakia have been organized around the principle of conflict pointing to a recognizable enemy. In 1938 government was based on a succession of semidemocratic structures, followed by the Nazi protectorate and, in Slovakia, a clerical fascist state. There was a brief resumption of democracy from 1945 to 1948, albeit with some qualifications, but a Communist dictatorship (excluding the interlude in 1968) ensured that political experience of democratic bargaining has not been great.

In effect, a mind-set of an adversarial character has been generated tending to regard opposing interests of whatever kind as illegitimate. In existing political conditions, a real danger threatens that one particular orthodoxy will be replaced with another, which cannot provide a solution to the problem of authoritarian heritage. This would perpetuate the cast of mind that is not conducive to bargaining and the mediation of interest on which a strong democracy should rest. Accepting that political parties in Czechoslovakia are continuing to operate in a relatively intolerant framework of discussion, there is a need to develop habits of thought through civic initiatives at the grassroots. Havel's backing of such initiatives is arguably based on his experience in the dissident movement and CF in its early days, when the shared experience of people with different political opinions operating over time generated a more democratic mindset derived at least partly from formalizing methods of mediation and debate.

The establishment of the market may also be causing difficulties for the post-Communist state. It is not by itself a guarantee of either liberty or democracy, and in certain circumstances it tends to suppress some citizens' interests, which contradicts the revolution's emphasis on social justice. Furthermore, it affects the parameters of democratic debate. The rationality of economic solutions may require that particular interests are regarded as unfulfillable or dependent on the implementation of the economic reform so as to postpone their formulation or operation. This, too, generates a mind-set with an emphasis on premises defined in a reductionist sense, in this case an economic one. It is doubtful whether this provides a satisfactory setting for the expression and realization of the interests of diverse groups.

As Havel warned and opinion polls now indicate, citizens have responded to the situation facing them in early 1992 by displaying increasing apathy toward democracy. This has not gone as far as it has in Poland, however, where 50 percent did not vote in the 1991 national elections, leading to a fragile coalition government. Nevertheless, as the citizens of Czechoslovakia lose trust in the government, there is a danger that elements of the "Weimar syndrome" will emerge, with isolated calls for a "government of strong hands." A December 1991 opinion poll, for instance, gave Miroslav Sládek's Republican party 23 percent in one region of northern Bohemia, though support for him is also tied to the racial problem.[22] The poll's area of influence should not be overstated however, particularly as Sládek's support nationally is nowhere near as great. Yet his movement has the potential to develop into an antidemocratic, fascist movement and provides a warning of what could happen.

Havel's support for civic initiatives and the principle of a referendum is an attempt to counterbalance the dominance of the political parties and the apparatus associated with them. Insofar as these also give people an opportunity to involve and organize themselves on issues of great public concern, it provides a potential for active citizenship.[23] The government's rejection of "populism" and its assertion of the supremacy of Parliament suggests an unwillingness to expand the rights of citizenship at the risk of a growing gulf between the rulers and the ruled. This is underlined by its domination of the public discourse, too, especially as regards the economy: It insists debates be limited to expertise involving professionals, thereby excluding the people. Increasing social and economic inequality is producing a growing resentment toward the new elites, not least because the origin of their fortunes is widely believed to be tied up with their former positions as privileged members of the old system. This gulf may deepen and prove unbridgeable, bringing about awkward political consequences.

The post-Communist state is in its third year, and the balance indicates positive developments, in particular the shift toward the market, the framework of democratic structures, and the rule of law. Problems have emerged—as expected—some of which are connected to the failure to keep some of the crucial elements of the original program. This has hampered attempts to maintain public optimism not only in regard to rising inflation and increasing unemployment but also as affects the political sphere. The spectacle of a set of relatively small political parties apparently obsessed with winning elections and the disproportionate impact of the changing economy—a matter likewise influencing public perceptions of social justice—has produced the sense of a chasm between the ordinary citizen and the government. The failure to build politics around civic initiatives and political pluralism in conditions of economic crisis has evoked a public response of noninvolvement resembling that under the normalization. It is clear that in the new system a tendency exists that does not encourage the recognition of politics as a rational process in which everyone has a stake. An eventual economic collapse could well encourage not only national conflict but even the emergence of a strong-arm government that would set back or overturn the process of transition.

Appendix A:
The Voice of the Street—
Slogans of the Revolution

One of the most immediate and memorable aspects of the revolution was the character and profusion of the slogans, most of which were produced by students and young people. The word *slogans* is slightly misleading if it is associated simply with the expression of demands of a political, social, or economic nature. Although many did make political demands, the slogans in Prague, Brno, and other cities did not have the earnest and sober, almost exclusively political character of those seen in the course of the revolutions in East Germany and, to a lesser extent, in Hungary. Instead, the slogans of the Velvet Revolution were striking for their graffiti-like quality—even if only a handful out of the thousands were ever written directly onto walls. Most involved wit as much as wisdom, oracular and gnomic statements, adages and epigrams, quotations and rhymes. Some were of a profoundly idealistic character reminiscent of the ethos of the Western youth culture of the 1960s and were not always connected with the events then unfolding.

One importance of the slogans lay in their role as an alternative means of information beyond the control of the regime at a time when people were only beginning to do something about censorship in the press. But equally significant was their ability to make people smile as much as ponder, so much so that, as one worker later said, "We didn't know what was going to happen in the first week. Everywhere doubt, confusion, and uncertainty. Then we read the slogans on walls, in the Metro, pasted up in shop windows. Simply everywhere. And we laughed and everything seemed better." This, of course, does not exhaust their significance as subtle expressions of popular desires and demands. Not all were witty; indeed, in translation some sound relatively banal, especially at this distance from events. In the twenty-first century, when the section of the archive in Prague where these slogans have been collected is opened, researchers will be able to make a more systematic classification and considered analysis of them. In the meantime, they are worth recording here as the embodiment of what some have preferred to call the "genial" or "merry" revolution.

It is, of course, not easy to render into English the precise nuances of the slogans, particularly when many rely as much on wordplay as rhythm and cadence and others encapsulate echoes of significant events in the national past. I have been quite selective and omitted many that make direct political and other demands, such as "An end to one-party government." I add a note where they are a response to a political or other kind of event. There is otherwise no attempt to put them into any kind of order: I simply reproduce them more or less as I recorded them.

Evil knows about good, but never good about evil.

He who doesn't know the truth and lies is an ignorant fool; he who knows the truth and lies is a criminal.

What good is a head for that isn't interested in its body?

Three sources and three components of Marxism: Elasticity [Bil'ak], Empty Rhetoric [Jakeš], Loss of Memory [Urbánek].

The street is the voice of the people.

Clean water, clean air, clean government!

We want a government and head of state made up of educated democrats.

Freedom is participation in power.

Democracy needs leaders, not feudal lords.

For a Christmas in a free republic.

We're on the wrong castle! [a call to demonstrate on Prague Castle, seat of the presidency, after the march to Vyšehrad November 17]

Students, you're still young . . . so we have a last chance—Parents.

When you can't solve problems in your offices, we must solve them on the street.

Mr. Adamec is gambling with the gentle revolution. [after the announcement of the notorious "coalition" with fifteen Communist ministers, also the topic of the next five slogans]

The construction of the new government we regard as a mockery of our demands—Student Coordinating Strike Committee.

Five new ministers, fifteen merry old men.

No support for the provisional government. [Lenin]

An end to the game of blindman's buff—off with the mask and let's get on with it!

You've had your fun, Mr. Adamec.

Today, the truth—tomorrow, freedom.

Czech and Slovak—it must be good; Dubček is our Robin Hood!

For Štěpán. [sign hanging on a miner's shovel]

Our children see that the emperor has no clothes.

Which fairy tale do the Communists like most of all?

Holy Anna! [the patron saint of Bohemia] Save us from the Czech Union of Women. [the students' reaction to the union's support for the police attack]

He speaks Czech better than Jakeš. [referring to a Hungarian student who had just given a speech]

The truncheon—the beating heart of the Communist party.

Long live the Communist party—in memory.

Abolish the People's Militia. They aren't popular.

Hang in there—if necessary, even until Victorious February. [the epithet for the Communists' capture of power in February 1948]

The governors do not stand above the law, but the law above the governors.

Is the CPC concerned for the future of the nation or in maintaining its own power?

With love, there is hope for the world.

Careful! A dangerous disease is spreading throughout the Ministry of the Interior—sudden loss of memory. [after the commission inquiring into the police attack had heard the first witnesses]

They say we won by the force of decency. But decency is at a stroke generally subjected to its lack if everybody fights only for himself.

1. What you don't wish for yourself, don't do to others.
2. At the same time, don't give way to turncoats.
3. But always make sure and with good will [that people are indeed turncoats before you condemn them]. A human being deserves that.

Members of the Federal Assembly, are you tired? It wasn't Vlasta Burian [the Czech Charlie Chaplin], Funes [the French comic], or Chaplin but Miloš Jakeš who made fun of you. Now we're laughing with Miloš. [a reference to Jakeš's making clowns of the MPs]

Remember the imprisoned as if you were imprisoned with them. Remember those who are suffering; suffering can come even to you.

We no longer have to beware—we don't want to live under surveillance.

We live to be happy and have a smile on our faces and not so that a one-party monopoly makes physical and psychological cripples of us—Vladimír Kolan and Martin Kendrych, Workers.

Whoever has to live in fear is not a free man.

Who does the StB serve?

We are class-conscious workers. We even make revolutions after working hours.

For the gentle growth of a revolution of decent people.

Prevent any attacks on members of the police.

If everybody acted in accordance with the principle "an eye for an eye," half of humanity would be blind. [Gandhi]

Idealists always win in the end.

Don't write slogans full of emotion and insults.

The students have taught us to think with our hearts and act with our heads.

With hasty leadership, the people will go into decline, but its protection lies in an abundance of advisers.

The first gentle revolution.

The battle cry for today—spread good humor.

Whoever lies, steals! [a reference to *Rudé právo* and Czech Television]

We only want what they told us we had a long time ago.

We have developed socialism for such a long time that we have become a Third World country.

Tough luck, comrades—the proletariat of all lands [that is, the Czech Lands] finally did unite. [when the workers united against rather than for the party]

To create the art of the possible with those who banned it is impossible.

We won't allow the Communists to subvert the republic!

And what about the 300,000 well-paid, useless apparatchiki? They live from our wages.

Take advantage of a special offer of year-round recreation, only for former members of the StB:
　Summer season: Ruzyně and Bory
　Winter season: Valdice and Špilberk
[These are the notorious hard-labor prisons where the 1950s purge victims and, later, dissidents were accommodated.]

We demand an audit of the property of the CPC.

Justice is a train that is always delayed.

Citizens! Don't forget to take your national pride with you when you go to Vienna. [poster displayed before 300,000 Czechs visited Austria for the weekend after the borders were opened]

And for us, Comrade Father Christmas, please bring everyone a shovel.

Whoever wants to change the world must start with himself, because it is better to light a candle than to curse the darkness.

The Central Committee played the cymbal and the worker danced.

We pensioners have had bitter experiences with the Communists! We no longer want them to govern us and to lie! We, the nonparty pensioners!

Even with new cards, it's possible to cheat. [referring to the 15:5 government]

Open the archives!

Forty German marks for 1 ton of toxic waste,
Forty German marks in a Swiss bank account,
Forty German marks for 1 ton of death.

Will Swiss bank accounts help to pay our foreign debts?

When you [the Communist party] go, who will lead the masses? [a mocking reference to Bolshevik ideology, which suggests that the masses are incapable of organizing themselves]

Life should be lived and not suffered.

With the continuous development of socialism, we have become a developing country.

Dwarfs believe that their size depends on the height of their plinths.

It is dishonorable not to go, but being carried away into the vortex of events, you ask yourself with wonder: How did I get here? [Seneca]

Communists have palaces while our children lie among cockroaches in hospitals.

Wanted: a good-quality nail file, not for the fingernails—M. Štěpán. [a joke making the rounds when it was fondly believed Štěpán would go on trial and be sentenced to prison]

People! Don't be frightened to say aloud what you've been thinking for the last forty years.

Truth will prevail—but it's a hell of a job.

I am for decentralization and respecting the specific character of Moravia. [in connection with the demand to revive the provincial Moravian government operative under Austria-Hungary, 1867–1918]

Dialogue = interrogate everybody!

The patience of the nation is not eternal.

Stop the press! Stop the press! Owners of weathercock [that is, the CPC] say revolution prepared long ago!

Ad: The CPC is accepting applications for a large number of cloakroom attendants. Apply under box name: Timeservers.

We want to treat you, but there's nothing to do it with. Help us!—The Medical Profession.

Hurrah! Our teacher no longer has to lie—Schoolchildren.

It's very hard to raise children so that they don't lie at home and they don't blurt out the truth outside.

For a life without a muzzle! [sign hanging around a dog's neck]

Intellect is invisible for those who have none. [Schopenhauer]

We don't want an emperor but a president. [in the context of the presidential campaign, when Cisář, meaning "emperor," was a candidate]

I'm not Pinocchio; I'm a Czech whom you've been leading by the nose for the last forty years.

Only Communists can discredit communism. [Lenin]

We demand the expulsion of comrades Štěpán and Jakeš from the ranks of expelled party members. [after they had been expelled from the CPC]

Moravian schools also want Moravian history.

We demand MPs disclose their tax returns.

Be as cautious as snakes and innocent as doves.

The only property that can be soiled but that cannot be taken away from anyone is quality—moral, ethical, or professional—and wisdom. No decree can remove wisdom. It just cannot be shifted—Jan Werich. [the most famous wit, raconteur, and cabaret artist in Czechoslovakia]

Once a person is in the world, he should look and see that he is there. And when he looks and sees that he is there and he is, so he should be what he is, and not what he isn't, as happens in many cases.—Jan Werich.

It is not enough simply to want—man must act; we always serve people if we serve humanity. [Goethe]

We are not comrades, but we, too, want to live freely.

We want our children to breathe clean air.

The StB is burning its archives. We demand an explanation.

We didn't know that the members of the police were studying television production at our schools. [referring to the appearance of the police at the film academy]

Why are the secret police supervising the technical side of things in the offices of Czechoslovak Television?

You can trample the candle, but you can't extinguish the light. [after the police attack]

Chapters from the life of a party functionary:
1959 — Train dispatcher in Bojkovice [a provincial, Moravian town].
1979 — Stationmaster in Bojkovice.
1982 — Secretary of CPC City Council, Brno.
1984 — First secretary of CPC City Council, Brno.
1988 — Member of the presidium of the Central Committee of the CPC.
1989 — General secretary of the Central Committee.
Prognosis:
1990 —Train dispatcher in Bojkovice.
[a comment in Brno on Urbánek's replacement of Jakeš]

Into the new year with a clean trough.

Decent people of the world, unite!! (And then keep your eyes peeled.)

Of course, you've got something to lose, but only your chains. [a play on Marx's famous statement in the *Communist Manifesto*]

Ad: Will anyone swap an unbound Lenin for a bound Štěpán? Box name: IMMEDIATELY.

A lion [the Czechoslovak national symbol] is a lion; even in a cage, it doesn't change into a donkey.

Come and join us! After all, we're YOUR children!

People! Be good to each other.

The Soviet Union—finally, our model. [This refers to the wish for the civic, press, and other freedoms emerging in the Soviet Union. A prominent party slogan during the normalization had been "The Soviet Union—the model for our social development."]

Don't forget the poor and forsaken.

We want no violence. [probably the most prominent and frequently repeated slogan of the revolution]

Whoever has done evil has no right to govern.

We want a government we don't have to be ashamed of!

Thank you to all provocateurs for keeping us on the alert.

Citizens! They ripped down all posters during the night. Hang up new ones. We're with you!—The employees of the Prague Metro.

We'll clean up for you. We want it tidy for Christmas—The Students.

Students! Stay in line: We all need one head.
We send you our greetings while baking our bread—The Bakers of Prague.

Havel president—Jakeš dissident.

Císař slept for twenty years. We're not voting for any Sleeping Beauty! [the general reaction of youthful Czechs to the old 1968 reformers]

Honecker on bread and water . . . and Štěpán and Jakeš still free?

Better shoes from Bat'a than a jacket from Bil'ak! [The former was a successful entrepreneur before World War II and the latter a tailor before joining the party.]

Comrades! For Christmas, a book to learn Romanian. [After Jakeš fell—but before the overthrow of Nicolae Ceausescu—the public thought of Romania as a fitting spot for dictatorial Communist leaders.]

Havel didn't keep quiet when we were frightened to speak out. Now it's our turn.

The flame of democracy is burning once again in our land; will the People's Militia now play the fireman?

Appendix B:
Documents of the Revolution

List of Documents

All documents collected and translated by B.W.

Several Sentences

The first months of 1989 have again clearly shown that, although the current Czechoslovak leaders forever invoke the words *perestroika* and *democratization,* in reality they mock everything that creates democracy or even remotely brings it to mind. They reject petitions and citizens' initiatives that they themselves have not organized as "coercive actions"; they condemn differing viewpoints as "antisocialist" and "hostile"; they break up peaceful popular demonstrations; they do not allow the people to contribute to the debates on new laws. At the same time, these same months have shown that civil society is shaking itself out of its lethargy and that more and more people have had the courage to publicly express their longing for social change.

This movement in society is coming onto a progressively more dangerous collision course with the inertia of power; social tension is growing and has started to threaten an open crisis, which none of us wants.

Accordingly, we appeal to the leadership of our country to understand that the time has come for real and substantial changes in the system and that these changes are possible and can be successful only if they are preceded by a genuinely free and democratic discussion. The first step toward any kind of sensible change, starting with a new constitution and ending with economic reform, must be a fundamental change in the social climate of our country, to which the spirit of freedom, trust, tolerance, and pluralism must return.

For that, in our opinion, it is necessary:

- that all political prisoners are released immediately;
- that freedom of assembly ceases to be restricted;
- that the various citizens' initiatives cease to be harassed and criminalized and that they are at last understood by the government as something they have long been in the eyes of the public, namely, a natural part of public

life and a legitimate expression of its diversity. At the same time, obstacles should not be placed in the way of the new, emerging citizens' movements, including independent trade unions, federations, and associations;

- that the mass media and all areas of cultural life are stripped of all forms of political manipulation and hidden censorship, leading to an open and free exchange of opinions, and that those means of communication hitherto operating independently of official structures are legalized;
- that the justified demands of citizens expressing religious belief are respected;
- that all schemes and completed projects designed to permanently alter the built and natural environment in our country and thereby to determine the life of future generations should be urgently submitted to the diverse judgments of specialists and the public;
- that a free discussion be opened not only into the 1950s but also the Prague Spring, the invasion of the five states of the Warsaw Pact, and the subsequent "normalization." It is sad that this subject is being discussed objectively in some countries whose armies in those days intervened in the internal developments in Czechoslovakia, yet in our own it is still taboo; and only so that those people in leading positions in politics and the state who are responsible for the twenty-year decline in all areas of social life would not have to step down.

Whoever agrees with this view can support it with his signature.

We appeal to the government not to treat this as it has been used to treating uncomfortable opinions. This would strike a fatal blow to the realization of the hopes we are seeking, namely, the hopes for a real social dialogue as the only way out of the blind alley in which Czechoslovakia finds itself.

STUHA: The Origin of the Independent Union of Students

(a) There is sense in founding an independent union of students. This union will:

1. coordinate actions at individual faculties.
2. organize student actions jointly.

Under Point 1 belongs, above all, the defense of persecuted students and the formation of self-administration; under Point 2, the publication of our own magazine, the organization of demonstrations and May festivals, and the expression of students' attitudes on international and domestic affairs.

(b) This union will be called STUHA; on the one hand, as an abbreviation of the words *student movement;* on the other, as it will not be easy, but difficult, and also because the tricolor is our badge.

(c) Before we officially request the registration of this union, we must have a sufficiently large support among students and we must be widely known.

(d) We can break into students' consciousness only by action. So we have decided to organize a petition against the teaching of Marxism-Leninism and to hold a demonstration on November 17.

Proclamation of the University Students
to the Workers and Peasants of Czechoslovakia

We, the university students of Czechoslovakia, protest most strongly against the brutal breaking up of the peaceful demonstration that took place on November 17, 1989, in Prague on International Students Day commemorating Jan Opletal, murdered by fascists. The Prague students' demonstration was absolutely peaceful. Nevertheless, the demonstrators were encircled by the forces of law and order and several times brutally beaten. To all appearances, this was not an attempt to restore public order but the meting out of physical punishment and with very serious consequences. This course of action is in contradiction to the function of the security forces, to current Czechoslovak law, and to accepted international treaties. Please understand that this was not simply an attack on students but at the same time an attack on your children, on the children of workers' and peasants' families.

We demand an inquiry without delay into the repressive action against the participants of the demonstration, the students. We therefore demand the formation of a suitable parliamentary commission of inquiry with the participation of the university strike committees and the subsequent punishment of the guilty, regardless of their present position and office. As we see no other way of expressing our disagreement and alarm at the present internal political situation in our country, nothing remains for us but to embark upon a week-long protest strike.

We appeal to you, workers and peasants, who with your daily work build the material basis for us to have an education and thereby prepare for our future occupations, to reflect on the serious moral, ecological, economic, and political problems of our society. As long as there are no radical changes in our economic and political life, these problems will grow and develop into a deep crisis that will not only affect us but also your own living standards and prospects.

Therefore we turn to you, because we have in mind not only our own difficulties but also many others to which we have completely closed our eyes and that are not possible to name in their entirety:

- We think of workers, men and women, working in conditions that insult human dignity, in textile factories, in the canning industry, in foundries, mines, and elsewhere;
- of young families without apartments;
- of pensioners and all the socially weak and needy;
- of the filth of corruption and the black economy that today affects everyone and leaves no area of our national life untouched;
- of the unearned privileges of the powerful;
- of the run-down state of our school system, health service, and buildings;

- of the inadequate opportunities for travel and contact with the outside world;

We turn to you to support the strike and our demands. You yourselves know your own problems and accordingly do not allow those with whom you do not agree to speak in your name.

We appeal to you to actively participate in the general strike on November 27, 1989, from 12 noon to 2 p.m. as an expression of your solidarity.

The Students of the Universities of Prague
November 20, 1989

Appeal to Our Fellow Citizens

After the repressive intervention of "the forces of order" on Friday, November 17, students have gone on strike, winning wide support. The response commits us not only to the punishment of the guilty but bears witness to the fact that there are unavoidable, structural changes in the political system, the method of organizing the national economy, and the general social climate in the interest of the renewal of the legal and civil responsibility of every individual. In order to achieve this, we consider it essential:

1. To constitute a commission in which the students' and citizens' initiatives will be represented to investigate all circumstances surrounding it, name the guilty parties, and submit objective information to the organs of the Ministry of Justice and the Czechoslovak public.

2. That those responsible for the present economic and social crisis, which we regard as the logical outcome of the devastation of basic national and general human values, immediately resign their functions, namely, Gustáv Husák, Miloš Jakeš, Alois Indra, Jan Fojtík, Miroslav Zavadil, Karel Hoffman.

3. That the first secretary of the City Council of the CPC, Miroslav Štěpán, and federal minister of the interior, František Kincl, who are fully responsible for all the brutal attacks of the last months, immediately resign.

4. That the Federal Assembly abolish the article in the constitution of the Czechoslovak Socialist Republic concerning the leading role of the party, which is in conflict with the democratic principle of the organization of the state.

5. That persons be immediately released who have been charged, sentenced, and are now serving sentences for riot as a result of the abuse of the criminal law and who are usually classified as political prisoners.

6. That international agreements relating to human rights, to which Czechoslovakia was a signatory in Helsinki and Vienna, are immediately adhered to.

7. That a nationwide discussion be opened, without time restrictions, about present conditions that will take into account all views concerning a solution to the catastrophic political, economic, and ecological situation.

In support of these demands, we appeal to all our fellow citizens to actively participate in the general strike on November 27, 1989, from 12 noon until 2 p.m. by which they can express their solidarity.

Open Letter of the Striking Students
to Comrades Miloš Jakeš, Gustav Husák,
Alois Indra, Karel Hoffman,
Jan Fojtík, Miroslav Štěpán,
Miroslav Zavadil, František Kincl

Esteemed comrades!

We ask you to consider that we shall be living in a completely different world from the one in which your generation has lived. You have lived for the ideas of the nineteenth century; we will be living in an information society.

You have fought against each other and against nature; we shall save the environment and defend each other.

You have lived in a period of class struggle; we shall live in a classless society. Comrades, we beg you to understand that it is impossible to implement perestroika with us because we simply do not believe you, and without the confidence of the younger generation above all others, you will never manage in your present capacities to bring perestroika to life.

We appeal to all Communists, to our parents, to all citizens who we know do not really believe in the competence of the present leaders of our society, to support our demand.

Esteemed comrades!

Please do not mistake the maintenance of your own positions of power with the defense of socialism. We have not lost faith in socialism nor in the regeneration of the Communist party. We have only lost faith in you, the present leadership of the party!

If you really have the interests of this country at heart, the interests of society, of the nations, if the fate of your own party really matters to you, the fate of socialism, of perestroika, the fate of the younger generation, that is, our fate, then leave! Leave, and by so doing you will help most of all to calm the current tense situation, by so doing you will help our people to concentrate fully on the difficult tasks that await them in future years, by so doing you will help the younger generation regain the confidence to rebuild the world of the twenty-first century in our country!

Thank you for giving us a hearing.

Thank you for respecting our request!

In the name of all the striking students of the universities and secondary schools of the Czechoslovak socialist republic.

The All-State Coordinating Student Strike Committee

The Eight Rules of Dialogue

1. Your opponent is not your enemy but a partner in the search for truth. The aim of our discussion is the truth, not intellectual competition. Participation in dialogue presupposes three duties: to the truth, to the other side, and to yourself.

2. Try to understand your partner. If you do not understand your opponent correctly, you can neither refute nor acknowledge his contention. Formulate his objections yourself so that it is clear you understand them.

3. Do not submit a contention as an argument without good reasons. In such a case, it is only your opinion, and your partner need not accept the weight of the argument.

4. Keep to the point. Do not avoid uncomfortable questions or arguments by leading the discussion off in another direction.

5. Do not insist on having the last word at any price. A mass of words does not make up for a faulty argument. Silencing an opponent does not mean a refutation of his argument or the negation of his ideas.

6. Do not disparage the personal dignity of your opponent. Whoever attacks the other side loses the right to take part in the dialogue.

7. Do not forget that dialogue demands self-control. In the end, we form our judgments with our intellect, not with our emotions. Whoever is incapable of controlling his feelings and passions, whoever is incapable of expressing his views calmly and intelligibly, cannot conduct a meaningful conversation with the other side.

8. Do not mistake a dialogue for a monologue. We all have the same right to express ourselves. Do not lose yourself in detail. Consideration for others also shows itself in the fact that you save time.

The Deposition of Lenka Schwammenhoterová

The whole demonstration went off peacefully. The crowd spontaneously chanted slogans expressing the wishes of the students and of all the assembled people. There were absolutely no exhortations against the state. I arrived before eight o'clock in the procession on National Avenue where the other roads were cut off by police units. There were no slogans calling for the overthrow of the republic. We chanted demands for the solution of the crying needs of our society. About half past eight, the police started to violently drag away the students just in front of us; they beat them indiscriminately with their truncheons.

Using bullhorns, the officers of the law called on us to disperse peacefully but at the same time cut us off from the other side. An armored transporter was on standby. Soldiers in red berets forced us against the walls of the houses so as to make room for them to beat up defenseless students. A terrible panic ran through the crowd that we would trample on each other. I have never experienced such a terrible fear because if anyone had fallen, the crowd would have trampled him to death. We were in an enclosed space from which there was no way out. We cried out, "Let us out; we don't want any violence; the world is watching you." We had to look on as they brutally beat our friends. Soldiers in red berets stood unconcernedly in pools of blood.

At about a quarter past nine, members of the police force with shields, truncheons, and trained Alsatian dogs formed a narrow alleyway through which we all had to pass. I went through with my arms above my head in complete calm, and I just waited for a member of the security forces to show his dislike for me and, according to his fancy, smash me over the head with his truncheon. I got a blow across my shoulder from behind. I couldn't raise my arms for the whole of Saturday and Sunday. Along Mikulandská Street and back to the Kaje-tanka student hall of residence, I met a lot of people who had been beaten up and were bleeding. I was horrified to see what the members of the security forces and soldiers in red berets were capable of.

I believe that no rationally thinking person can remain indifferent to this brutal suppression of a peaceful student demonstration.

Proclamation of the Founding of Citizens Forum

On November 19, 1989, at 10 p.m. at a meeting in the auditorium of the Prague Činoherní Klub, Citizens Forum was constituted as the spokesman for the part of Czechoslovak society that has become progressively more critical of the policy of the present Czechoslovak leadership and that was deeply shocked by the brutal massacre of a peaceful student demonstration. Participating in the work of this forum are Charter 77, the Club of Independent Intelligentsia, the Movement for Civil Freedoms, Artforum, Revival, the Independent Students, the Czechoslo-vak Democratic Initiative, the Committee for the Defense of the Unjustly Prose-cuted, the Independent Peace Association, Open Dialogue, the Czechoslovak Center of the Pen Club, several members of the Czech Socialist party, the Czech People's party, the church, artistic and other associations, some former and present members of the Communist party, and other democratically inclined citizens. Citizens Forum feels itself competent to negotiate immediately with the state leadership concerning the critical situation in our country, to express the present demands of the public, and to seek ways to their solution.

Citizens Forum wishes to open a negotiation, which should be the beginning of a nationwide discussion about the future of Czechoslovakia, with talks about the following pressing demands openly formulated by society at large:

1. That those members of the presidium of the Central Committee of the Communist party who were directly implicated in the planned intervention of the five states of the Warsaw Pact in 1968 and who are responsible for the long years of devastation in all areas of social life immediately resign their positions. This concerns namely Gustáv Husák, Miloš Jakeš, Jan Fojtík, Miroslav Zavadil, Karel Hoffman, and Alois Indra. The destructive policy of these people, who for years have rejected any kind of democratic dialogue with society, has inevitably led to the terrible events of the last few days.
2. That the first secretary of the Communist party City Council in Prague, Miroslav Štěpán, and the federal minister of the interior, František Kincl,

who are responsible for all the police interventions against peacefully demonstrating citizens, immediately resign.

3. That a commission is constituted that will look into the facts of these interventions, find out who the culprits are, and recommend that they be punished. Citizens Forum must be represented on this commission.
4. That all prisoners of conscience are immediately released, including those detained in connection with the latest demonstrations.

Citizens Forum requests that this proclamation be published in all the official Czechoslovak media.

Citizens Forum considers that its emergence and work corresponds to the will of the 40,000 who have so far signed the petition "Several Sentences," and is open to all sections and forces in Czechoslovak society on which our country depends, to initiate the process of finding ways by peaceful methods to a democratic social order and with it, prosperity.

For Citizens Forum:
Ing. Rudolf Battěk, Petr Čepek, Václav Havel, Milan Hruška,
Prof. Dr. Milan Jelínek, Milan Kňažko, Dr. Lubomír Kopecký, Jiří Křižan,
Václav Malý, Martin Mejstřík, Petr Oslzlý, doc. Dr. Libor Pátý,
Jana Petrová, Jan Ruml, Prof. Dr. Věnek Šilhán, Ondřej Trojan,
Ing. Josef Vavroušek C.Sc., Saša Vondra
Prague, November 19, 1989

Citizens Forum on the General Strike

The general strike called for November 27, 1989, is a political protest strike and has no other aims. To ensure that the strike causes no material or other damage, we recommend this course of action:

1. The strike will be called and directed by a strike committee of the company, office, or other institution.
2. The strike will begin at the same time everywhere on November 27, at 12 noon.
3. The length of the strike will be determined by the strike committee according to the character of production in industrial concerns and according to the character of the work in offices and other establishments; the strike will last at the longest until 2 p.m.
4. The beginning of the strike will be made known by the strike committee in a suitable way.
5. In the health service, public transportation, and service industries that safeguard the essential needs of communities, towns, and commercial life, we recommend calling a general strike and, according to the conditions of work, manifesting the strike in a suitable way.

6. Concerning the preparations, launch, and course of the strike, the factory and all other strike committees should inform the National Strike Coordinating Committee of Citizens Forum.

7. In the enterprises where a strike committee has not been founded, the employees can join the strike in the way they themselves choose.

Citizens Forum
November 22, 1989

Students to the Workers

WORKING PEOPLE!!!!!!!!!!

The spontaneous offers of secondary school and university students to help in production, health care, to help wherever necessary to reinforce your ranks, are growing. Seventy students from the philosophy faculty of the Charles University have offered their help for tomorrow, November 23, 1989, in hospitals and medical centers.

We suggest that every striking student work one shift without payment. Companies and other organizations who need any such help, please contact us!

The two-hour general strike cannot threaten the operation of the national economy but will become society's expression of agreement with the demands of the striking students.

The Students of the Philosophy Faculty

Statement of the Basic Organizations of the Communist Party of Czechoslovakia and the Socialist Union of Youth of the State Security Forces of the Prague Police to the Presidium of the Central Committee of the Communist Party

We, Communists of the basic organization of the party in the police force in the Ninth District of Prague, turn to you in the presidium of the Central Committee of the Communist party, as Communists and members of the police force firmly supporting the principles of Marxism-Leninism and believing it our duty to do everything for the protection and development of socialism in our homeland. The events of recent days oblige us to take up a position with the aim of achieving a political solution to the problem that has arisen in the state and society.

Given the inactivity of us Communists, it is no longer possible to leave the initiative to the opposition, which is represented by various legal and illegal structures. Further hesitation could lead to far-reaching and awesome consequences in the evolution of the whole of our society. Likewise, it is no longer possible to use us, the officers of the law, to cover up unsolved political and other problems.

Hence we demand and suggest:

1. That the Communist party immediately take up an objective and definite line on the situation in state and society and publicize it in the media, as we regard the attitude of the party leadership as inadequate.
2. The immediate summoning of a conference of the Central Committee of the party that would concern itself with finding a definite solution to the problem.
3. Bearing in mind that trust in the ability of the present leadership of the party to deal with the situation has been weakened, we demand the introduction of essential changes of personnel in the party leadership, above all in the presidium, with a view to renewing the party's capacity for action in the spirit of Marxism-Leninism.
4. From our information, it is clear that not all participants in the strikes and demonstrations have a negative attitude to the socialist system and not all reject the leading role of the party; accordingly, in the spirit of Gottwald's slogan, "Forward with the masses," we demand an open discussion between the leading representatives of the party and state, workers and youth. To do this, it is necessary to make use not only of the media but, above all, personal contacts between party officials and the broad masses.
5. We recommend the calling of an extraordinary congress of the party at the earliest possible moment, which would contribute to the stabilization of society on the tenets and principles of Marxism-Leninism. Delegates to this congress will be voted directly from the ranks of the basic organizations of the party.
6. Wholesale interventions by the security forces will be undertaken only with the agreement and responsibility of party officials in the presidium.
7. The basic organizations of the party must be kept informed of internal political developments.

The Committee of the Basic Organization CPC
of the Police Department, Prague 9 [signatures]

The Basic Organization of the SUY of the Police Department, Prague 9, supports the statement of the Basic Organization of the CPC from November 22, 1989, and, at the same time, hopes that the Central Committee of the SUY will help to guide the evolution of recent events, above all among the young, and will not allow itself to be carried along or manipulated by antisocialist elements, who are understandably using this process.

The Committee of the Basic Organization of the SUY
and the leader of the members' groups of
the Police Department, Prague 9 [stamp and signature]

What We Want:
The Program and Principles of Citizens Forum

Our country has found itself in a deep moral, spiritual, ecological, social, economic, and political crisis. This crisis is testimony to the ineffectiveness of the hitherto existing political and economic system. All mechanisms essential for society to react to changing domestic and foreign conditions have been discarded. The self-evident principle that whoever has power must also accept responsibility has not been respected for many decades. All three fundamental powers in the state—the legislative, the executive, and the judicial—have merged into the hands of a narrow, ruling group consisting almost exclusively of Communist party members. The foundations of the legal state have thereby been destroyed.

The Communist party monopoly in filling all important posts has created a system of subjection that has paralyzed the whole of society. People are thereby condemned to the role of mere executors of the orders handed down from on high. They are denied political, civil, and human rights. The centralized management of the economy operating under the command system has been a conspicuous failure. The promised restructuring of the economic mechanism has been slow, inconsistently applied, and not accompanied by appropriate political changes.

These problems will not be changed by replacing those persons in positions of power or by the retirement of a handful of politicians from public life.

Citizens Forum is striving for the following objectives:

1. *The Law.* The Czechoslovak republic must be a legal, democratic state in the spirit and traditions of Czechoslovak statehood and of internationally valid principles expressed above all in the international treaty on civil and political rights.

A new constitution must be worked out in this spirit, in which the relations between citizens and the state must be more precisely regulated. Only a newly elected constituent assembly can pass such a constitution. The exercise of civil rights and freedoms will be reliably ensured by a developed system of legal guarantees. The independent judiciary will also include constitutional and administrative courts.

The whole Czechoslovak legal system will gradually be brought into agreement with these principles and become binding on all citizens and also on the organs and officials of state.

We insist that the wrongs done in the past occasioned by politically motivated persecution be put right.

2. *The Political System.* We demand fundamental, consistent, and permanent changes in the political system of our society. We must remake or renew democratic institutions and mechanisms that make possible the real participation of all citizens in the administration of public affairs and at the same time provide effective barriers against the abuse of economic and political power. All existing and newly emerging political parties and other social and political associations must therefore have equal conditions for participation in free elections at all

levels of government. This assumes, however, that the Communist party abandon its constitutionally guaranteed leading role in our society and likewise its monopoly of the means of communication. Nothing prevents it from doing so tomorrow.

Czechoslovakia, though remaining a federation, will be a union of both nations and all nationalities with equal rights.

3. *Foreign Policy.* We must take steps so that our country regains an honorable place in Europe and the world. We are a part of Central Europe, and hence we wish to maintain good relations with all our neighbors.

We count on becoming part of the process of European integration. We would also prefer to give priority to the idea of the Common European Home over that of the Warsaw Pact and Comecon. Maintaining our sovereignty as a state, we nevertheless wish to revise agreements that were inspired by the unreasonable ambitions of the leading representatives of the state.

4. *The Economy.* We must abandon the previous system of economic management. It takes away all appetite for work, squanders its results, devastates natural resources, destroys the environment, and deepens the wholesale backwardness of Czechoslovakia. We are convinced that it is not possible to improve this method of management by piecemeal reforms.

We wish to create a market undeformed by bureaucratic intervention. Its successful functioning is conditioned by the monopoly positions of today's great concerns and by the formation of genuine competition. This can only emerge on the basis of the parallel existence of different kinds of ownership with equal rights and with the gradual opening of our economy to the world.

The state naturally will maintain a series of indispensable functions. It will guarantee general conditions of enterprise, the same for all, and introduce a macroeconomic policy of regulation to control inflation, the growth of our foreign debt, and impending unemployment. Only the state can guarantee the essential minimum of public and social services and the protection of the environment.

5. *Social Justice.* It is essential that conditions emerge in society for the development and application of everybody's abilities. The same conditions and chances should be extended to everybody.

Czechoslovakia must become a socially just society in which the people receive help in old age, in sickness, and in times of hardship. However, a growing national economy is the essential prerequisite for such a society.

The church, the community, firms, and the most varied state and voluntary organizations can contribute to the origin of a diverse network of social services. This will thereby extend opportunities for the application of the precious sense of human solidarity, responsibility, and love for your neighbor. These humane principles are essential, particularly today, for our national fellowship.

6. *The Environment.* All of us must seek a way to the renewal of the harmony between human and nature. We will strive for a gradual rectification of the damage we have done to the environment in the last decades. We will attempt to return the original beauty of nature to the countryside and to the places where people live, to ensure the more effective protection of nature and natural resources. We will see to it that in the shortest possible time the basic conditions

of life are substantially improved, that the quality of drinking water is guaranteed, likewise fresh air and essential food. We shall insist on a basic improvement in the system of health care that will be directed not only at destroying the previous sources of pollution but above all at the prevention of further damage.

At the same time we shall have to change the structure and objectives of the economy and thereby, above all, to lower the consumption of energy and raw materials. We are aware that this will involve sacrifices that will affect every one of us. This all demands an alteration in our hierarchy of values and life-style.

7. *Culture.* Culture cannot simply be a matter for artists, scientists, and teachers but must be a way of life for the whole of civil society. It must free itself from the shackles of whatever ideology and overcome the artificial division from world culture.

Art and literature must not be restricted, and opportunities for publication and contact with the public must be made more extensive.

Let us put science and research in the place where they belong in society. Let us exclude not only their naive and demagogic overestimation but also the humiliating position that made them a servant of the governing party.

Let a democratic school system be organized on humanist principles without a state monopoly of education. Society must value teachers in all kinds of schools and must give them space to apply their own personalities. It is necessary to return historical rights to the universities, which once guaranteed them their independence and academic freedom, not only for the faculty but also for the students.

We regard the education of our society as the most valuable national asset. Upbringing and education must lead to independent thought and morally responsible behavior.

This is what we want. Today our program is short. We are, however, working on its finalization. Citizens Forum is an open association of citizens. We therefore appeal to everybody who can contribute to this work to take part.

Prague, 6 p.m. November 26, 1989

Resolution of the Public Meeting of the Workers of Kolben-Daněk, Polodovice, Prague

As a result of the events of November 17 to 21, the workers of the machine-tool factory Kolben-Daněk met and adopted these resolutions:

1. We absolutely disagree with the brutal intervention of the security forces of November 17, 1989, against the participants in a peaceful student demonstration.
2. We demand the formation of a nonparty commission of inquiry with the participation of representatives of the Czechoslovak public and those students concerned.
3. We further demand the truthful publication of the results of the investigation and the severe punishment of the guilty persons.

4. We demand that all those employed in the media are given the opportunity to keep the public truthfully and reliably informed.

5. We express our complete support for the joint statement of the Town Council of the Socialist Union of Youth and of the City University Council of the Socialist Union of Youth from November 19, 1989, and also of the presidium of the Central Committee of the Czech Socialist party and of the Committee of the Czechoslovak Public for Human Rights and Humanitarian cooperation.

6. We do not agree with the statements of the Czechoslovak Socialist Republic, the Czech Socialist Republic, and the Slovak Socialist Republic of November 20, 1989, on the situation that arose in Prague on November 17, 1989.

7. We are convinced that the only possible way out of the present situation is a genuine, open dialogue involving all of society.

8. We express our complete solidarity with the striking students and the theater companies.

9. We demand the legalization of independent initiatives.

10. We demand that an invitation be submitted for the abolition of the People's Militia and for them not to use their weapons.

11. We demand the holding of free elections.

12. In support of these demands we are prepared to stop work on November 27, 1989, between 12 noon and 2 p.m.

1,410 workers took part in the gathering. One abstained from voting, two were against. 1,407 voted in favor of this resolution.

The participants of the meeting
For the information of: The Revolutionary Trade
Union Movement; the Central Trade Union Council;
the Local Committee of the Communist party;
the Central Committee of the Communist party;
the governments of Czechoslovakia, the Czech Lands,
and Slovakia; the Directorate of Kolben-Daněk;
the Central Committee of the Socialist Union of Youth;
all national newspapers; Czechoslovak Television and Radio

Declaration of the Secretariat of the Central Committee of the Socialist Union of Youth

The Secretariat of the Central Committee of the SUY fully supports the view of the SUY university students of November 17 and the declaration arising out of the joint meeting of the presidia of the Prague City Committee of the SUY and of the University Council of the SUY held on November 19.

We stand behind the demand for an objective examination of the actions of the security forces on Friday evening on Prague's National Avenue, for the immediate formation of a commission of the Federal Parliament to establish all the facts surrounding these events. We support the speeding up of the framing of the amendment of the law of assembly and association and of the criminal code. The strict application of antiquated legal norms in this field does not correspond with the needs of the time nor to the gravity of the present situation. A majority of young people are calling for and supporting fundamental and essential political reforms in our society, sometimes perhaps with little judgment and with the overcritical attitude of youth, but nevertheless honestly. We regard a political solution to the current situation as essential and just possible, if only because on Friday evening in the same way as has happened several times in recent months, young people, all members of the Socialist Union of Youth, confronted each other on the street. We condemn violent demonstrations, whether from one side or the other. We consider violence in this case to be undemocratic and not corresponding to the politics of perestroika and the democratization of society.

We accepted the conclusions of the seventh and ninth meetings of the Central Committee of the CPC. Yet definite actions for their implementation lag behind the words. We consider it necessary once again to emphasize that it is not possible in our society for certain subjects to be forever forbidden, for certain norms to be forever appropriate. Not only does the present situation run counter to this but also to the concept of the formation of a Common European Home, the basis of socialist perestroika introduced in April 1985 by the Communist party of the Soviet Union. It is necessary to discuss this openly and objectively, above all with young people.

A solution to the current crisis is impossible without a dialogue among all who care for the fate of our socialist homeland. Otherwise, the confidence of the public in the reality and honesty of the aims of perestroika and democratization is and will be shaken. We appeal to everyone who has an interest in such a dialogue. It is in full agreement with the policy of the united children's and youth organizations and with the decisions of the recent national conference of the SUY.

The secretariat of the Central Committee of the SUY is conscious of the gravity of the situation, especially in the universities and secondary schools. We appeal to all our members, young people, to consider and conduct themselves with caution. For the benefit of our country, the Czechoslovak socialist republic.

The Secretariat of the Central Committee of the SUY
November 20, 1989

Declaration of the Czechoslovak University Committee of the Socialist Union of Youth

The presidium met at an extraordinary meeting on November 21, 1989, to formulate a position on the current political situation among the students in the Czech Socialist Republic.

We support the proclamation of the secretariat of the Central Committee of the Youth Union of November 20, 1989, and the opinions of the students that it is now necessary to move from words to actions. At the same time, we support the demands of the strike committees deriving from the declaration of the City Committee of the Council of the Union of Youth in Prague, and we distance ourselves from all extremism.

We appeal to the governments of the Czechoslovak Socialist Republic, MPs in Parliament, and the Czech National Council to open an immediate dialogue with the representatives of the strike committees. We consider this as the point of departure for the solution of the present situation.

We appreciate the opening of the investigation into the causes of the intervention of the security forces on November 17, 1989, and the contribution of the general procurator.

We will be discussing the demands of the students today with the Ministry of Education, Youth, and Physical Training, and we shall inform the public of the results without delay.

The Presidium of the Czech Universities Council
Passed unanimously

Declaration of the Presidium of the District Committee of the Socialist Union of Youth, Karvina

The presidium, at its meeting of November 21, 1989, concerned itself with events in connection with November 17 and asserts that:

1. It fully identifies itself with the proclamation of the government of Czechoslovakia printed in *Rudé právo* on November 21, 1989.
2. It does not agree with the approach of young people, especially students, in Prague and in other towns in the republic. Further, it cannot agree with the proclamation of the Central Committee of the Union of Youth expressing support for the views of the Czech University Committee of the union of November 17, 1989, and the declaration arising out of the joint meeting of the presidia of the City Committee of the union and the City University Council of the union in Prague on November 19, 1989.
3. It demands a constructive dialogue between young people in schools of all kinds and the leading representatives of our society, but without emotion, strikes, or provocative actions.

We stand for the view that the justified demands of young people expressed at the national conference of the union be rapidly met and not the demands from "the street," from young people who have been manipulated by people, enemies of our social system.

Carried unanimously by the District Committee of the Youth Union,
Karvina Český Těšín, November 21, 1989

Proclamation of the Meeting of the Members of the People's Militia of Kolben-Daněk, Sokolovo, Held on November 23, 1989

We have read the newspaper, *The Voice,* of the members of the state security forces in the Ninth District of Prague, the views of our comrades in arms, which were published yesterday by *Mladá fronta,* and we completely identify ourselves with them. Indeed, we have felt for some time already similar inadequacies, and despite our frequent reminders to the party organs, even those as high as the Central Committee and the general secretary, we have only rarely received a satisfactory reply without, however, having had these failures rectified.

In this unusually complicated and serious situation, caused above all by the incapacity and self-satisfaction of several functionaries in leading positions in our socialist country, we demand the immediate resolution of those problems to which attention has justifiably been drawn in the present period. Although this is not a simple matter, it is realistic to solve a series of problems immediately and the others gradually according to their difficulty and feasibility.

In conclusion, we consider it necessary to emphasize that we are fulfilling our task in defending and guarding the building of socialist society and the achievements of the working class down to the last detail. We will never take steps against working people nor working youth, including the student community; rather, we will work to build socialism in common and work toward perestroika.

Suggestions for an immediate solution at the meeting of the presidium of the Communist party on November 24, 1989:

1. The shortening of military service to eighteen months from the period of basic training. Improving the social conditions of families of soldiers doing their military service and alternatively allowing community service as a substitute for it.

2. Recommend that the government immediately lower the tax paid by the whole of the younger generation and progressively increase taxation where above-average salaries are earned.

3. We recommend the immediate reform of the system of personnel in the state and party apparat—whoever fails to work responsibly for society must be replaced by capable and committed young people—and to solve thereafter the personnel problem at the party congress.

4. The party must not be frightened of the truth, even if it is sometimes hard and unpleasant—it is absolutely necessary to tell the truth in the press, radio, and television. It is necessary to publicize the video recordings of the police intervention of November 17 and, after the state prosecutor's investigation, to publish its results in the mass media.

5. It is necessary to reduce the bureaucratic apparatus immediately in all organs of the party—with the greater part of this work being done by the basic organizations.

6. Conscientiously and with full responsibility meet the suggestions of the basic organizations without the responses being filtered out through the intermediary organs of the party.

7. The People's Militia is an organ for the defense of the state and is identified with the most mature members of the party. We demand the maximum degree of knowledge and closer relations between the units and their headquarters. Do not allow the units of the People's Militia to be misused and thereby discredit it before the whole of society. Use the units of the People's Militia only in the event of a direct threat to the socialist system.

The Members of the Factory Units of the People's Militia,
Kolben-Daněk, Sokolovo

The Internal Organization of Citizens Forum

1. Citizens Forum [hereafter CF] is a spontaneously emerging movement of citizens united in their efforts to find a way out of the crisis in our society. Nobody is excluded from this movement who agrees with the principles and program of CF published on November 26, 1989, and who, above all, rejects the maintenance of the political system of only one governing force. As its basic aim, CF regards the opening of society as a prerequisite for the origin of political pluralism and for the holding of free elections in our country.

2. It is possible to found local CFs anywhere on the basis of region or working or interest groups with citizens, but not with institutions. We recommend that membership in CF be expressed by means of a signature on the founding documents of the local CFs; further, we recommend the setting up of an informal, coordinating group to whom citizens can turn and, in addition, the election of its representatives.

3. The relations of the coordinating center and the local CFs:

(a) The coordinating center and the local CF form a unity joined only by the active citizens' commitment of its members. CF has no hierarchy whatsoever but is rather a horizontal network, with all local CFs joined to one coordinating center.

(b) The coordinating center is only an information and coordinating center and in no sense a controlling center. Its task is to collect information from local CFs, pass it on, and keep everyone informed about past and future actions. All local CFs work completely independently.

(c) The coordinating center represents CF in negotiations with central, state, and international institutions and, above all, on the basis of the suggestions and recommendations of the local CFs.

4. The function of CF's information system:

(a) For the provision of information links, it is necessary to inform the coordinating committee in writing of the basic details regarding the local CFs: the company, parish, interest group from which the local CF originated; the exact address, telephone number, the names of the representatives, the number of members, at least approximately. This data will be filed centrally.

(b) Contact with the coordinating center: for a period of three weeks beginning November 28, 1989, files, information, and advice will be available at Špálova Gallery, Národní třída, 11000 Prague 1, tel. 22 47 09. The new address and telephone number of the coordinating center will be announced in good time.

(c) The transmission and communication of information between individual, local CFs and the coordinating center will be provided in the form of a newsletter distributed from the center by means of the mass media or, in exceptional instances, by telephone.

5. The objective of the local CFs is the voluntary mobilization of citizens in political and in everyday life. Therefore, the coordinating center does not want and cannot give orders to the local CFs; rather, it will offer suggestions and recommendations.

6. We believe that the local CFs will be capable of pursuing these areas of activity.

(a) The local CFs should help clarify attitudes of citizens in a broadly based democratic discussion. This debate should lead to political differentiation, which is an indispensable prerequisite for a democratic and pluralistic political system.

(b) Local CFs can only concern themselves with local solutions that have not been satisfactorily dealt with by existing political structures. This can lead to citizens' self-government or the transformation of the bureaucratic apparatus into a democratic one.

(c) Local CFs can organize strikes, demonstrations, or other actions in support of their demands or, alternatively, for the whole of CF if these actions are essential. Local CFs are a continuation of the strike committees until the period when all the demands of CF have been met.

(d) Local CFs will support all citizens where, in contact with the existing undemocratic structures, civil rights broadly defined are being interfered with. Local CFs are hence the means of citizens' self-defense.

Citizens Forum
Prague, November 28, 1989

The Demands of the Citizens' Initiatives, the Public Against Violence, and the Coordinating Committee of Slovak Universities

1. We demand free elections as the basis for the transformation of the Slovak National Council into a real parliament of the Slovak nation in which all sections of our society will be represented.

2. We demand guarantees for the complete freedom of expression. Journalists, elect this very day the leaders of your editorial boards, which will guarantee this freedom.

3. We demand freedom of enterprise, of assembly, of association, movement, conscience, and other civil rights and liberties.

4. We demand the abolition of the leading role of the CPC embodied in the constitution and corresponding changes in the constitution.

5. We demand the removal of ideology from the educational system and culture and the separation of culture from state institutions.

6. We demand guarantees of the impartiality of the courts and of the office of the public prosecutor and the formation of a genuine legal state.

7. We demand the complete separation of church and state.

8. We demand free trade unions and an independent student organization.

9. We demand the legalization of all forms of ownership.

10. We demand a consistent democratic federation of Czechs and Slovaks and the legal regulation of the rights and position of the nationalities on the principle of complete equality.

11. We demand absolute guarantees of the right to a healthy environment.

12. We demand an equal chance for all in the elections and for their path through life.

November 25, 1989

On the Work of Citizens Fora

Citizens, a majority from the countryside, are turning more and more frequently to us with questions how they should express their social and political attitudes in the present situation and how they can contribute to the formation of a democratic system in our country. Many people expect the Prague Citizens Forum—as a kind of "center"—to answer these questions by directing and determining how to proceed in individual cases. However, the reality is such that the Prague Citizens Forum expresses in general the interests of civil society; it cannot prescribe remedies for citizens' activities. This is not possible as much for logistic reasons as those of principle. One group cannot achieve democracy by itself, be it the most representative, as it demands the personal engagement of every one of us. Accordingly, we will restrict ourselves to several comments that will perhaps help in a way such that personal engagement could be better organized in our common efforts for freedom and democracy.

1. In all towns, villages, and likewise in factories, companies, and places of work, it is essential to found Citizens Fora and strike committees. Citizens Forum is any group of people that announces—either at an official gathering or at a meeting called at someone's initiative—that they agree with the basic proclamation of Citizens Forum from November 19, 1989, with its four demands.

2. This newly founded Citizens Forum should ask the state organs and social organizations for material assistance for their activity—accommodation, telephones, photocopying equipment, access to local government and factory printing facilities, even to the radio.

3. One of the most important tasks of Citizens Fora at the present is to inform their fellow citizens, collect their demands, and submit them to the local and central organs of power.

4. As the state power is attempting in many places to either boycott Citizens Forum or otherwise thwart its efforts, it is necessary to find an effective substitute solution and, at any price, disseminate reliable information, among other things, the homemade production of posters, proclamations, and newsletters. Don't let them frighten you!

5. Individual Citizens Fora must strive for the quickest and closest possible cooperation. Publicize the telephone numbers of individual activists and the places they congregate. These details are important even for us in Prague and in Moravia, where they will be offered to those people constantly telephoning in and asking for contacts.

6. All newly emerging groups, Citizens Fora, strike committees, politically oriented associations must strive, quite apart from their mutual links, to build a stronger internal structure. To push through their demands, they should choose and elect a spokesperson and representatives. By adopting this democratic procedure, the structure of a citizens' movement covering the whole of society will gradually emerge.

7. Inform us of your activities, problems, and above all, of every attack, even the slightest one, from the previous organs of state power. Their publication is a basic condition for the gradual and complete elimination of all acts of arbitrary despotism.

Our telephone number: Citizens Forum, Olomouc 23316
November 29, 1989

Facts on the Current Situation in Czechoslovakia

1. Czechoslovakia occupies forty-ninth place in the world as regards the proportion of its inhabitants with college or tertiary education. (The intelligentsia represents only 6 percent of the population as a whole.) By this yardstick, we are just behind Nepal, which has 6.7 percent. In other countries, this figure is much higher, for instance, the Soviet Union has 8 percent; East Germany, 13 percent; the United States, 39 percent; Canada, 40 percent.

2. As regards expenditure on education expressed as a proportion of GNP, in the last twenty years, we have fallen from twenty-second to seventy-second place in the world. The source for the first two statistics is the UNESCO Statistical Yearbook and *Mladá fronta,* November 1988; author of the article, Jaroslav Kalous.

3. Czechoslovakia is in first place in Europe as regards the pollution of the environment. Every year, there are 25 tons of waste fallout for every square kilometer of land. For the purpose of comparison, Sweden has 0.6 tons. Source: Czechoslovak Press Agency, published November 9, 1989.

4. Thirty-two percent of all the territories of our state are contaminated. Such a percentage is unprecedented throughout Europe. Source: Rudolf Hegenbart, director of the Armed Services Section of the Central Committee of the Communist party, in an interview for *Izvestija,* June 1989.

5. The overall speed of economic development in Czechoslovakia is on the same level as Algeria and Peru and well beneath the level of Portugal. Source: Ďurkovič, member of the Central Committee of the Communist party of Slovakia.

6. A comparison of mortality rates in twenty-eight European states reveals that Czechoslovakia is in second place for death rates of the adult population, in first place for male mortality, and also in first place for oncological diseases. Source: Institute of Social Medicine.

7. During the past forty years, Czechoslovakia has fallen from tenth to fortieth in the world as regards productivity per person. Source: Novosti [Soviet Press Agency], AFP [French Press Agency], March 1989.

What Kind of Program is Possible?

1. Political democracy, not democratization.

2. A market economy, not merely economic reform.

3. Support for local initiatives, above all pressure for independent candidates to formulate their programs and thereby demonstrate their competence.

4. The courage to take unpopular steps going beyond the parameters of partial initiatives, specifically, wide retraining and social programs, programs at the price of a temporary lowering of living standards, a program for the defense of the environment, a health program.

For those who have reservations that the two-hour general strike will damage our economy: As far as damage to this system is concerned, it will be the best investment in the last forty years.

When normal studies are resumed at normal universities and colleges in a normal Czechoslovakia, I will be very glad to offer you normal lectures on normal economic forecasting.

Miloš Zeman
Institute of Economic Forecasting

Proclamation of the Democratic Forum of Communists

The Democratic Forum of Communists hereby submits the following proposals for discussion that were accepted at its meeting on November 27, 1989.

1. The abolition of the leading role of the party established in the constitution.
2. We reject the present standpoints of the party and its new proposals; we suggest the working out of statutes with a view to the formation of a party of a democratic type.
3. We demand the abolition of the People's Militia. In a democratic society, no political party can maintain armed units.
4. We demand the immediate working out of an action program of the party, to which we would make our contribution.
5. We demand that the extraordinary congress of the Communist party be brought forward to December 20, 1989; we demand the election of candidates directly from the basic organizations.
6. We condemn the intervention in 1968 of the armies of the Warsaw Pact and similarly the document "Lessons of the Crisis."
7. We demand the abrogation of the results of the vetting of members of the CPC after 1968. We will offer an opportunity for former members to return to the party.
8. We demand the complete rehabilitation of citizens unjustly discriminated against by the so-called normalization.

At the meeting, serious consideration was given to the question of the relationship between the Democratic Forum of Communists and Citizens Forum. We wish to resolve this at our next meeting, which will take place at the House of Political Education of the City Council in Prague, Celetná 13, on Thursday, November 30, 1989, at 4:30 p.m.

Appendix C:
Public Opinion During the Revolution

TABLE 1 Frequency with Which People Followed Basic Information Sources (in percent)

	November 22–24, 1989			December 10–12, 1989		
	Almost Daily	Less Often	Not at All	Almost Daily	Less Often	Not at All
Czechoslovak media	87	12	1	95	5	0
Western media	36	25	39	15	35	50
Media in socialist countries	16	14	70	10	18	72

Notes: In November, 447 people were in the sample; in December, 1,107 citizens; in both cases those polled were from the whole of Czechoslovakia. In the week November 17–24, 25 percent of another sample said they trusted Czechoslovak media sources most; 23 percent, the Western media; 2 percent, socialist countries' media; 13 percent, information from friends, acquaintances, etc.; 10 percent, "did not believe anything"; 28 percent were unable to judge what to believe.

TABLE 2 Views on What Would Damage or Benefit the Situation (in percent)

What Would Benefit		What Would Damage	
Personnel changes at the top of CPC	88		
Working properly and continuing with perestroika	85	Strikes	58
Calm and discretion	84	Crushing the opposition	74
Official negotiation with the opposition	81		
Demonstrating against previous policies	55	Demonstrating in support of previous policies	59

Note: Results summarized from surveys conducted throughout Czechoslovakia after November 17, 1989.

TABLE 3   Areas of Social Life in Which People Saw Problems (in percent)

	Major Problems	Minor Problems	Almost No Problems	Don't Know
Environment	98	2	0	0
Economy	92	2	0	6
Health system	90	7	1	2
Political system	88	8	2	2
Quality of top management	78	15	1	6
Education	76	16	2	6
Public morality	70	24	2	4
Social security	63	28	3	6
Human rights	58	31	6	5
Culture	47	37	8	8
Foreign travel	45	39	12	4
Religious freedom	29	39	19	13

Note: Results taken from a survey of 401 respondents, November 20–22, 1989.

TABLE 4   Opinions on Future Social Development (in percent)

	November 23–24, 1989	December 9–12, 1989
Czechoslovakia should follow:		
A socialist path	45	41
A capitalist path	3	3
Something in-between	47	52
Doesn't matter or can't judge	5	4

Note: The sample was 709 for the first survey and 1,107 for the second, both from the whole country.

TABLE 5   Opinions on Three Foreign Policy Suggestions in the December Action Program of the CPC (in percent)

	Clear	Likely	Not Likely	Not Clear	Don't Know
Warsaw Pact membership is an important condition for the defense capability of this country	16	31	25	15	13
Foreign policy should rely mainly on friendship with the USSR	5	28	35	25	7
Czechoslovakia should cooperate economically mainly with socialist countries	6	16	46	27	5

Note: Results taken from a nationwide survey of 1,107 respondents, December 9–12, 1989.

TABLE 6   Opinions on Reprivatization (in percent)

	Definitely Yes	Likely Yes	Likely No	Definitely No	Don't Know
The large-scale manufacturing industries should be returned to private hands as well as small units, restaurants, etc.	8	14	33	40	5
Large-scale collectivized agriculture should return to private hands	4	9	29	54	4

Note: Survey held from December 9–12, 1989; 1,107 respondents from throughout the country.

TABLE 7   Opinions of the Leading Role of the Party (in percent)

	Republic	Czech Lands	Slovakia	Prague
The leading role is:				
Very necessary	2	2	3	1
Necessary	12	9	19	9
Hardly necessary	23	18	32	16
Unnecessary	59	67	44	71
Don't know	4	5	2	2

Note: Survey conducted from November 29 to December 1, 1989; 456 respondents in Czechoslovakia (301 in the Czech Lands, 155 in Slovakia) and 289 in Prague.

TABLE 8   Views on Whether the National Front Parliament Is the Basis of the Political System (in percent)

	October 1988	December 1989
Definitely yes	21	13
Probably yes	37	25
Probably not	19	25
Definitely not	8	20
Don't know	15	17

Note: Results from the whole of Czechoslovakia; 1,914 citizens responded in 1988, 1,107 in 1989.

TABLE 9   Groups That Give Basis for Hopes for the Future (in percent)

	October 12–17	November 29–December 1	December 9–12
Social Democrats	34	46	49
Czechoslovak Socialists	32[a]	47[a]	47
Czechoslovak People's party	32[a]	36[a]	44
CPC	40	21	16
Origin of independent trade unions	35	59	62
Previous Revolutionary Trade Union Movement	41	17	14
Charter 77	23	40	42

Note: In October, 206 people were polled; in November–December, 456; in December, 1,107.

[a]Among respondents in Czech Lands only.

Sources: All tables adapted from Dragoslav Slejška et al., *Sondy do veřejného mínění* (Survey of public opinion) (Svoboda, 1990).

Appendix D:
Václav Havel—
A Biographical Cameo

Václav Havel was born on October 5, 1936, into a well-to-do, middle-class family. Both his paternal grandfather and his father were successful architects and builders. Havel's privileged background left him with a certain sense of isolation; he has stated that his childhood experiences generated a lifelong opposition to unearned privilege and to unjust and inequitable social barriers. His family lost all their property after the Communists took power in 1948, and they became one of the many prime targets of social persecution in the class struggle that marked the new regime.

Havel's class origins thereafter worked against him, and he had a long and difficult struggle to complete his formal education. He had to leave school at the age of fifteen and for the subsequent five years found employment as a laboratory technician. Nevertheless, he managed to attend evening classes—organized, paradoxically, for the new worker elite—and matriculated in 1954. Unable to win a place to study philosophy, art history, or film studies at the university, he turned to the Technical Institute, where his study of transportation economics enabled him to put off military service but did not otherwise interest him. After a further attempt to study at the Film Institute in 1957 had failed, he spent the following two years in military service. Once out of the army, he found employment as a stagehand in the ABC Theater in Prague. A year later, he moved to the theater On the Balustrade, working for eight years as a stagehand, lighting technician, administrative secretary, and producer. This theater, with which he most strongly associated himself, put on his first major plays—*The Garden Party* in 1963, *The Memorandum* in 1965, and *Increased Difficulty of Concentration* in 1968. While employed in the theater, he studied part-time, graduating with a degree in drama from the philosophy faculty at Prague University. Havel never joined the Communist party but was quite active in the Prague literary scene

---

Biographical details from V. Havel, *Dálkový výslech* (Long-distance interrogation) (Melantrich, 1989); Havel, *Do různých stran* (In different directions) (Lidové noviny, 1989); Havel, *Living in Truth*, ed. J. Vladislav (Faber and Faber, 1976).

and its politics throughout the 1960s. During the Prague Spring, Havel became involved not only in the politics of the Writers Union but also in various public efforts to speed up the process of democratic reform. In the summer of 1968, he decided to resign from On the Balustrade.

After the Soviet invasion of Czechoslovakia, he maintained a high public profile, opposing the onset of the normalization. Over the next twenty years, he assumed one of the leading roles in the manifold dissident movement; his consistent and unflinching opposition caused the regime to persecute him with ever increasing severity. He could neither publish nor have his plays produced, and in 1971 all his works were placed on the index of banned books and became inaccessible to the general public. He continued to be subjected to various forms of police harassment and at times to formal criminal proceedings. Toward the end of 1976, he was among those who were instrumental in organizing Charter 77, and he became one of its first three spokesmen. His first prison term lasted from January to May 1977. In October of the same year, after a two-day trial, he was found guilty of "damaging the interests of the republic abroad" and sentenced to fourteen months imprisonment, though the sentence was suspended for three years. Havel again spent time in jail between January and March 1978, following his conviction for "preventing a public official from executing his duties." Subsequently, he became one of the founding members of the Committee for the Defense of the Unjustly Prosecuted and took an active part in its activities. Along with other leading members, he was again arrested in May 1979 on a charge of subversion and in October 1979 was sentenced to four and a half years in jail. He contracted a serious illness in prison and was released in February 1983, a few months before he was due to complete his sentence. Undeterred by constant police surveillance and frequent arrests, he returned to active participation in the dissident movement until the revolution of 1989.

Throughout the twenty years of the normalized regime, Havel had continued to write plays that were performed abroad with great success. These included *The Beggar's Opera, Audience, A Private View, Protest, A Hotel in the Hills, Mistake, Largo Desolato, Temptation,* and *Slum Clearance.* He also wrote a number of important essays in which he formulated his political philosophy and addressed the crucial political questions of the day. Among the most significant are "The Power of the Powerless," "Politics and Conscience," and "An Anatomy of Reticence." In these essays, he developed his ideas about "antipolitical politics" and the importance of setting an example by living in truth.

Notes

Chapter 1

1. R. Richta, *Civilizace ne rozcestí* (Svoboda, 1967).

2. Interview with J. Šabata, *East European Reporter*, vol. 3, no. 3, 1988. He noted: "The wording of the Protocols, though bad enough, wasn't necessarily the worst part of it. What was really the worst was that, while Dubček's speech [August 31] was intended for the public, the Moscow Protocols were to remain secret."

3. The Vysočany Congress met on August 22, 1968, the day after the Soviet invasion, at a factory in a Prague suburb. This extraordinary congress of the CPC was brought forward from September to discuss the crisis. As the highest body of the party, it condemned the invasion, appealed to the world for help, and elected a new leadership from which all conservatives were excluded. Leading reformers were brought into the Politburo, and most importantly, the congress elected Dubček as party leader. The exclusion of the conservatives terminated any direct influence of the Soviet Communist party on the CPC.

4. KAN was the club of politically active non–party people. K231 was an organization of former political prisoners jailed under Article 231 of the criminal code.

5. Dubček was sent as ambassador to Turkey in January 1970. He was quickly recalled and expelled from the party, thereafter spending many years as a forestry official in Bratislava.

6. Milan Šimečka, *Obnovení pořádku* (The restoration of order) (Index 1979), pp. 26–28.

7. V. Kusin, *From Dubček to Charter 77* (Q-Press, 1978), p. 55. "Deletion" from the party did not bring anywhere near as powerful forms of social and economic discrimination as expulsion. It often allowed those affected to remain in their jobs, though there were precious few, if any, chances of upward progress.

8. Ibid., p. 76.

9. Ibid., p. 174.

10. Václav Havel et al., *The Power of the Powerless*, ed. John Keane (Hutchinson, 1985), pp. 27–29.

11. See M. Kusy, "Chartism and Real Socialism," in Havel et al., *Power*, pp. 163–167.

12. Kusy, "Chartism," p. 164.

13. Slogan recorded by B. W. in Brno on November 28, 1989.

14. Kusy, "Chartism," p. 164.

15. P. Pithart, "Social and Economic Developments in Czechoslovakia," part 2, *East European Reporter,* vol. 4, no. 2, 1990.

16. The term *Czech Lands* summarizes the so-called historic provinces, namely, Bohemia, Moravia, and Silesia.

17. M. Myant, *The Czechoslovak Economy: 1948–1988* (Cambridge Univ. Press, 1989), p. 261.

18. The Declaration of Charter 77 dated January 1, 1977, is in H. Gordon Skilling, *Charter 77 and Human Rights in Czechoslovakia* (George Allen and Unwin, 1981), pp. 210–211.

19. Sergei Kovalev, "Sovereignty and International Obligations in Socialist Countries," *Pravda,* September 26, 1968, and U.S. Senate, *Czechoslovakia and the Brezhnev Doctrine* (1969), pp. 67–68.

20. Central Committee thesis for the Nineteenth All-Union Party Conference, *Soviet News,* June 1, 1988. See Gorbachev's speech.

21. Gorbachev to the Congress of People's Deputies on May 30, 1989, *Soviet News,* May 31, 1989.

22. Gorbachev's report on the seventieth anniversary of the October Revolution, *Soviet Weekly,* November 7, 1987.

23. *Soviet News,* November 27, 1985. At his press conference in Geneva on November 21, 1985, Gorbachev observed: "When I was in England last December, I recalled a phrase of Palmerston's. He said that Britain had no eternal enemies nor eternal friends, only eternal interests. . . . I agreed with that judgement. . . . When about 200 states are involved in the international arena, each of them strives to promote its own interests, but to what extent are they promoted? It depends on taking the interests of others into account in the course of co-operation."

24. M. Gorbachev, *Perestrojka* (Collins, 1987), p. 195.

25. See Gorbachev's interview with the Italian Communist newspaper, *L'unita,* reprinted in *Soviet News,* May 27, 1987.

26. *Soviet Weekly,* January 7, 1987.

27. *Soviet News,* May 27, 1987.

28. Gorbachev to the Nineteenth All-Union Conference of the CPSU, June 28, 1988, *Soviet News,* July 6, 1988.

29. In 1943 in the Katyn Forest in Poland, the Germans discovered mass graves containing the bodies of several thousand Polish army officers who were reputed to have been missing since shortly after the Nazi invasion of the Soviet Union. After establishing committees of inquiry, both the Germans and the Soviets blamed each other for the massacre.

30. *Soviet News,* March 1, 1989.

31. Ibid., April 26, 1989.

32. Ibid., October 11, 1989.

33. Ibid., November 24, 1989, and October 29, 1989.

34. Ibid., December 9 and 13, 1989.

Chapter 2

1. Dragoslav Slejška, Jan Herzmann, Václav Forst, Stanislav Hampl, Jana Himmlová, Miluše Rezková, Jitka Slavíková, Jiří Šubrt, and Ivan Tomek, *Sondy do veřejného mínění* (Survey of public opinion) (Svoboda, 1990), p. 56.

2. *Rudé právo* (Red justice), October 28, 1988.

3. The Helsinki agreement, signed by the United States, Canada, and all the European countries in 1975, established various measures intended to maintain security and foster cooperation. The CSCE conferences, which concentrated on human rights, were a product of this accord.

4. See Appendix B, "Several Sentences."

5. *Rudé právo,* November 28, 1990.

Chapter 3

1. The word *stuha* was chosen at least partly for its mischievous play on words. Apart from its original derivation—from *Stu*dentské *h*nutí (Students Movement)—it referred to the tricolor that most students wore in their lapels at demonstrations. In another transformation, *ztuha* means "with difficulty."

2. See the contribution of Martin Benda in *Studenti psali revoluci* (Students wrote the revolution) (Univerzum, 1990), p. 17f.

3. See Appendix B, "The Deposition of Lenka Schwammenhoterová," which was only one of many.

4. The information that provided the basis for much of this chapter was culled variously from conversations with some of the leading students, from *Mladá fronta* (Young front) of November 17, 1989, and other national newspapers from November 18 on, and from cyclostyled documents distributed throughout Prague by students and other interested parties after the police attack. They are in my possession and available for inspection. [B.W.] See also the article "Předlouhé odumírání komunismu" (The long drawn-out dying of communism), *Mladá fronta,* November 17, 1990.

Chapter 4

1. Radio Prague, 9 p.m. news, November 18, 1989, and *Rudé právo,* November 18, 1989.

2. See Appendix B, "Appeal to Our Fellow Citizens."

3. Radio Free Europe, 8 p.m. news, November 18, 1989.

4. *Rudé právo* (Red justice), November 18, 1989.

5. *Práce* (Work), November 19, 1989.

6. Ibid., November 20, 1989.

7. See Appendix B, "Proclamation of the University Students to the Workers and Peasants of Czechoslovakia."

8. The coalition of opposition groups went under the name of Občanské Fórum, which was translated in the press center of the movement as Civic Forum.

They were likely unaware that in British English this conveys a gloss redolent of Victorian municipal institutions and of the individuals peopling them, far removed from the central ideas of the movement. As the name *Citizens Forum* arguably conveys more accurately the essence of its openness and its nonparty, nonclass character, we use this term throughout.

9. See Appendix B, "Proclamation of the Founding of Citizens Forum."

10. *Rudé právo,* November 20, 1989.

11. See Appendix B, "Declaration of the Secretariat of the Central Committee of the Socialist Union of Youth."

12. *Mladá fronta* (Young front), November 20, 1989.

13. Radio Star, 8 p.m. news, November 20, 1989.

14. See Appendix B, "Statement of the Basic Organizations."

15. See, for example, the address of the general secretary of the party, Jakeš, to the Union of Soviet-Czechoslovak Friendship, *Rudé právo,* November 20, 1989.

16. *Lidová demokracie* (People's democracy), November 20, 1989.

17. See "The Preparatory Congress of the National Congress of the Communist Party Factory Committees," in ibid.

18. *Mladá fronta,* November 20, 1989.

19. *Informační servis* (Information Service), 1, November 20, 1989.

20. See Appendix B, "Statement of the Basic Organizations."

21. The nervousness of the population was compounded by alarming news of supply problems that surfaced when the Prague Bakeries and Flour Mills asked for conscripts to help bake bread.

22. *Rudé právo,* November 21, 1989.

23. Petr Holubec, ed., *Kronika sametové revoluce* (Chronicle of the Velvet Revolution), vol. 1 (Czechoslovak Press Agency, 1990), p. 2f.

24. Proclamation of Czechoslovak Television of November 22, 1989, *Svobodné slovo* (Free word), November 23, 1989.

25. *Mladá fronta,* November 22 and 23, 1989.

26. "Prohlášení Zakladných organizaci" (Proclamation of the basic organizations), *Práce,* Novemer 23, 1989.

27. "Anarchie a rozvrat" (Anarchy and subversion), *Rudé právo,* November 21, 1989.

28. See Martin Benda et al., *Studenti psali revoluci* (Students wrote the revolution) (Univerzum, 1990), p. 99.

29. See Appendix B, "Resolution of the Public Meeting of the Workers of Kolben-Daněk."

30. *Stráž lidu* (Guardian of the people), November 24, 1989.

31. "Předlouhé odumírání komunismu" (The long drawn-out dying of communism), *Mladá fronta,* November 17, 1990.

32. See *Report of the Commission of Enquiry on the Events Surrounding November 17,* published October 1990.

33. See Appendix B, "Appeal to Our Fellow Citizens."

34. An average monthly salary was 2,500 to 3,000 crowns. The value of the dollar fluctuated at official, private, and trade rates and on the black market. On

the official market, a dollar was worth 15 crowns at this time; on the black market it would bring closer to 40 crowns.

35. This statistic was provided by a ranking officer in the police force in a private conversation.

36. *Mladá fronta,* November 23, 1989.

37. Ibid.

38. Ibid.

39. Ibid.

40. See Appendix B, "Citizens Forum on the General Strike."

41. Under the old regime, the National Assembly was a single-chamber parliament. After the federalization of 1968, it became a two-chamber legislature with a chamber of the nations and one of the people. In reality, then, it became a federal assembly, though in common usage it is referred to as the National Assembly.

42. See Appendix B, "What We Want."

43. *Práce,* November 23–24, 1989.

44. Dragoslav Slejška, Jan Herzmann, Václav Forst, Stanislav Hampl, Jana Himmlová, Miluše Rezková, Jitka Slavíková, Jiří Šubrt, and Ivan Tomek, *Sondy do veřejného mínění* (Survey of public opinion) (Svoboda, 1990), p. 48.

Chapter 5

1. See Appendix B, "Proclamation of the University Students to the Workers and Peasants of Czechoslovakia."

2. Ibid., "Citizens Forum on the General Strike."

3. Ibid.

4. *Mladá fronta* (Young front), November 25, 1989.

5. Dragoslav Slejška, Jan Herzmann, Václav Forst, Stanislav Hampl, Jana Him-mlová, Miluše Rezková, Jitka Slavíková, Jiří Šubrt, and Ivan Tomek, *Sondy do veřejného mínění* (Survey of public opinion) (Svoboda, 1990), p. 45.

6. This refers to the Czech Lands only. See ibid., p. 50. A survey conducted from November 20 to 22, 1989, showed that only 29 percent of respondents regarded religious freedom as a "great problem."

7. Ibid., p. 63.

8. See Appendix B, "Facts on the Current Situation in Czechoslovakia."

9. See the daily press from October 27, 1989.

10. *Práce* (Work), November 11, 1989.

11. Channel 1 News, 7:30 p.m., November 25, 1989.

12. See Appendix B, "Proclamation of the Democratic Forum of Communists."

13. The exact figure was 58 percent, involving 447 respondents from the whole of Czechoslovakia, 260 in Prague. See Slejška et al., *Sondy,* p. 48.

14. Ibid., p. 47.

15. Petr Holubec, ed., *Kronika sametové revoluce* (Chronicle of the Velvet Revolution), vol. 1 (Czechoslovak Press Agency, 1990), p. 18.

16. *Rudé právo* (Red justice), October 28, 1989.

17. *Práce,* November 28, 1989.

18. Slejška et al., *Sondy,* p. 47.

19. Ibid.

20. Slejška et al., *Sondy,* p. 51. On November 24, 45 percent wanted "a socialist way"; this declined to 41 percent by December 9. Those favoring "a third way" rose from 47 percent to 52 percent over the same period.

21. As of December 1, 1989. *Sondy,* p. 57.

22. Slejška et al., *Sondy,* p. 59. This was higher than any other movement or party, though Citizens Forum was not represented in the survey.

23. *Rudé právo,* November 29, 1989.

24. Slejška et al., *Sondy,* p. 51f.

25. Ibid.

26. Holubec, *Kronika,* vol. 1, p. 24.

27. At the official exchange rate, this would come to about $20 million; on the black market it would mean roughly $7.5 million.

28. Daily news on Radio Star, December 8, 1989. Although the majority had guessed right in leaving the party, given the trend of events, those who joined the CPC at this point were either utterly confused or perhaps expected a revived, reformist party to be around the corner and worth supporting.

29. *Mladá fronta,* November 28, 1989.

30. Holubec, *Kronika,* vol. 2, p. 4.

31. Ibid.

32. Holubec, *Kronika,* vol. 2, p. 6.

33. The elder Baťa was the most successful entrepreneur in the First Republic. Even today his name has great symbolic implications for the people.

34. Slejška et al., *Sondy,* p. 63. On December 12, 1989, Havel was lagging well behind Komárek in popularity, roughly 18 percent favoring him. Thereafter, he experienced a meteoric rise, so that by December 22, 75 percent wanted him to be the next president.

Chapter 6

1. Dragoslav Slejška, Jan Herzmann, Václav Forst, Stanislav Hampl, Jana Himmlová, Miluše Rezková, Jitka Slavíková, Jiří Šubrt, and Ivan Tomek, *Sondy do veřejného mínění* (Survey of public opinion) (Svoboda, 1990), p. 63.

2. Reinhard Heydrich, who served as *Reichsprotektor* from 1941 to 1942, was notorious for his pitiless application of Nazi policies in the protectorate. He was killed by Czech parachutists.

3. *Host do domu* (A guest in the house), vol. 15, no. 15, 1968–1969.

4. Milan Kundera, "A Kidnapped West, or Culture Bows Out," *New York Review of Books,* November 18, 1984.

5. "Život jako umění možného" (Life as the art of the possible), *Svědectví,* (Testimony), vol. 19, 1985, p. 75.

6. H. Gordon Skilling, *Czechoslovakia's Interrupted Revolution* (Princeton Univ. Press, 1976).

Chapter 7

1. Dragoslav Slejška, Jan Herzmann, Václav Forst, Stanislav Hampl, Jana Him-mlová, Miluše Rezková, Jitka Slavíková, Jiří Šubrt, and Ivan Tomek, *Sondy do veřejného mínění* (Survey of public opinion) (Svoboda, 1990), p. 63.

2. Ibid. This likely shows that the CPC retained a proportion of the "hard" support.

3. Report of the Research Institute of Trade, January 1990.

4. *Lidová demokracie* (People's democracy), January 2, 1990.

5. See the first draft of State Planning Commission, Ministry of Finance, *Strategie radikální ekonomické reformy* (Strategy of radical economic reform), no. 90/663/90–2.

6. See n. 3 above.

7. *Lidová demokracie,* April 17, 1990.

8. Ibid.

9. Published in *East European Reporter,* vol. 4, no. 2, 1990.

10. Věra Pospíšilová, "Džungle roste rychle" (The jungle is growing quickly), *Lidové noviny* (People's newspaper), April 29, 1990.

11. See Václav Havel et al., *The Power of the Powerless,* ed. John Keane (Hutchinson, 1985), and Havel's New Year's speech in *Lidová demokracie,* January 1, 1990.

12. Interview with Richard Sacher in *Lidová demokracie,* January 1, 1990.

13. Havel's New Year's speech.

14. Čalfa's speech in *East European Reporter,* vol. 4, no. 2, 1990.

15. See J. Smrčka, "Švedská mýty a realita aneb švedský model v krízi?" (Swedish myths and reality; or, the Swedish model in crisis?), *Fórum,* vol. 1, no. 15, May 8, 1990.

16. *Guardian,* April 14, 1990.

17. State Planning Commission, *Strategie.*

18. Interview with Ota Šik, Havel's economic adviser, in *Mladá fronta* (Young front), April 26, 1990.

19. *Právní encyklopédie soukromých podnikatelů* (A legal encyclopedia for entrepreneurs) (Svobodová, Vaněk, Forejt, Trizonia, 1990).

20. Stephany Griffith-Jones, "Czechoslovakia's Economic Reforms: How Can the EEC Best Help Sustain Them?" (Unpublished paper, Institute of Development Studies, University of Sussex, Autumn 1990).

21. This is about 5 percent of the average monthly income.

22. Election Manifesto of Citizens Forum, May 1990.

23. "Unemployment Set to Rise in the New Democracies," *Guardian,* April 29, 1990.

24. *Lidová demokracie,* January 2, 1990.

25. "Školské zákony schválené" (Education laws ratified), *Lidová demokra-cie,* May 5, 1990.

26. "Bude zdravotnictví zdravé?" (Will the Health Service be healthy?), *Mladý svět* 32, 37.

27. "Léky nemáme" (We don't have any medicines), *Reflex,* May 22, 1990.

28. Election Manifesto of Citizens Forum.
29. State Planning Commission, *Strategie.*
30. Election Manifesto of Citizens Forum.
31. Čalfa's speech in *East European Reporter,* vol. 4, no. 2, 1990.
32. Unpublished figures of the Ministry of the Interior.
33. Ibid.
34. Ibid.
35. See Saša Vondra, "A View from the Castle," *East European Reporter,* vol. 4, no. 2, 1990.
36. Memorandum on the European Security Commission.
37. "Czechs Press for Full EEC Membership," *Guardian,* May 5, 1990.
38. "Havel Proposes New European Order," *Guardian,* January 26, 1990.
39. Opinion poll published in all Czech papers, March 29, 1990.
40. Results published in daily press June 7, 1990.

Chapter 8

1. See the interview with Ota Šik in *Mladá fronta* (Young front), April 26, 1990. His complaints are touched upon in Chapter 7.
2. See the article by M. Hradil in *Rudé právo* (Red justice), June 26, 1990.
3. Ibid.
4. *Expres,* July 18, 1990.
5. Interview with Vladimír Dlouhy in *Lidové noviny* (People's newspaper), June 13, 1990.
6. *Zemědělské noviny* (Agricultural news), September 12, 1990.
7. See Federal Ministry of Strategic Planning, *Návrh zásad státni politiky v rozvoji informatizace* (A bill for the basis of state policy in the development of information technology), no. 91.662/90V, November 25, 1990.
8. *Hospodářské noviny* (Economic news), February 15, 1990.
9. Ibid., November 22, 1990.
10. *Guardian,* February 2, 1991.
11. *Občanský deník* (The citizen's daily), October 12, 1990.
12. *Mladá fronta,* October 2, 1990.
13. *Hospodářské noviny,* September 11, 1990.
14. Ibid., January 28, 1991.
15. Ibid., March 7, 1991.
16. Ibid.
17. At the official exchange rate for that time, 17 billion crowns was worth about $1.2 billion; on the black market the value was about $425 million.
18. Ministry of Finance, "Zpráva FÚS o ekonomickém a sociálním vývoji ČSFR v roce 1990" (The report of the Federal Statistical Office on the economic and social development of the Czechoslovak Federative Republic for 1990), *Hospodářské noviny,* March 12, 1991.
19. Ministry of Finance, "Informace pro podníky o ekonomických podminkach roku 1991" (Information for companies on economic conditions for 1991), *Hospodářské noviny,* March 8, 1991.

20. Unsigned editorial in *Credit Line,* March 6, 1991.
21. *Hospodářské noviny,* March 8, 1991.
22. *Práce* (Work), March 6, 1991.
23. *Hospodářské noviny,* February 15, 1991.
24. *Mladá fronta,* September 12, 1990.
25. *Expres,* July 18, 1990.
26. *Lidové noviny,* June 13, 1990.
27. *Mladá fronta,* October 25, 1990.
28. *Lidové noviny,* October 15, 1990.
29. *Květy* (Flowers), March 1, 1991.
30. *Občanský deník,* November 2, 1990.
31. *Lidové noviny,* March 2, 1991.
32. Ibid., November 28, 1991.
33. *Mladá fronta,* March 11, 1991.
34. Ibid., March 14, 1991.
35. Ibid.
36. *Mladá fronta,* March 11, 1991.
37. Report of the general procurator, *Hospodářské noviny,* March 12, 1991.
38. See Jiřina Šiklová in *Maxima,* no. 4, 1990.
39. *Mladá fronta,* January 14, 1991, reproduced the List of Rights.

Chapter 9

1. *Mladá fronta* (Young front), July 27, 1991.
2. Ibid.
3. Figures for late January 1992 showed the following: In the Czech Lands, the CDP garnered 21 percent, CSD 13 percent, CPBM 7 percent, the Liberal Social Union (a coalition of the CFP, the Greens, and CSP) 7 percent, CDP(C) 5 percent, and CM 4 percent; 25 percent of those polled were undecided. In Slovakia the MFDS received the support of 27 percent of the respondents, CDM 15 percent, PDL 10 percent, SNP 10 percent, CDU/VPN 4 percent, and SMM/HCDM 4 percent.
4. Vaclav Havel, *Letní přemítání* (Summer reflections) (Odeon, 1991), p. 39.
5. "Nevyšla výzva občanů" (The appeal of the citizens came to nothing), *Hospodářské noviny* (Economic news), January 27, 1992.
6. *Hospodářské noviny,* January 27, 1992.
7. *Rudé právo* (Red justice), July 23, 1991.
8. *Rudé právo,* July 20, 1991. See the speech of the chairman of the Citizens Democratic party parliamentary club, F. Houška.
9. Ministry of the Interior, *Návrh zákona, kterým se stanovým podmínky pro výkon některých funkcí v organech a organizacích české a slovenské federativní republiky české a slovenské republiky* (Draft law to determine the conditions for the exercise of certain functions in the organs and organizations of the Czech and Slovak federal republic and in the Czech and Slovak republics), no. KR-452/L-91.

10. Jičínský is an MP and leading lawmaker, and Rychetský is deputy prime minister and a leader of CM.

11. *Právo lidu* (Right of the people), August 9, 1991.

12. *Mladý svět* (Young world), third week of August 1991.

13. *Lidová demokracie* (People's democracy), September 3, 1991. According to the results of an opinion poll, 54 percent of the sample favored continuing the *lustrace,* but two-thirds of the sample believed this to be a means of political struggle that diverted attention from the problems of society. Further, 59 percent agreed that the National Assembly paid too much attention to it, whereas 30 percent disagreed and 11 percent were undecided.

14. *Rudé právo,* February 26, 1991.

15. *Hospodářské noviny,* September 20, 1991.

16. *Credit Line,* August 21, 1991.

17. See "Předběžná zpráva, FÚS" (Interim report of the Federal Statistical Office), *Hospodářské noviny,* September 18, 1991.

18. Ibid., September 19, 1991.

19. *Svobodné slovo* (Free word), August 30, 1991.

20. Havel's New Year's speech, *Hospodářské noviny,* January 1, 1992.

21. Ferdinand Peroutka, *Budování státu, 1918–1921* (The building of the state), 4 vols. (Borový, 1936).

22. All Czech newspapers carried this report on December 18, 1991.

23. *Hospodářské noviny,* January 1, 1992.

Selected Bibliography

Ash, T. G. *The Uses of Adversity.* Granta, 1989.
_____ . *We, the People.* Granta, 1980.
Brzezinski, Z. *The Sovet Block.* Harvard Univ. Press, 1967.
Dawisha, K. *Eastern Europe: Gorbachev and Reform.* Cambridge Univ. Press, 1988.
Dyker, D., ed. *The Soviet Union Since Gorbachev.* Croom Helm, 1987.
Erikson, W. *Lighting the Night: Revolution in Eastern Europe.* Sidgwick and Jackson, 1990.
Ermath, F. *Internationalism, Security, Legitimacy.* Rand, 1969.
Fejto, F. *A History of the People's Democracies.* Penguin, 1971.
Golan, G. *The Czechoslovak Reform Movement.* Cambridge Univ. Press, 1971.
_____ . *Reform Rule in Czechoslovakia.* Cambridge Univ. Press, 1973.
Goldfarb, J. *Beyond Glasnost.* University of Chicago Press, 1989.
Gorbachev, M. *Perestroika.* Collins, 1987.
_____ . *Socialism, Peace and Democracy.* Zwan, 1987.
Hasagowa, T., and Pravda, A., eds. *Perestroika: Soviet Domestic and Foreign Policies.* Sage, 1990.
Havel, V. *Dálkový výslech* (Long-distance interrogation). Melantrich, 1989.
_____ . *Do různých stran* (In different directions). Lidové noviny, 1989.
_____ . *Letters to Olga.* Faber and Faber, 1988.
_____ . *Living in Truth.* Ed. J. Vladislav. Faber and Faber, 1976.
Havel, V., et al. *The Power of the Powerless.* Ed. John Keane. Hutchinson, 1985.
Hutchings, R. *Soviet–East European Relations: Consolidation and Conflict, 1968–1980.* University of Wisconsin Press, 1983.
Jones, R. A. *The Soviet Concept of Limited Sovereignty from Lenin to Gorbachev: The Brezhnev Doctrine.* Macmillan, 1990.
Joyce, W., Ticktin, H., and White, S., eds. *Gorbachev and Gorbachevism.* Frank Cass, 1989.
Judson Mitchell, R. *Ideology of a Superpower.* Hoover Institute, 1982.
Kaplan, K. *The Short March.* C. Hurst, 1987.
Keane, J. *Democracy and Civil Society.* Verso, 1988.
_____ , ed. *Civil Society and the State.* Verso, 1988.
Krystufek, Z. *The Soviet Regime in Czechoslovakia.* Columbia Univ. Press, 1981.
Kundera, M. *The Art of the Novel.* Faber and Faber, 1986.
_____ . *The Book of Laughter and Forgetting.* Penguin, 1983.
Kusin, V. *From Dubček to Charter 77.* Q-Press, 1978.

————. *The Intellectual Origins of the Prague Spring.* Camridge Univ. Press, 1971.

Light, M. *Soviet Theory of International Relations.* Harvester-Wheatsheaf, 1987.

Masaryk, T. G. *The Making of a State.* George Allen and Unwin, 1927.

McCauley, M. *The Soviet Union Since Gorbachev.* Macmillan, 1987.

————, ed. *Gorbachev and Perestroika.* Macmillan, 1990.

Mlynář, Z. *Československý pokus o reformu, 1968* (Czechoslovak attempt at reform, 1968). Index, 1975.

————. *Mraz přichází z Kremlu* (Night frost from the Kremlin). Index, 1978.

Myant, M. *The Czechoslovak Economy: 1948-1988.* Cambridge Univ. Press, 1989.

————. *Socialism and Democracy in Czechoslovakia: 1945-1948.* Cambridge Univ. Press, 1981.

Olivová, V. *The Doomed Democracy.* Sidgwick and Jackson, 1972.

Ostrý, A. *Československý problém* (The Czechoslovak problem). Index, 1972.

Page, B. *The Czechoslovak Reform Movement: 1963-1968.* B. R. Grüner, 1973.

Pelikán, J. *Příspvěvek k dějinám KSČ* (Contribution to the history of the CPC). Europa, 1970.

————. *Socialist Opposition in Eastern Europe.* Alison and Busby, 1970.

Pielkalkiewicz, J. *Public Opinion Polling in Czechoslovakia: 1968-69.* Praeger, 1972.

Remington, A., ed. *Winter in Prague.* MIT Press, 1969.

Remington, R. *The Warsaw Pact.* MIT Press, 1971.

Richta, R., ed. *Civilization at the Crossroads.* Svoboda, 1989.

Schopflin, G., and Woods, N., eds. *In Search of Central Europe.* Polity Press, 1989.

Selucký, R. *Czechoslovakia: The Plan That Failed.* T. Nelson and Sons, 1970.

Shawcross, W. *Dubček.* Hogarth Press, 1990.

Skilling, H. Gordon. *Charter 77 and Human Rights in Czechoslovakia.* George Allen and Unwin, 1981.

————. *Czechoslovakia's Interrupted Revolution.* Princeton Univ. Press, 1976.

Sládeček, J. [Petr Pithart]. *Osmašedesátý* (Sixty-eight). Index, 1980.

Steele, J., ed. *Eastern Europe Since Stalin.* David and Charles, 1974.

Steiner, E. *The Slovak Dilemma.* Cambridge Univ. Press, 1973.

Suda, Z. *Zealots and Rebels.* Hoover Institution Press, 1980.

Šik, O. *Jarní probuzení—lluze a skutečnost* (Summer awakening—illusion and reality). Polygon, 1989.

Škvorecký, J. *The Cowards.* Penguin, 1972.

————. *Mirákl* (Miracle). 68 Publishers, 1972.

For Part Two

Primary Sources

Handbills of Student Strike Coordinating Committees, November 17–December 28, 1989

Cyclostyled documents of Citizens Forum, November 19–December 31, 1989

Informační servis (Information Service; newspaper of Citizens Forum), nos. 1–40

Agitation and Information Broadsheets of

Democratic Forum of Communists
Obroda
Left Alternative
Social Democratic party
Basic organizations of the Communist party of Czechoslovakia, the Revolutionary Trade Union Movement, and the Socialist Union of Youth

Newspapers (from November 15 to December 31, 1989)

Hornický sever (The mining north), CP regional paper for those engaged in coal-mining in northern Bohemia
Lidová demokracie (People's democracy), organ of the Czechoslovak People's party
Mladá fronta (Young front), organ of the Socialist Union of Youth
Mladý svět (Young world)
Práce (Work), organ of the Revolutionary Trade Union Movement
Průboj (Struggle), party daily in northern Bohemia
Rudé právo (Red justice), organ of the Czechoslovak Communist party
Severočeský deník, North Bohemian daily news
Stráž lidu (Guardian of the people), party daily in Moravia
Svobodné slovo (Free word), organ of the Czech Socialist party
Tribuna (Tribune), theoretical journal of the Central Committee of the CPC, published in Prague
Večerní Praha (Prague Evening news)

Commemorative Publications

Holubec, Petr, ed., *Kronika sametové revoluce* (Chronicle of the Velvet Revolution), 2 vols. (Czechoslovak Press Agency, 1990)
Studenti psali revoluci (Students wrote the revolution) (Univerzum, 1990)

Video and audio recordings of news broadcasts

Recordings of interviews

For Part Three

Newspapers (from January 1990 to February 1991)

Hospodářské noviny (Economic news)
Květy (Flowers), a women's magazine
Lidová demokracie

Lidové noviny (People's newspaper)
Mladá fronta
Mladý svět
Občanský deník (the citizen's daily)
Obzor (Horizon)
Práce
Rudé právo
Svobodné slovo

*Private conversations with members of Citizens Forum, the Student Strike
   Coordinating Committee, and the Communist party*

About the Book and Authors

This vivid portrayal of the "Velvet Revolution" describes the dramatic social and political changes that heralded the collapse of the Czechoslovak Communist party—one of the last Stalinist regimes to fall in Europe—and the emergence of the pluralist, parliamentary democracy that superseded it.

Wheaton and Kavan set the stage by examining the state that was built for and by the so-called Red Aristocracy after the Soviet invasion in 1968. They identify the key features of this system of "normalization," including the *nomenklatura,* which was more or less instrumental in bringing about the collapse of civil society. The authors describe the devastating social and economic effects of communism during this period and then chronicle the reemergence of civil society in a climate warmed by Gorbachev's program of perestroika and the collapse of the powerful leadership in the German Democratic Republic.

The authors then describe the Velvet Revolution itself: the police attack on Black Friday; the strike by university students and actors in Prague; the formation of Citizens Forum, in which the playwright Václav Havel has been prominent; and the mobilization of protest against the Communist party—which developed into a mass, popular, and, in its own way, nationalist revolution. The book pays special attention to the problems posed by nationalities and national minorities, the conflicting attitudes of urban and rural dwellers, the role of the Communist party and the failure of force, and the sea change in public activity.

The authors conclude by assessing the legacy of the revolution and examining the foundation of the Czech and Slovak Federative Republic. They analyze the establishment of democratic structures; the founding of new and the emergence of old political parties; the ebb and flow of the debates on new economic, social, and international policies; and Czechoslovakia's place in Europe and the world.

Bernard Wheaton, one of the few Western observers in the country during the nonviolent change of government in November 1989, and Zdeněk Kavan, himself a Czech, interweave first-hand descriptions with interviews of student leaders, press accounts, and scholarly analysis of the historical antecedents of the revolution to bring the extraordinary events of 1989 to life. The narrative is enriched with political cartoons and photographs.

Bernard Wheaton is a historian and private researcher who regularly works in the Historical Archive of the Charles University, Prague. **Zdeněk Kavan** teaches international relations at the University of Sussex, England.

Index